Praise for *Epic Content Marketing*

There's a reason some of the best companies in the world have used content marketing as a critical component of their growth. It provides long-term leverage. This is the definitive guide to doing content marketing well—and making it epic.

> —**Dharmesh Shah**, cofounder and CTO, HubSpot

Strategy, operations, tactics, inspiration: It's all here, packaged for you as your guide to a modern content marketing age.

> —**Ann Handley**, *Wall Street Journal* bestselling author of
> *Everybody Writes*

Intelligent, clear, and comprehensive. Pulizzi and Piper's monumental contribution to the modern marketing landscape cannot be missed. The second edition of *Epic Content Marketing* is the only book every content creator must read and then read again.

> —**Andrew Davis**, global keynote speaker and bestselling author

Organizations that educate and inform instead of interrupt and sell attract interested people and grow business! Joe and Brian show you how to implement the ideas of content marketing so you can build passionate fans too.

> —**David Meerman Scott**, bestselling author of 12 books,
> including *Fanocracy* and *The New Rules of Marketing & PR*

This book is a fantastic resource for content marketers of all levels. Whether you're just getting started or super advanced, it is useful, helpful, and relevant. Joe and Brian do a phenomenal job of capturing what makes content marketing a foundational discipline in any modern marketing mix.

> —**Amanda Todorovich**, Executive Director, Content Marketing,
> Cleveland Clinic

The quintessential guide to content marketing strategy, operations, and success. Every business needs content marketing—thus every businessperson needs this new edition of *Epic Content Marketing*.

> —**Jay Baer**, *New York Times* bestselling author

If there was ever a textbook for the practice of content marketing, *Epic Content Marketing* is it.

> —**David Siegel**, CEO of Meetup and author of *Decide & Conquer*

An easy-to-digest blueprint for what you must know about content marketing. Not only does it clearly lay out what actions to take today, but it also gives us a road map into the future of content marketing.

—**A. Lee Judge**, founder of Content Monsta

Joe and Brian just put a new shine on a classic marketing text! Essential for any marketing library.

—**Mark Schaefer**, author of *Marketing Rebellion*

Packed with useful resources and real-life examples, this is a must-read for every marketing team. Joe and Brian break down not only how to effectively create and execute a content marketing strategy, but also why it works. You will be inspired and motivated to take your marketing efforts to the next level.

—**Ruth Carter**, content marketing speaker, author, entrepreneur, and attorney

It's rare that a business book balances both the rebellious spirit and real-world practicality of what it's like to be a modern marketing professional.

—**Robert Rose**, leading global advisor for content marketing

The newly revised version of *Epic Content Marketing* has what every content marketing chef wants and needs: more, better, newer recipes. In the second edition, you'll get a ton of new recipes and ideas for improving your content marketing in useful, compact ways—just like a real cookbook.

—**Christopher Penn**, Chief Data Scientist, Trust Insights

EPIC CONTENT MARKETING

SECOND EDITION

BREAK THROUGH THE CLUTTER WITH A DIFFERENT STORY,
GET THE MOST OUT OF YOUR CONTENT,
AND BUILD A COMMUNITY IN WEB3

JOE PULIZZI
BRIAN PIPER

NEW YORK   CHICAGO   SAN FRANCISCO   ATHENS   LONDON
MADRID   MEXICO CITY   MILAN   NEW DELHI
SINGAPORE   SYDNEY   TORONTO

1 2 3 4 5 6 7 8 9   LCR   28 27 26 25 24 23

ISBN   978-1-264-77445-6
MHID   1-264-77445-1

e-ISBN   978-1-264-77549-1
e-MHID   1-264-77549-0

Library of Congress Cataloging-in-Publication Data
Names: Pulizzi, Joe, author. | Piper, Brian (Web content consultant), author.
Title: Epic content marketing : break through the clutter with a different story,
   get the most out of your content, and build a community in Web3 / Joe Pulizzi
   and Brian Piper.
Description: New York : McGraw Hill, [2023] | Includes bibliographical references
   and index.
Identifiers: LCCN 2022050350 (print) | LCCN 2022050351 (ebook) | ISBN
   9781264774456 (hardback) | ISBN 9781264775491 (ebook)
Subjects: LCSH: Marketing--Social aspects. | Social media. | Internet marketing. |
   Target marketing.
Classification: LCC HF5415 .P756 2023 (print) | LCC HF5415 (ebook) |
   DDC 658.8—dc23/eng/20221019
LC record available at https://lccn.loc.gov/2022050350
LC ebook record available at https://lccn.loc.gov/2022050351

McGraw Hill books are available at special quantity discounts to use as premiums and sales promotions or for use in corporate training programs. To contact a representative, please visit the Contact Us pages at www.mhprofessional.com.

McGraw Hill is committed to making our products accessible to all learners. To learn more about the available support and accommodations we offer, please contact us at accessibility@mheducation.com. We also participate in the Access Text Network (www.accesstext.org), and ATN members may submit requests through ATN.

Joe—For Pam, the oldest and Adam . . .

We have each other. That is how we win.
Lando (w/slight alteration)

Brian—For Anthony, Shannon, Michael, Patrick,
Elizabeth, Peter, and Adam . . .

Do or do not, there is no try.
Yoda

Contents

Part I
Content Marketing—There and Back Again . . . and Again

PART II
Defining Your Content Niche and Strategy

PART III
Managing the Content Process

Part IV
Making Content Work

PART V
Web3

PART VI
What's Next?

Introduction

Greatness is won, not awarded.

GUY KAWASAKI

When we started writing the second edition of this book, we thought we'd be able to approach it as most second edition authors have—refresh the statistics and update the observations from the first edition. We progressed to Chapter 3 before we realized that simply wouldn't be enough. The entire landscape changed so much in the past 10 years that a content refresher would be a disservice. We decided to throw it all away and start over.

That's right. We had to completely revamp this new edition of *Epic Content Marketing*. Don't get us wrong . . . the key content pillars are still a part of this book, but so much has changed in a decade. Today content marketing is a key staple in almost every organization on the planet, from the largest tech companies to the smallest of content entrepreneurs. Take that and add in new social channels, improved and automated technology, innovative content processes, and fresh business models—plus a whole new movement called the "creator economy." If you're new to content marketing, we have you covered. The first three parts of the book cover the content marketing frameworks every content marketing strategy requires. But even for veteran content marketers, you'll see new stories and case studies that illustrate some of the latest concepts and applications.

The final parts of the book dive deeper into the mechanics of promoting and optimizing your content and feature new chapters that address techniques such as community building as well as emerging technologies such as artificial intelligence. We also address critical concepts around buying and selling content businesses and measuring content marketing departments in different ways. And whether you are a content entrepreneur creating content for your personal brand or working in a large organization using your skills at scale, you'll benefit from the totally new outlook on community building and new marketing tactics that Web3 has introduced to the world.

THE SECRET

Your customers don't care about you, your products, or your services. They care about themselves.

Before you go any further in this book, you must accept this truth as the first step. Most of us feel we have something wonderful and revolutionary to offer people. We really don't . . . at least not anything more than customers can probably find elsewhere. If that's true, how do we get customers to pay attention to us, trust us, ultimately buy something from us, and keep coming back for more?

WHY EPIC?

Content marketing is not new, and it is getting cluttered—contaminated, if you will. Globally, 97 percent of businesses use content marketing as part of their marketing strategy, according to SEMrush's "The State of Content Marketing, 2022 Global Report."

A search for the term "content marketing" in Google will return more than 2.8 billion results. How do we break through this clutter?

We need to be epic with our content marketing. We need to do it better. We need to focus more on our customers and less on our products. Yes, you heard that right: to sell more, we need to be marketing our products and services less.

CHANGE YOUR STARS

Since the first edition of this book was published, there have been some amazing examples of companies and content entrepreneurs leveraging content marketing to shift the traditional methods of connecting with audiences, building communities, and creating trust. We will explore many of those in this book.

Everything we have learned from working with hundreds of companies and growing numerous businesses through the art and science of content marketing is in this book. You have given us a gift by buying this book. We will return the favor and make sure it is not a waste of your time.

HOW TO READ THIS BOOK

Delivering the right content to the right audience is a key concept for effective content marketing. That being said, we've written this book for a few different audiences and have some suggestions on how those audiences might get the most out of this book.

If you are just starting your content marketing journey and education, read the entire book! Regardless of whether you're a content entrepreneur, creating content to build the audience for your small business, or a content marketer for a large brand or company, looking to build better connections with your customers, soak up as much information about content marketing as you can.

If you are an experienced content marketer, look at the table of contents and start where you think you'll find the information most relevant to you. The foundation from the first edition is there, but each chapter has been altered to reflect the changes in those areas over the past decade. The last four parts of the book are almost completely new, as many of the technologies and capabilities addressed in those sections didn't exist when the first edition was written.

People often ask how long their blog posts or newsletter articles should be. The answer is always this: "As long as it needs to be." And that's exactly what you'll find in this book. Some chapters are very short, others not so much. Regardless, each one will provide some insight to help you think differently about your business or give tangible advice on developing your own content marketing process.

Remember the Jack Palance character, Curly, from the movie *City Slickers*? Remember the "one thing"? You know that one thing that is the secret of life? Our goal is for you to take away that one thing from this book that will make a difference in your business.

Some of the ideas and concepts in this book will be new. Some will be familiar, which you may want to skip. Please feel free to jump around. Find the one thing that will help you grow your company and create either more or better customers.

GROW

Whether you are a CMO at a Fortune 500 company, own the smallest of small businesses, or are a content entrepreneur and you want to grow your business, this book is for you. Size is not an issue. Whatever your title or role, if you are part of the marketing process to generate revenue (to help make or sustain a sale), this book is for you.

Many chapters include the following for your reference:

- **Epic thoughts.** These are issues to keep in mind. To help you think differently about your marketing. Concepts that will help change your stars.
- **Epic resources.** This book references hundreds of books, articles, blog posts, movies, and comments from friends and influencers. Several of the key resources that helped that specific chapter come together will be included at the end of each chapter.

Good luck, and thank you for deciding to take this epic journey with us.

HOW THIS BOOK CAME TO BE

FROM JOE PULIZZI

If you read the first edition of this book or any of my other books, you might know my story. For those of you who don't, here's the short version.

In March 2007 I left a six-figure executive position at the largest independent business media company in North America to bootstrap a startup called Content Marketing Institute (CMI).

In 2015, we just missed $10 million in sales. In June 2016, we sold our company for $20+ million to a billion-dollar, London-based events company. To achieve this type of growth and recognized success with little to no traditional advertising, we had to develop a new business model around content creation and distribution.

Even while this idea of content marketing is now a recognized industry term, most business owners have no playbook to do this properly. I talk to people every day from businesses that waste an incredible amount of time on social media tactics without first having the content marketing strategy to make it work for the business.

After selling CMI, I took a year sabbatical, wrote a marketing mystery novel (*The Will to Die*), and focused on our speech therapy nonprofit, the

Orange Effect Foundation. And then Covid hit. I wrote the second edition of my book *Content Inc.*, relaunched the podcast, developed an email newsletter, and started The Tilt, specifically for content entrepreneurs, to provide a business model that can help them find success by understanding how to navigate the "business side" of content.

In May 2022, we launched the Creator Economy Expo (CEX), an education and networking conference focused on how serious content creators can become successful content entrepreneurs.

The content marketing landscape has changed dramatically in the past 10 years since I wrote the first edition of *Epic Content Marketing*. There are new channels, opportunities, technologies, tools, and techniques for both content entrepreneurs and businesses creating content. With all these changes, it still comes down to creating epic content, and we want to help you learn to do that.

FROM BRIAN PIPER

I started developing websites, creating e-learning content, and optimizing digital content performance in 1996. I wasn't a particularly passionate or talented developer, but it was a job that I could do to help pay my bills and support my hobbies. I read the first edition of *Epic Content Marketing* back in 2014 and immediately recognized that it was the path for me. I marched right down to the new VP of marketing at the company I worked for and convinced her that she needed to put me on her team to handle digital marketing. I would have said "content marketing" rather than "digital marketing," but at the time, she wouldn't have known what I was talking about and probably wouldn't have given me a chance.

I went to my first Content Marketing World (a CMI event) in 2017 and tracked down Joe to take a selfie with him and thank him for changing my career path with his book. I spent the next several years focusing on using data and strategy to optimize content for the companies that I worked for, training other people how to create content that performs, and consistently increasing organic traffic and brand awareness each year. I started presenting at industry conferences and running workshops and consulting with other institutions on content strategy and content data, and in 2020 I presented at Content Marketing World (virtually). I spoke in person in 2021 and spent some time talking with Joe, beyond the annual selfie, and started diving into the Web3 world and the creator economy.

Two weeks after Content Marketing World, I joined an online book club discussion about *Content Inc.* with Joe and a few other people. I asked when he was going to update *Epic Content Marketing*, and he proposed that we coauthor the next edition. So here I am. The book that changed my career path almost 10 years ago is changing it again as I build my personal brand and start creating content for myself.

Acknowledgments

FROM JOE PULIZZI

This book would not exist without Brian Piper. He spent months trying to convince me that a new version of this book was what the world needed. I guess we will find out if he is correct.

To the amazing businesses and individuals featured in this book: This model is yours. Thank you for inspiring me each day to do better.

To the entire TILT community for helping to make this book possible.

To Laura/Jim, Becky/Marc, and Kristin/JK for making every minute of this journey a blast.

To my two amazing kids. Never settle. Ask questions. I'm so proud of both of you.

To my immediate family, Terry and Tony Pulizzi, Lea and Steve Smith, Tony and Cathy Pulizzi, Sandy McDermott, Sandy Kozelka, Ryan and Amy Kozelka, and Laura Kozelka for all your love and support.

To Pam. My best friend. With you, every day is better than the last. I love you. Most (obviously)!

Philippians 4:13

FROM BRIAN PIPER

To my kids, who inspire and motivate me to be a better person every day, keep chasing your dreams and being true to yourselves. Watching you grow, learn, and become your own people has been one of the most rewarding parts of my life.

To my mother, Kathryn Buckstaff, who showed me that I could do anything and be anyone I wanted, you were my best friend and I miss you every day. You always inspired me, believed in me, and supported me even when I made bad decisions.

To my father, Travis, who taught me the value of consistency, of showing up on time every day, and working harder than anyone else, thank you for always being there when I needed you.

To my amazing wife, Jenn, the love of my life and the most incredible person I've ever met, your love, unwavering support, and strength of character mean more to me than you know. Not to mention all the time you spent reading, editing, and taking care of everything for the past few months.

Finally, to Joe, this is all your fault. The first edition of this book changed my life, career, and business, which is what you said (in Chapter 7) that you wanted it to do. The best part of this entire journey has been working with you. Thank you for your time, your mentorship, and most of all your friendship.

PART I

Content Marketing— There and Back Again . . . and Again

CHAPTER 1

What Is Content Marketing?

BY JOE PULIZZI

Ninety percent of leadership is the ability to communicate something people want.
DIANNE FEINSTEIN

A good definition of content marketing is this:

> Content marketing is the marketing and business process for creating and distributing valuable and compelling content to attract, acquire, and engage a clearly defined and understood target audience—with the objective of driving profitable customer action.

Content marketing can happen across every channel—videos, blogs, newsletters, social, in-person events, and consistent virtual conversations. Don't limit yourself to where you can create valuable content marketing opportunities. The key is to drive a particular audience to take action based on the story that you tell.

CONTENT MARKETING: FOR NONBELIEVERS

Your customers don't care about you, your products, or your services. They care about themselves, their wants, and their needs. So content marketing can also be thought of this way:

> Content marketing is about creating interesting information your customers are passionate about, *so they actually pay attention to you.*

This definition is my favorite (with kudos to bestselling author David Meerman Scott for helping popularize this), and the hardest for marketers and business owners to deal with. So often we marketers believe that our products and services are so special—so amazing—and we think that if more people knew about them, all our sales problems would be solved.

Remember that your customers are just trying to solve their problems and answer the questions they have. We see example after example of businesses using this model to create content that answers the audience's questions and then turning that into increased revenue and new business models.

Just look at River Pools and Spas. It was a fiberglass pool installation company that almost went out of business in 2009. Then the owner, Marcus Sheridan, decided to start answering every question his customers ever asked, posting the answers on his blog. Now the company is the world's largest provider of information on fiberglass pools, its installation business is global, and it is even manufacturing its own fiberglass pools. Content marketing not only improved the company's product sales, but also created an entirely new set of business opportunities.

Another incredible example of a small business using content in a creative way is Sweet Farm. Sweet Farm is a nonprofit animal sanctuary and sustainable plant farm. Back in 2019, it was a small farm that hosted corporate team-building events and volunteer programs to educate the local community about the importance of farm animal rescue and sustainable agriculture.

When Covid hit, visits were canceled, and the company's revenue plummeted. It got to the point where Sweet Farm would have to start letting employees go. With its back to the wall, the company came up with a brilliant idea: a live content model that addressed the needs of virtual audiences around the world, Goat-2-Meeting. Sweet Farm let users make an appointment to bring a farm animal into its virtual meetings. With all the online fatigue people were experiencing and the amount of time people were spending in virtual meetings, Sweet Farm capitalized on this with its incredible solution.

In two years, Sweet Farm has provided 10,000 virtual events to over 350,000 people on every continent, where attendees paid from $65 to $750 to share the virtual stage with an animal. Did this save its business? Absolutely. No employees were let go as well. But more than that, Sweet Farm delivered on its mission to educate and drive change toward a more sustainable planet. All by telling a consistent story in a differentiated manner.

MARKETING BY SELLING LESS

Basically, content marketing is the art of communicating with your customers and prospects without selling. In other words, it is noninterruption marketing. Instead of pitching your products or services, you are delivering information that makes your buyers more intelligent or perhaps entertaining them to build an emotional connection. *The essence of this strategy is the belief that if we, as businesses, deliver consistent, ongoing valuable information to buyers, they ultimately reward us with their business and loyalty.*

Don't get me wrong; there is a time for sales collateral, feature and benefit marketing, and customer testimonials about why you are so awesome. If you are like most companies, you have plenty of that content. The problem with that type of content is that it is only critical when your prospect is ready to buy. What about the other 99 percent of the time when your customers aren't ready to buy? Ah, that is where content marketing pays its dues.

INFORM OR ENTERTAIN

Twenty years ago, I had the opportunity to have lunch with Kirk Cheyfitz, then CEO of Story Worldwide, a global content agency. His words at that lunch have always stuck with me.

"Inform or entertain," Cheyfitz said. "What other options do brands have when communicating with their customers and prospects? Brands serve their customers best when they are telling engaging stories."

Actually, you have four choices. First, you can inform and help your customers live better lives, find better jobs, or be more successful in the jobs they have now. Second, you can also choose to entertain and begin to build an emotional connection with your customers. These two choices help you build a following (like a media company does . . . but more on that later).

Your third choice is to develop lackluster content that doesn't move the needle. This is content that could be self-serving and promotional. It could also be content that you want to be useful or entertaining, but because of quality, consistency, or planning issues, it's ignored by your customers.

Your fourth choice is to spend money on traditional marketing, such as paid advertising, traditional direct mail, and public relations. Again, there's nothing wrong with these activities, but this book will show that there may be a better way to use those advertising dollars.

CONTENT MARKETING VERSUS SOCIAL MEDIA MARKETING: WHAT'S THE DIFFERENCE?

These days, people are much more familiar with the term "content marketing" (see Figure 1.1), but many people still confuse content marketing with social media marketing. There are a few distinct differences.

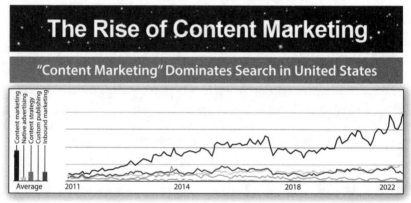

FIGURE 1.1 In 2022, "content marketing," as a term, has significantly outperformed every other industry term as a percentage of Google searches. (*Source: Google Trends*)

Indeed, content marketing often involves social media. And of course, in social media, marketers use content to get their messages across. But although there is plenty of overlap between content marketing and social media marketing, they are actually two distinct entities, with different focal points, goals, and processes. To help clear the confusion, let's look at the major ways in which they differ.

CENTER OF GRAVITY

In social media marketing, the center of gravity—the focus of the marketing activity—is located within the social networks themselves. When marketers operate social media campaigns, they are operating inside Facebook, Twitter,

Instagram, TikTok, and so on. As they produce content, they place it inside these networks.

In contrast, the center of gravity for content marketing is a brand website (your ultimate platform; see Chapter 16 for more), whether it be a branded web address, such as ClevelandClinic.com, or a microsite for a specific initiative, such as the Clinic's Health Essentials (health.clevelandclinic.com). Social networks are many times vital to the success of content marketing efforts, but in this case, Facebook, Twitter, and Instagram are used primarily as distribution mechanisms that take you back to the content on the brand's website, rather than serve as containers of the content itself.

TYPES OF CONTENT

In social media marketing, content is built to fit the context of the chosen social platform: shorter messages or threads for Twitter; contests, quizzes, and games for Facebook; 20-second entertainment reels for TikTok; and so on. *With this type of marketing, brands model their behavior after that of the individuals using social networks.*

On the other hand, in content marketing, the context of websites permits much longer forms of content. Brands can publish blog posts, videos, infographics, and e-books, just to name a few formats. *With this type of marketing, brands model their behavior after that of media publishers.*

RENTED LAND

One of the biggest problems with social media is that you don't control the platform. You're essentially building your content strategy on rented land. At any time, your landlords can decide they don't like the message you're sending, the people you're connecting with, or how you're engaging with other content, and they can evict you.

They can temporarily shut down your account, remove your posts, and control how your content gets shared or monetized. These are private platforms, and they can (and will) do what they want to drive revenues and profit. That means you could be blocked tomorrow (if you say something they don't like). Or they could change the rules (which they do almost daily).

You are also dependent on the platform not going down. In October 2021, Facebook went down for six hours. With more than 3.5 billion users, many of whom relied on the channel for their business and income, this was a serious wake-up call.

The outage also affected Facebook's subsidiary channels including Messenger, WhatsApp, Instagram, Mapillary, and Oculus. This resulted in users who ran their businesses through any of those channels seriously reconsidering the importance of having their own channel that they control.

Discord, the popular discussion forum, and Alphabet's YouTube both were silenced multiple times in 2022. Users and content creators could do nothing but watch and wait.

OBJECTIVES

While both social media marketing and content marketing can be used for a multitude of purposes, social media marketing generally tends to focus on two main objectives. First, it is used for brand awareness by generating activity and discussion around the brand. Second, it is used for customer retention and satisfaction; brands can use social channels as an open forum for direct dialogues with customers, often around issues or questions that consumers have.

In contrast, content marketing's website-based center of gravity (think "owned" or "controlled") enables it to focus more on demand (or lead) generation and subscriber growth. As quality content brings prospects to a brand's site, that brand can develop a relationship with the prospects and nurture them toward a lead conversion or purchase.

EVOLUTION OF ONLINE MARKETING

We need to think of social media marketing and content marketing less as two isolated options and more as interrelated parts of marketing's ongoing evolution. The internet has unleashed a revolutionary ability for every brand to communicate directly with its customers—without the need for a media industry intermediary.

Social media marketing is the natural first step in this process. Access to users is direct (users spend lots of time on social networks), and content is generally formatted into shorter chunks, which makes the publishing process relatively easy.

But as brands become more familiar with their new role as publishers, the natural progression is to move toward content marketing. Yes, the bar here is higher: in content marketing, brands must produce longer-form, higher-quality content and build audiences on their own sites—they must become true media publishers. But the rewards and results are arguably more powerful. Brands can engage more deeply with their customers through content marketing efforts. And by driving consumers to its own website, a brand has a greater opportunity to gain leads and move them down the conversion funnel.

As we all pioneer this "new" strategy of content marketing, a shared definition of what we do relative to approaches like social media marketing is invaluable.

THE NEW WORLD OF CONTENT MARKETING

Let's take a look at the first content marketing definition one more time, but this time remove the "valuable and compelling":

> Content marketing is the marketing and business process for creating and distributing content to attract, acquire, and engage a clearly defined and understood target audience—with the objective of driving profitable customer action.

That's the difference between content marketing and the other informational garbage you get from companies trying to sell you "stuff." Companies send out information all the time; it's just that most of the time informational garbage is not very compelling or useful (think "spam"). That's what makes content marketing so intriguing in today's environment of thousands of marketing messages per person per day. *Good content marketing makes a person stop, read, think, and behave differently.*

THE DIFFERENCE BETWEEN *CONTENT* AND *CONTENT MARKETING*

Not a day goes by that some marketer somewhere around the world doesn't try to figure this out. Here's the answer.

Some experts say that content is any word, image, or pixel that can be engaged with by another human being. In the context of this book, content is *compelling content that informs, engages, or amuses.*

What makes content marketing different from simple content is that content marketing must do something for the business. It must inform, engage, or amuse *with the objective of driving profitable customer action.*

Your content may engage or inform, but if it's not accomplishing your business goals (for example, customer retention or lead generation), it's not content marketing. The content you create must work directly to attract and/ or retain customers in some way.

CONTENT MARKETING NEXT

Yes, you really can create marketing that is anticipated and truly makes a connection! You can develop and execute "sales" messages that are needed, even requested, by your customers. Content marketing is a far cry from the interruption marketing we are bombarded with every minute of every day. Content marketing is about marketing for the present and the future.

Content marketing has changed dramatically in the last 10 years. There are more content creators putting out content on more channels than ever before. There are new technologies that allow content creators to build community and monetize their content, and their brand, to generate income in entirely new ways. Media companies are blurring the lines between content marketing and entertainment. Companies are purchasing and creating their own media companies to acquire audiences like never before.

As you move forward, think about this question: If you stopped delivering content to your customers, would they notice? In my experience, most marketers and content creators would say no, they would not notice. No matter where you are in your content marketing journey, knowing this presents an amazing opportunity. Let's do this.

EPIC THOUGHTS

- Content is just . . . content, unless it's driving behavior change in your customers and prospects toward a business goal. Then it's called "content marketing."

- Your marketing needs to be anticipated, loved, and wanted. This is the new world we live in today.

- Your content marketing strategy comes before your social media strategy—yesterday, today, and always.

EPIC RESOURCES

- Google Trends, "content marketing" search, https://trends.google.com/trends/explore?date=2011-02-07%202022-03-07&geo=US&q=content%20marketing,native%20advertising,content%20strategy,custom%20publishing,inbound%20marketing.

- Sydney Page, "The Latest Thing on Zoom Meetings: A Live Goat," accessed July 9, 2022, https://www.washingtonpost.com/lifestyle/2021/02/05/goat-zoom-meeting-surprise/.

CHAPTER 2

The History of Content Marketing

BY BRIAN PIPER

A generation which ignores history
has no past and no future.
ROBERT HEINLEIN

CONTENT MARKETING IN THE EIGHTEENTH CENTURY

There was once a young printer named Benjamin who was looking for ways to promote his printing house. He had written stories, been a publisher of a newspaper, and even tried writing and printing his own newspaper, all with little success. Then, on December 28, 1732, he started publishing an almanac filled with useful information that answered questions his readers had.

Poor Richard's Almanack (see Figure 2.1) went on to sell as many as 10,000 copies a year in the 25 years that it was published. It was second in sales only to the Bible. It was filled with valuable and relevant information, but the thing that made it stand apart from the other almanacs available at the time was the wit and style of the creator.

His name was Benjamin Franklin.

Benjamin Franklin's "Poor Richard's Almanack"

FIGURE 2.1 *Poor Richard's Almanack* was first published in 1732 by Benjamin Franklin and was distributed to as many as 10,000 people per year until 1758. (*Source: benjamin-franklin-history.org*)

A GLORIOUS PAST

And Benjamin Franklin was just the beginning. Here are a few more examples of how content marketing has been used and how it has evolved over the years. This list certainly doesn't include all the examples but features some key moments.

- **1801. The bookstore Librairie Galignani (in Paris) starts printing *Galignani's Messenger* (in English).** This daily newspaper was created to feature notable authors, and the bookstore started community-building initiatives like opening a reading room.
- **1861. Samuel Wagner creates the *American Bee Journal*.** His friend, the Rev. L. L. Langstroth, was an advisor and contributor and used the publication to feature the benefits of his movable frame hive. The journal halted publication for four years during the Civil War, but has been educating beekeepers ever since.

- **1867. Harvard Steam Boiler Inspection and Insurance Company develops** *The Locomotive*. Dedicated to steam power and industrial safety, this publication is the oldest company magazine that has been continually published in the United States under the same name.
- **1887. Charles Scribner's Sons develops** *Scribner's Magazine*. This magazine published articles and stories by many famous authors, providing glimpses into their personal lives. Almost half the pages in the magazine were reserved for advertising.
- **1888. Johnson & Johnson publishes** *Modern Methods of Antiseptic Wound Treatment*. This step-by-step guide on how to perform sterile surgeries was distributed to doctors, surgeons, and pharmacists. Around 85,000 copies were distributed in the first few months and more than 4.5 million copies over the next few years.
- **1895. John Deere releases** *The Furrow*. Created to help farmers become more prosperous and profitable, *The Furrow* is the largest circulated farming magazine in the world. It's printed in four languages and delivered monthly to millions of farmers in 115 different countries.
- **1900. Michelin develops** *The Michelin Guide*. This 400-page guide, now with its iconic red cover, helps drivers maintain their cars and find decent lodging. In its first edition, 35,000 copies were distributed for free.
- **1904. Jell-O recipe book pays off.** Jell-O distributed free copies of a recipe book that contributed to sales of over $1 million by 1906.
- **1924. Sears launches WLS (World's Largest Store) radio station.** The station helped keep farmers informed during the deflation crisis with content supplied by the Sears-Roebuck Agricultural Foundation.
- **1930s. Procter & Gamble (P&G) begins foray into radio serial dramas.** This extremely successful initiative, featuring brands such as Duz and Oxydol detergents, marked the beginning of the "soap opera."
- **1939. Robert L. May writes** *Rudolph the Red-Nosed Reindeer.* Ann Handley, author of *Everybody Writes*, does an amazing presentation on how this book launched Robert May's career. Originally written for Montgomery Ward, 2.4 million copies were distributed to shoppers nationwide. May later purchased the rights from

Montgomery Ward and made "Rudolph" a global sensation through television syndication.

- **1968.** *Weight Watchers Magazine* **was founded.** This was one of the first consumer magazines distributed via newsstands and at supermarkets.
- **1987. LEGO launches** *Brick Kicks* **magazine.** Now *LEGO Life Magazine*, this print and digital magazine is delivered five times per year to children around the world.
- **2001. Penton Custom Media begins using the term "content marketing."**

GOOD STORIES LAST FOREVER

As mentioned in Chapter 1, the content marketing industry has taken off, but it's important to realize where brands have been. Brands have been telling stories for centuries. That endeavor started when brands had just a few channels, and it continues today, even as brands can choose from literally hundreds of media channels for marketing.

Telling a quality story to the right person at the right time always cuts through the clutter. There will be another new channel tomorrow, and another one the next day. It's easy to be seduced by the new. As smart content marketers, we need to keep in mind that channels come and go, but good stories (and storytelling) last forever.

EPIC THOUGHTS

- Content marketing is not new. Brands have been telling epic stories for centuries. The difference? It's more critical now than ever to get it right.

- *The Furrow* magazine by John Deere is one of the largest circulated magazines to farmers in the world. Could you be the leading provider of information for your customers?

EPIC RESOURCES

- Addison Rizer, "A History of Poor Richard's Almanac," Book Riot, accessed June 16, 2022, https://bookriot.com/poor-richards -almanac-history/.

- Galignani, "Galignani Since 1520," accessed June 16, 2022, https://www.galignani.fr/galignani-since-1520/ssh-5250.

- *American Bee Journal*, "History," accessed June 16, 2022, https:// americanbeejournal.com/history/.

- HSB, "Publications," accessed June 16, 2022, https://www .munichre.com/hsb/en/press-and-publications/publications.html.

- Modernist Journals Project, "Scribner's Magazine," accessed June 16, 2022, https://modjourn.org/journal/scribners-magazine/.

- Johnson & Johnson, *Modern Methods of Antiseptic Wound Treatment*, accessed June 16, 2022, https://ourstory.jnj.com/ modern-methods-antiseptic-wound-treatment.

- *The Furrow*, accessed June 1, 2022, https://www.deere.com/en/ publications/the-furrow/.

- Michelin, "About Us," accessed June 16, 2022, https://guide .michelin.com/us/en/about-us.

- Internet Archive, "Jell-O Recipe Book (1905)," accessed June 16, 2022, https://ia801307.us.archive.org/25/items/jello-recipe-book/ jello-recipe-book.pdf.

- The Tilt, "Ann Handley—How to Make Writing Your Superpower," accessed June 16, 2022, https://www.thetilt.com/topic/session-1 -ann-handley.

- Joe Pulizzi, "The History of Content Marketing" (Infographic), ContentMarketingInstitute.com, July 1, 2016, https:// contentmarketinginstitute.com/2016/07/history-content -marketing/.

CHAPTER 3

Why Content Marketing?

BY JOE PULIZZI

People don't buy what you do;
they buy why you do it.
SIMON SINEK

When you have a question or a problem, where do you go for the answer? Most likely a search engine such as Google.

When you are browsing through your favorite social networking site, what do you tend to share? Perhaps interesting stories, clever images, or funny videos?

When you are working out, do you possibly listen to entertaining podcasts or to the latest business audiobook?

When you are doing research to book a hotel room or perhaps buy some new business software, what do you look for? Maybe a research or comparison report for the software?

In each case, it's content that solves our problems, makes us laugh, or gives us the idea for our next journey. Jon Wuebben, author of *Content Is Currency*, states that "through content, you connect. Content is the currency that powers the connection. It speaks to us, makes us want to share it, and motivates people to buy."

Simply put, all those wonderful social media channels we have today are useless without epic content.

SOLUTIONS FOR CUSTOMERS

In 2008, I partnered with Newt Barrett to write *Get Content Get Customers* (McGraw-Hill). Two paragraphs toward the beginning of the book are still relevant 15 years later:

> Marketing organizations are now realizing that they can create content whose quality is equal to or better than what many media companies are producing. Moreover, they are seeing that they can deliver tangible benefits to prospects and customers by offering relevant content that helps produce solutions to some of the toughest problems their prospective buyers are facing.
>
> By delivering content that is vital and relevant to your target market, you will begin to take on an important role in your customers' lives. This applies to your online, print, and in-person communications. And this is the same role that newspapers, magazines, TV, radio, conferences, workshops, and Web sites have played in the past. Now it's time for your organization to play that role.

CUTTING THROUGH THE CLUTTER

Today we have the same opportunity we had 15 years ago, but the stakes are higher. Yankelovich, a marketing research firm, states that consumers were exposed to about 500 marketing messages per day in the 1970s. In 2021, consumers are bombarded with as many as 10,000 or more.

But consumers aren't tuning out—they are becoming highly selective. According to MarTech, in 2020 the average B2B (business-to-business) buyer engages with 13 pieces of content before making a buying decision.

This number will continue to increase as consumers engage in even more media. According to Statista, the penetration of smartphones is more than 85 percent in the United States alone. That means almost all of us have content-gathering tools with us at all times.

And let's face it: we have a relationship problem with our phones. Nomophobia, the fear of not having your cell phone, has been growing dramatically in the past few years. Here are a few stats:

- 47 percent of US smartphone owners consider themselves "addicted" to their cell phones. (Reviews.org)
- 83 percent of Americans feel uneasy leaving their cell phones at home. (Reviews.org)
- On average, in 2022, Americans check their smartphones once every four minutes. That's approximately 344 times each day. (Reviews.org)
- In 2020, 45 percent of Americans said they would rather give up sex for a year than give up their phones. (Small Business Trends)

And according to a 2019 Statista survey, over 76 percent of cell phone owners engage in content on their cell phones *while* they watch video or television content. This means that even though your customers are being inundated with content 24/7, *they can and do let messages through that they want and need.*

THE CASE FOR CONTENT MARKETING

When the first edition of this book came out, it was a struggle to convince traditional marketers and brands that using content and storytelling was a legitimate marketing strategy. People would often ask if "content marketing" was a buzzword and if it would last.

In the last decade, more brands have seen the value of content marketing, but it's still a relatively small industry compared with advertising.

But the last three years have seen some dramatic changes.

The global pandemic, the great resignation, and the widespread adoption of remote work have changed the way we live, work, and communicate. The growing number of content entrepreneurs and the increase in brands looking to buy media companies and acquire communities have created opportunities for content marketing at all levels.

THE CONTENT CREATION REVOLUTION

If you follow the stock market at all, then you understand what a correction is. Technically, a correction in the stock market happens when stocks (as a whole) decline at least 10 percent over a relatively short period of time, usually after a good run-up in stocks (called a "bull market").

Over the last 60 years, we've seen (for the most part), a bull market in paid media. Most marketing programs have revolved around paid media of some kind. Even today, while online channels account for 56 percent of marketing budget spend, more than 60 percent of that is spent on paid channels according to Gartner.

When I worked at Penton Media in the early 2000s, I had the opportunity to discuss marketing budgets with several B2B marketing executives. There was heavy investment in trade show exhibits, print advertising, and sponsorships. The remaining dollars went to public relations. The pennies on the floor went to owned media (content marketing).

It was clear back then, and it is even clearer today, that most brands were (and are) overweight in paid media and underweight in owned media. The movement (make that the *revolution*) of content marketing is a necessary correction in the marketplace. Brands of all sizes are making a huge organizational shift toward content creation.

REASONS FOR THE SHIFT

There are many reasons for this shift. Here are a few to chew on:

- **No technology barriers.** In the past, the publishing process was complex and expensive. Traditionally, media companies spent hundreds of thousands of dollars on complex content management and production systems. Today anyone can publish for free online in five minutes (seconds?) or less.
- **Talent availability.** Journalists are no longer wary of working for non-media companies. Many journalists have left their jobs working for traditional media organizations and stepped into roles in content marketing. In addition, with a new generation growing up producing content on their phones, there is a wider talent pool available who know how to develop engaging content.
- **Content acceptance.** You don't have to be the *Wall Street Journal* to have engaging content that is shared. Consumers are deciding on the spot what is credible and what is not. Brand trust has become a big priority for consumers. According to the "Trust Barometer Special Report" (research published by Edelman in 2020), "53 percent of respondents say 'whether you trust the company that owns the brand or brand that makes the product' is the second most important factor [after price] when purchasing a new brand."

  And recent research by 5W Public Relations shows that 83 percent of millennials want to buy from companies that align with their beliefs and values, 65 percent have boycotted a company because of their stance on an issue, and 71 percent will pay more for a product if they know that some of the proceeds go to charity.

- **Social media.** Social media won't work for most brands without valuable, consistent, and compelling information creation and distribution. If brands want to be successful in social media, they need to tell captivating stories first. According to Statista, more than 92 percent of businesses use social media for marketing to customers. This type of penetration means that more organizations are trying to figure out what kind of content to put into those social media channels.
- **Google.** One of Google's recent major algorithm (how Google determines its search engine rankings) updates, MUM (Multitask Unified Model), shows that the company is putting more and more importance on quality content. Google is trying to provide the most valuable answer to a user for a specific search and is looking across the entire landscape of content (text, audio, video, etc.). So if you want to be found in search engines today, it's almost impossible to game the system (sometimes called "black hat search engine optimization") without a solid content marketing strategy.
- **Covid.** Few things have had the type of global impact that we've experienced with the pandemic. The increased reliance on digital channels and remote technologies, combined with the lack of connection and solitude everyone was experiencing, has created an even greater need for brands to use content to form those connections with their community.

Don't get me wrong, I'm not a traditional marketing hater. I believe that an integrated program of paid, earned, and owned media works best. Content marketing works best when it's integrated into the entire marketing organization (more on that later). But simply put, most of us are still overweight in paid media. Until we see more substantial resources shift to the owned media side of the house, the correction will continue.

EVERYONE IS NOW A CONTENT CREATOR

More and more companies, especially tech companies, are creating (or buying) their own media teams to connect with their audience and provide content they need. Salesforce, HubSpot, JP Morgan, and many other technology and financial services companies are actively growing their content assets through organic growth and the acquisition of media and creator brands.

In a tweet in 2020, Dharmesh Shah, the CTO and cofounder of HubSpot, said: "Modern media companies have a software company embedded inside. Next-gen software companies will have a media company embedded inside."

Brian Armstrong, the CEO of Coinbase, wrote a blog post specifically talking about companies becoming their own sources of truth to combat misinformation spread through traditional media or social media channels. Armstrong commented, "The tools for distribution have become democratized, and every company can become a source of truth."

Apple, Amazon, and John Deere have all discovered the value of creating media to grow their audience and generate revenue. In fact, 2021 saw a streaming service, Apple TV+, win an Academy Award for best picture for the first time ever, only three years after launching the service. In 2022, most Oscar winners came from movies that initially launched on streaming networks.

DOES TRADITIONAL MEDIA HAVE A FUNDING PROBLEM?

A few years ago, the IAB (Interactive Advertising Bureau) held a one-day event on the state of the media business as it pertained to content marketing. During the event, one publisher stood up and announced: "We simply do not have the resources that our advertisers have. We cannot hire the quality journalists and do the amount of research necessary for the amount of funding (advertising) we get. But at least all my journalist friends who were terminated for budget reasons are finding homes on the brand side."

We have seen this statement take hold and shape the media industry in the past 10 years. More and more journalists have moved into content creator positions for product and service companies or begun to build their own audiences as content entrepreneurs.

Advertising spend in traditional media has dropped sharply due to the much more effective targeted and personalized advertising that is available through digital platforms. As more publications rely more heavily on reader subscriptions, those publications must cater to the public demand for relevant news, often changing headlines or coverage based on input from social media.

According to the 2022 Edelman Trust Barometer, nearly half of the 36,000 people surveyed see the media and government as divisive forces in society, while they see businesses and NGOs (nongovernment organizations) as unifying forces. That survey also showed that 58 percent of respondents will buy or advocate for brands based on the brands' beliefs and values. In short, people want businesses to lead and be credible. Creating trust among customers hinges on putting out honest content about a brand's beliefs.

This is especially critical for local businesses. An article in the *Washington Post* stated that "about 2,200 local print newspapers have closed since 2005 and the number of newspaper journalists fell by more than half between 2008 and 2020." This dramatic reduction in the number of local newspapers has created "news deserts" across the United States and forced many people to find other sources of local news.

The Edelman Trust Barometer also showed that people have a higher level of trust for their own company's CEOs and coworkers. For the second year in a row, "My employer" media is the most trusted source of information among respondents, and information quality is the most powerful trust builder across institutions.

The point is this: *traditional media outlets no longer have the trust or financial resources to compete with corporate media sources*, providing companies of all sizes with incredible opportunities to build trust with their brand, connect with their audience, and create a community of loyal consumers.

This same convention applies to content entrepreneurs. If you consistently create valuable, honest, and engaging content, you can grow your community and create followers that will trust your opinions and take your advice.

Indeed, today we truly are all publishers.

HUNTING AN AUDIENCE

The hope is that by now you have figured out that publishing is not dead. Far from it; in fact, publishing has never been stronger. What is dying is the business model of solely ad-supported content. This leaves an opportunity for you—if, and only if, you put the processes in place to tell valuable and helpful stories for your customers and prospects.

Brand publishers (non-media companies such as Intel, DuPont, or the local plumbing company), media companies, and content entrepreneurs have the same goal. That goal is to build an audience, one that loves your content so much that it leads to subscription. That, in turn, leads to finding ways to monetize that audience.

Brand publishers and content entrepreneurs are challenged with trying to get found in search engines, drive leads, and figure out social media. All that hinges on creating helpful, valuable, and compelling stories that position them as trusted experts in their fields. That content, if worthy, will convert casual, passerby readers into loyal ones. In turn, those loyal readers may then be converted into loyal customers.

Media companies and content entrepreneurs are trying to do the same thing—*exactly the same thing.* The only difference is how the money is generated from the content (more on this in the next chapter). In my recent book, *Content Inc.*, second edition, I talk about the importance of consistency in content frequency. "To be great, you have to show up. Then you have to be interesting. *Every. Single. Time.* In short, the job of marketing is no longer to create customers; it is (to paraphrase Peter Drucker) to "create *passionate subscribers* to our brand."

An underlying theme throughout this book is about attracting and keeping an audience. Once the audience is built, that is when the magic happens. That is when marketers see long-term results. Content marketing without a loyal audience is not content marketing at all. Your content can't accomplish much without an engaged audience or community. And even though this book presents some thoughts about how media companies are competing with you for the same audience, they can be powerful partners to help you grow and sustain your audience.

THE BUSINESS MODEL OF CONTENT MARKETING

There have been many examples of content marketing throughout the years. John Deere sells tractors to farmers, but John Deere is also a publisher. Deere creates and distributes content just like any media company in the agricultural space. But the business model behind it is very different from the model that media companies use.

There is only one thing that separates the content developed by a media company and content developed both by brands such as Intel, John Deere, and Walmart and by content entrepreneurs: *how the money comes in.*

For a media company, content is created to make money directly from the creation of the content through *paid content sales* (direct purchase of content, like a subscription) or *advertising/sponsorship sales* (someone sponsors the content that is created, similar to what we see in newspapers and magazines or commercials).

For a non-media company, content is created, not to profit from the content directly, but to attract and retain customers (to sell more or create more opportunities to sell more). *Content supports the business* (see Figure 3.1), but it is not *the* business model (meaning that non-media companies are not required to make revenues directly off the content itself).

In all other respects, the content creation activities are generally the same. This is important to understand. Non-media companies and individual creators compete with traditional media for attention and retention, just as you compete with the regular competitors in your field.

FIGURE 3.1 Content marketing goals (*Source: Content Marketing Institute/ Marketing Profs*)

THE TILT BUSINESS MODEL

The Tilt, a company Joe founded, profits directly from the production of content. Although we position ourselves as an education and training organization, we leverage a media business model. This includes:

- **Email newsletter content.** The Tilt creates daily web content and delivers that content twice a week to subscribers for free. Companies that want to reach The Tilt's audience of content entrepreneurs pay for advertising and sponsorship opportunities.
- **Sponsored courses.** The Tilt produces educational "mini" courses that are funded by a corporate partner.
- **Paid courses.** We created longer-form instructional courses that subscribers can pay for directly (these are nonsponsored).
- **In-person events.** In 2022 we launched the Creator Economy Expo (CEX). We produce in-person content that attendees pay to get access to (paid content) and that sponsors support to interact with their prospects (the attendees).

Although The Tilt employs a number of content marketing tactics, we are, in a business model sense, a media company.

SEPARATE BUT INTEGRATED

We've just spent a fair amount of time telling you how different content marketing is as a business model. For some small businesses and content entrepreneurs, a content marketing approach may be all you need.

But if you work in a company of any size, this "different" approach will need to be integrated into *all* the other marketing you do. As Robert Rose says in the next chapter, "Content marketing is *a part of the integrated marketing mix*—not separate from it."

Over the past decade we've spent so much time evangelizing for the practice, sometimes we believe it can stand alone. Well, it usually cannot. Content marketing is made better by advertising, events, and public relations. And social media, sales, and loyalty programs are made better by content marketing.

In the next chapter, you'll understand where you are as an organization to either develop or alter your content marketing business case, which today is not a side project, but a plan that should be directed at (and involve) the marketing from the entire organization.

EPIC THOUGHTS

- Your customers are exposed to over 10,000 marketing messages per day. Are your messages cutting through the clutter and making an impact?

- In the past, entering the content creation and distribution business was filled with all kinds of barriers. Today all the barriers to entry are gone . . . paving the way for you (if you choose).

- The future of media is not the media; it's brands like yours. Like it or not, your competitors are starting to wake up to this fact.

EPIC RESOURCES

- Jon Wuebben, *Content Is Currency*, Nicholas Brealey Publishing, 2012.

- Joe Pulizzi and Newt Barrett, *Get Content Get Customers,* McGraw-Hill, 2009.

- Siteefy, "How Many Ads Do We See a Day?," accessed June 16, 2022, https://siteefy.com/how-many-ads-do-we-see-a-day/.

- Martech, "B2B Buyers Consume an Average of 13 Content Pieces Before Deciding on a Vendor," accessed June 16, 2022, https://martech.org/b2b-buyers-consume-an-average-of-13-content-pieces-before-deciding-on-a-vendor/.

- Statista, "Smartphones in the U.S.—Statistics & Facts," accessed June 16, 2022, https://www.statista.com/topics/2711/us-smartphone-market/.

- Reviews.org, "2022 Cell Phone Usage Statistics: How Obsessed Are We?," accessed June 16, 2022, https://www.reviews.org/mobile/cell-phone-addiction/.

- Smallbiztrends.org, "66% of Americans Check Phone 160 Times a Day, Here's How Your Business Can Benefit," accessed June 16, 2022, https://smallbiztrends.com/2020/03/2020-mobile-phone -usage-statistics.html.

- Statista, "Most Popular Smartphone Activities of Second Screen Users in the United States While Watching TV as of January 2019," accessed June 16, 2022, https://www.statista.com/ statistics/455377/smartphone-usage-while-watching-tv/.

- Gartner, "The State of Marketing Budget and Strategy 2022," accessed June 16, 2022, https://emtemp.gcom.cloud/ngw/ globalassets/en/marketing/documents/marketing_budgets _2022_research.pdf.

- Edelman, "Trust, the New Brand Equity," accessed June 16, 2022, https://www.edelman.com/trust/2021-brand-trust/brand-equity.

- 5WPR.com, "Consumer PR Culture Report | PR Firm Research Report: 5W Public Relations," accessed June 16, 2022, https:// www.5wpr.com/new/research/5wpr-2020-consumer-culture -report/.

- Statista, "US Social Media Marketing Usage Rate in the United States from 2013 to 2022," accessed June 16, 2022, https://www .statista.com/statistics/203513/usage-trands-of-social-media -platforms-in-marketing/.

- Edelman, "Trust Barometer Special Report: Brand Trust in 2020," accessed June 16, 2022, https://www.edelman.com/research/ brand-trust-2020.

- Twitter, "Dharmesh on Twitter: Modern Media . . . ," accessed June 16, 2022, https://twitter.com/dharmesh/status/ 1313859320493285376.

- Edelman, "2022 Edelman Trust Barometer," accessed June 16, 2022, https://www.edelman.com/trust/2022-trust-barometer.

- *Coinbase Blog*, "Announcing Coinbase Fact Check: Decentralizing Truth in the Age of Misinformation," accessed June 16, 2022, https://blog.coinbase.com/announcing-coinbase-fact-check-decentralizing-truth-in-the-age-of-misinformation-757d2392d61a.

- *Washington Post*, "Local News Deserts Are Expanding: Here's What We'll Lose," accessed June 16, 2022, https://www.washingtonpost.com/magazine/interactive/2021/local-news-deserts-expanding/.

- Joe Pulizzi, *Content Inc.*, 2nd ed., McGraw-Hill, 2021.

CHAPTER 4

The Business Case for Content Marketing

BY ROBERT ROSE

Luck is not a business model.
ANTHONY BOURDAIN

It feels like we've been down this road before, doesn't it?

In 2011, and the last time we were coming out of an economic challenge, it was all about "innovation." In fact, when Joe and I wrote *Managing Content Marketing* in 2011, our very first chapter noted this, saying:

> Building the business case for innovation is a huge piece of starting to introduce an innovative process like content marketing into an organization. Why? Because it's quite simply getting permission to fail. There's no way to prove return on investment (ROI) before you innovate because by definition it hasn't been proven before. In order to build more innovative and disruptive processes in your marketing, you have to have the capability to tolerate more failure.

We then went on to suggest building small experiments or pilot programs, and then outlined a plan for building the business case, innovation, and plan.

Five years later, when I wrote *Experiences: The 7th Era of Marketing* with my colleague Carla Johnson, the case for content marketing was wrapped distinctly in the blanket of getting "organized" with something we were already doing. We said:

> Marketing departments are currently working separately to highlight the company's value by creating more digital experiences than ever before. What must change is the structure of the strategy that delivers a cohesive, connected, and consistent portfolio of experiences that integrates everything a brand does (physical or otherwise) to help create the total customer experience.

Put simply, we won the argument in 2011 to go do cool, innovative stuff, so we just started doing it. But in fact, by 2018, we'd done too much cool stuff—and some of it was great, and some of it was poor. But all of it was disorganized.

And that brings us to another five years gone by.

IT'S THE OPERATION GAME

Remember the wonderful game Operation? It was a game where you had to carefully remove bones and organs from a patient on a table. And if you slipped up and touched the metal walls, the patient's nose would light up and buzz.

In a nutshell, that's content marketing these days.

Here's an anecdotal bit of evidence when it comes to building the current business case for content marketing.

In 2019, my consulting group helped 35 businesses develop a business case and strategy for content as a function in the business. At least 25 (83 percent) were primarily focused on developing a better lead-generation engine. Four (13 percent) were focused on brand and purpose-driven strategies. And the remaining one (4 percent) was focused on loyalty and better customer experiences post-sale.

By the way, all of them are firmly in the camp of "We're doing this because we have to be more organized, measured, and scalable."

In 2022, we worked with 52 companies on their content marketing operations. Thirty-nine of them (75 percent) were focused on how content marketing can help enhance every part of the business funnel. In other words, it was no longer a question of whether content marketing was an innovative practice. It is. And it's no longer a question of how we can get more organized around any one experience in the customer's journey. It's all of them.

The business case and need now is to determine how we institute content marketing as a functional operation and not just a series of one-off campaigns.

The strategy/challenge is focused on two key (and different) questions:

1. How do we successfully build (or merge as the case may be) the teams of content strategy (governance, processes, structured content, data, and technology) with content marketing (creating valuable, purpose-driven, content experiences)?

2. How do we scale this new operation to make it efficient, measurable, and manageable?

The business case has changed. And you better be sharp about it because you're about to get yelled at (maybe you'll be yelling at yourself if you're a content entrepreneur).

If your current business case is to prove the concept to your boss by showing how competitor X has an amazing blog, competitor Y won an award for its white paper program, or competitor Z is driving better awareness with its print magazine, you'll mostly get shrugged shoulders and a lifted eyebrow.

You see, many marketers are still answering, "Why should we do content marketing?" believing the folks in the C-suite are skeptical. *They aren't.* They're wondering why it's taken so long for us to get there.

In other words, we're asking for a new model car, and the CEO is saying, "What the hell have you been doing with all the parts that we've been buying?"

THE BUSINESS CASE FOR STRATEGIC CONTENT OPERATIONS

Make no bones about it—this pushback hits every aspect of any content strategy we want to stand up. Just as an example, our last two advisory engagement inquiries weren't about why the business should launch a content marketing approach. In both cases, the CEO of that company had issued a directive to launch strategic content as a core piece of the company's marketing strategy. But that same CEO challenged the members of the team to not *add* to the existing costs, but instead find a way to do it within all the content they were already producing. And to make the resources available to do that, they had to fix the entirety of the content as a strategic function.

"Beware," one of them said. "Our CEO now doesn't believe we can do this. They believe we already have too much content." But the thing is, once we dig in, it's not that the CEO doesn't believe in content marketing. Nor is it that they don't understand what content marketing is. They are skeptical about why no one has bothered to think strategically about all this stuff in the first place.

Let's look at the common pushbacks to implementing content—and specifically content marketing—as a strategic function that we're hearing these days and address them one by one.

LET ME COUNT THE WAYS

In Content Marketing Institute's 2022 research across thousands of marketers at businesses large and small, we examined which factors marketers attributed to a minimal or lack of content marketing success. By a huge margin, the top two factors were content creation challenges and strategy issues.

This is where the "we-already-suck-at-it" pushback comes from senior management. Why should management invest *more* in content when your brand struggles with the content you're already creating?

Of course, no one actually says this part out loud. In business, we tend to couch our reservations in much softer terms like "pushback" or "concerns." We hear things like:

> "There is already too much content. Shouldn't we reduce the amount of content we are creating?"

> "Content marketing costs too much. Isn't social/search advertising/ paid media more efficient?"

> "How can we compete? I don't know if we're capable of creating differentiated content. Isn't there that thing called 'content shock' out there?"

> "We can't tie the content marketing approach to revenue. Where's the data? How will we measure this?"

Let's acknowledge that every single one of these concerns is or has been true at different times. Now let's address each one and figure out how to make the business case.

THERE IS ALREADY TOO MUCH CONTENT

Here's an interesting twist that we've found across the hundreds of clients we've worked with over the last couple of years. Almost none of them create too much content. Yup, you read that right—almost none of them. But almost all of them create too many assets.

What, what? What do we mean by that?

We are trained (as marketers and business practitioners) to think container first, content second. We start with "I need a web page," "I need an email," or "I need a blog post." Then we go right to creating content for that container. It's inefficient and is entirely limited by our content production (as opposed to creation) capabilities.

This focus on content production is a symptom of not having codified any type of strategic content operating model. Yes, we can build a smart "factory" of content, but unless there's a specific purpose behind what we put on the assembly line, the widgets won't ever be valuable, and we won't know when we're making too many.

The answer to the "There is already too much content" objection is to acknowledge it and respond that this is the primary business opportunity for putting a strategy behind it. One of my favorite questions to ask a CFO to make a business case for content is, "How much did you spend on content last year?" The answer (if it can be answered at all) is that it's almost certainly the biggest expense that's not actually tracked by the company.

We *must* get our arms around this. Developing an operational model for content is the critical piece that will enable us to track not just how much we are spending on content, but how much we will spend for the planning, activation, and measurement of all the content we will produce. This will allow us to know how much content is enough, because that little voice in the brain that asks "Are we actually creating too much content?" is correct in what it's implying. It's rarely not that we are making too much different content. We are simply stuck in a cycle of duplicating assets in different containers in a never-ending rinse-and-repeat cycle.

That brings us to the second objection.

CONTENT MARKETING COSTS MORE

Somewhere in the collective consciousness of marketing—especially digital marketing—"paid media" became the de facto standard for how much things should cost. Any new approach that comes along is put through the same filter: Is it cheaper or more expensive than advertising? If it's cheaper, it must be worth doing, and if it's more expensive, it's not.

The troubling thing about the question is that it assumes two things: (1) "advertising" and the costs associated with it are as good as it's going to get and won't degrade further, and (2) we are pitching content marketing as a replacement for paid media (*spoiler alert:* this is the biggest culprit for the business case challenge).

In other words, it may (or may not) be true that content marketing is more expensive than advertising today. But what if advertising completely fails one day, and we haven't invested in an alternative form of marketing? Or what if (and hear me out just a second) advertising on its own actually costs more than we truly admit?

That brings us to the second (and bigger) erroneous assumption—we are proposing it as a replacement for advertising. This isn't true. Content marketing provides multiple ways to draw value, and *all* of them are interdependent on public relations, paid media, sales, and loyalty programs.

Content marketing is *a part of the integrated marketing mix*—not separate from it. When we present the approach of content marketing, it should not be as a set of campaigns that are meant to replace (or be cheaper than) a paid media advertisement. In fact, quite the opposite. The content marketing approach is about the development of the *product of content,* with which we will integrate all other types of marketing, including paid media.

At its heart, a great content marketing program is a content product operation that builds, activates, and promotes our customer experiences, which ultimately benefits the sale of our other products and services. This is why the great content marketing experiences that you're showing the C-suite are almost always publishing platforms like blogs, resource centers, events, or print magazines. They are meant to be an integrated part of your content operation and measured in similar ways.

But that means we must treat them with the same skills, budgets, care, and feeding that we do our products. An amazing blog, a differentiated podcast, and a killer thought leadership program should be as important as the products we sell, if not more important. This is because they *are* demonstrative of the value of the products we sell.

That then leads us to the third objection.

HOW CAN WE COMPETE?

If our business was hurting, and the head of product management came to the CEO and said, "We can't create great products," how might the CEO react?

What if that situation was reversed? In either case, the head of product management may be looking for a job. The ability to create great products and services is *core* to our business.

If we're treating content seriously, why would we expect anything less? The only reason this assertion will be true is if we don't try hard or care.

Remember, nobody has truly figured this out. You are *not* late. Not yet. As an example, PR firm Edelman and LinkedIn recently conducted research about the potential of thought leadership for B2B marketing. Almost half (48 percent) of decision makers spend an hour or more per week engaged in thought leadership. Only 15 percent of those same decision makers rated the quality of the thought leadership as "excellent." Further, only 29 percent of them said they gain valuable insights more than half the time.

This all means that the current bar for thought leadership (and content marketing in general) is pretty darn low. If we're not providing thought leadership for our industry, the real question is who is? Are we going to rely on our competitors to set the bar for what "smart" looks like in our business?

And then take it another step. Maybe you think you can't create better content than the media businesses in your industry. Think about that for a second. Most likely, you have more resources (or maybe truly differentiated talent) than any media company out there.

Joe and I have been involved in hundreds of content marketing engagements. Many of those engagements were with media companies. Oh, how the media companies would complain about lack of resources and only "wish" to have half the resources of a product company. We found the only reason why media companies outperformed product or service companies is because of a smarter strategy (with fewer resources).

That brings us to our last objection that I'll cover here.

WE CAN'T TIE CONTENT MARKETING TO REVENUE

The short answer here is, then don't.

There are myriad ways to associate content marketing with business value (see the Chapter 20 on measurement). Revenue is but one. If you can tie any of your marketing and advertising to revenue, then you can tie content marketing to revenue.

But if we dig deeper, the real assertion here is that content marketing is "too fuzzy" to associate with a sale, and thus it's hard to draw a straight line to revenue. Now this may be true, but it's not an argument for not doing content marketing. This is simply a challenge to how we design our measurement program—and ensure we apply the proper goals to our content operation. Show me a company that struggles to measure content marketing, and I'll show you a company that struggles to measure marketing.

Put simply, a blog that is meant to support brand awareness should not be measured by how many leads it produces. Likewise, assets stored in a fully gated resource center to drive leads should not be measured by how much it powers awareness through search engine optimization.

Each of the various content operating models will have different (and distinct) measurement goals (see Chapter 20). This is why it's so critical to understand that operating model.

This is what we're really driving for: a business case for a content operating model.

YOU'RE IN GOOD COMPANY

Here's something that will either comfort you or keep you up at night. Ready for it?

You're not alone. Nobody has this completely figured out yet. Nobody. Well, OK, maybe except for a few of the case studies in this book.

We've spilled gallons of digital ink over the years talking about how content marketing isn't a new thing for businesses. It's been around for hundreds of years. We point to the *Michelin Guide,* John Deere's *The Furrow* magazine, and even the *LEGO Life Magazine* as prime examples. But I can tell you that over the years I've talked with and/or consulted with every one of those companies, as well as so many others that serve as "case study" fodder at conferences, and all of them, without exception, are just like the rest of us: feeling our way, exploring, on a journey to make the business case. Every. Single. Day. As the leader at one of the most frequently mentioned content marketing case studies said to me in 2022, "I wish my boss could see all the times we're mentioned as a case study. I'm still fighting for budget every single month."

But guess what? This struggle is not a sign that content marketing isn't working. It's a sign that it's just become a normal part of marketing.

The big rock we must get over—the business case of today—is that the classic content marketing adage that "We need to act like a media company" is mostly misunderstood. It's not that we need to create stuff that helps us market ourselves as a media company would. No. *The goal is that we need to operate as a media company does.*

That's what we're building a business case for—a scalable operational model of content that's as important as any product or service we offer in the market, an operation that helps power everything in modern marketing.

When making our renewed business case for content, remember that no single new marketing approach is going to change the business. But one new approach to marketing can be the reason the business changes.

EPIC THOUGHTS

- Content marketing is not something that should be separate from other marketing. It's our responsibility to integrate it, when it makes sense, with the other parts of marketing to a particular audience.

- Today the CMO is actively pushing for a content marketing strategy. Maybe your organizational problem is that your CMO doesn't know why a thorough content marketing strategy hasn't been completed yet with the assets currently in use.

EPIC RESOURCES

- Robert Rose and Joe Pulizzi, *Managing Content Marketing: The Real-World Guide for Creating Passionate Subscribers to Your Brand*, Content Marketing Institute, 2011.

- Robert Rose and Carla Johnson, *Experiences: The 7th Era of Marketing*, Content Marketing Institute, 2015.

- Content Marketing Institute, "B2B Content Marketing [New Research for 2022]," accessed July 9, 2022, https://contentmarketinginstitute.com/2021/10/b2b-power-content-marketing-research/.

- LinkedIn Marketing Solutions, "2021 Edelman-LinkedIn B2B Thought Leadership Impact Study," accessed July 9, 2022, https://business.linkedin.com/marketing-solutions/b2b-thought-leadership-research.

CHAPTER 5

Content Marketing: Interviews with Top Players

BY BRIAN PIPER

Growth and comfort do not coexist.

GINNI ROMETTY

If you've ever seen the movie *Jerry McGuire*, you remember the blue mission statement. This is the moment in the movie when Jerry McGuire (played by Tom Cruise) wakes up in a cold sweat and writes what he believes is the future direction for his sports agency: one with fewer clients, more customer service, and more individual attention on the athletes.

Amanda Todorovich had that vision when she started working at the Cleveland Clinic.

CASE STUDY: CLEVELAND CLINIC

In 2012, Cleveland Clinic launched the *Health Essentials* blog to provide expert answers to health-related questions. In 2013, Amanda took over the blog, and for the past 10 years, she has created a revenue and brand awareness–generating media company within the organization as well as one of the premier case studies for content marketing. Amanda is now the executive director of content marketing at Cleveland Clinic.

INTERVIEW WITH AMANDA TODOROVICH

Brian: You started working at the Cleveland Clinic 10 years ago. How did you create the focus on content marketing and build to where you are today?

Amanda: It's been quite a journey. I started in February of 2013, and I was really hired for the blog and to lead social media. I had a team of about three people. They didn't know quite where we could take it, but they knew they were onto something. The blog was doing well, getting about 250,000 visits a month.

I came in and started asking a lot of questions about how they were deciding what to write. And as it turned out, they had this crazy spreadsheet that was collecting a bunch of requests from internal stakeholders for future blog post topics. They were running around, stressed out and anxious about how to prioritize and keep people happy, while trying to get help from the physicians to be interviewed in the posts.

My immediate reaction was to throw this out the window. This spreadsheet was not going to do it. We initially created a system to understand who the audience was we were trying to attract and what they wanted to learn about from Cleveland Clinic. And that's what got our physicians excited, because they too wanted to provide the information their patients wanted to know, and they needed our help communicating it.

We did that early on. About six months after I got there, we were at a million visits a month. And then about a year later, we were around 3 million visits a month. Today it averages anywhere from 10 million to 13 million visits a month just for the blog. But as we grew, there were questions like, what else can we do with this? How else can we leverage it?

We started monetizing in small ways about 2015. We partnered with Verywell Health and did that for quite a while. We expanded over time as my role evolved a bit too. Today I am responsible for pretty much all the digital content for Cleveland Clinic. Everything on the entire website, beyond the blog, and all of our social media, podcasts, video, voice, all of it.

The team has also grown and evolved a lot through the years. It wasn't that we added people or added positions overnight. A lot of it was changing marketing, integrating existing staff and teams, and eventually promoting and involving other leaders within and kind of spinning off stuff. Because at certain points in time, it felt like everything became content marketing. And that's not true, right? Not all content is content marketing.

We expanded the monetization strategy to be inclusive of our health library content, as well as our physician blog, and have been growing that piece of what we do substantially over time. And we switched our monetization and publishing partner this year. It's no longer just fun and gravy; it's built into the budget, and we treat content as a business. It's evolved a lot from just a fun experiment to something meaningful to the organization.

Traffic . . . I can't, I don't even know how to explain. Covid obviously did some crazy things to healthcare, and we saw a lot of upsides to that. *Health Essentials* had a record year in 2020. And we were publishing more content than any of us had ever done in our careers. It was the most intense year of my life.

What's interesting is that 2021 and 2022 are even bigger. And not with a Covid focus. It's everything else. At the beginning of 2021, I was giving a presentation to our executive team on where we were with our health library content and our content marketing efforts. It was sort of routine to talk about the impressive growth. We're doing amazing.

And our CEO said to me, "This is really great, but our biggest competitor is still doing more than we are." And he challenged me and asked what it would take to become the undisputed leader in digital healthcare content. And I said, "Oh, um, a lot. We're a great big team, but we are not what they are. And we're also not structured quite like all the publishers that we're really competing with in this space."

We presented a plan that had a five-year strategy. He said, "Good, but I want it in two years. Come back in 10 days and tell me what it takes to do it in two years."

We did that. The healthcare industry is still trying to recover financially from Covid. And when we made this ask, I never thought it would get approved. It was sort of like pie in the sky—this is my dream team, and it's never going to happen. But we'll put it together, and we'll answer their question.

We did. And it got approved, kind of unanimously by our executive team in the first quarter of last year. And what it meant was adding about 60 FTEs to my team. And we've hired most of those already. And a lot of it has to do with expanding our content marketing presence.

The health library is an area where we need to be more comprehensive, and it's not even just about being competitive; it's about being that trusted go-to source of information for people. Our strategy is being there in every moment of need.

If you're looking for something that's going to help you take care of your-self and your family, Cleveland Clinic shows up. And it's not just that we want you to make an appointment with us, because most of the time you won't, depending on where you live. But we want to be known as that source that has that answer. And that we do it in a way that's truly credible and it's not about us.

When you read a *Health Essentials* article or you read a health library article, there's never any mention of Cleveland Clinic. The content itself is meant to be useful, helpful, and relevant to people all over the world. And that has been true since the day I stepped in the door and started working on *Health Essentials*. Our core strategy hasn't really changed. It's just scaled dramatically.

And the institution has bought in and supported content the whole time because they've seen the growth. Everybody knows that digital is the future. It really is where people start their journey with us. Even if they're going to call for an appointment, they still go to the website to find the phone num-ber. You must make sure that you have the best foot forward, and that we're starting the journey for patients with great information that's accurate and reviewed by our medical experts.

Everything my team does is a true partnership with medical experts. We don't publish anything without their review. It's grown; it's scaled. It's gone from a blog and a handful of social media accounts, to a blog, every social media channel, podcasts, videos, voice, and an expansive website that is on track to get more than a billion visits this year.

Brian: How do you coordinate that sort of expansive effort across so many channels with so many people?

Amanda: What we're doing right now is on a scale unlike anything I've ever experienced. The collaboration and involvement of many other teams and departments is essential to the success of this and our ability to deliver the content we must. I spend a ton of my time personally going around present-ing the plans, the strategy, the approach, and talking about why this matters, so that when my team is coming to ask for your help, to interview you, or to have you review something, you know where it's coming from.

And I think that's an important part . . . that everybody needs to see the North Star. What are we trying to do? And why does this matter to our patients? To other industries? To your customer? And why is this significant or important?

I think that it's also about inclusivity. It's not just my team telling everybody what to do. It's conversations around how we do it. It's conversations about what those partners and stakeholders need from us to be able to help more. It's experimenting with different models and approaches to collaboration and being a bit open-minded. It doesn't always have to be the way it's always been.

We test and iterate on everything. And we involve as many different people as we can because we need a lot of help, especially from our highest-level leadership. Having the CEO endorse a project, having the CMO stand behind you and support you when you need someone to lean a little harder on this particular group or this particular area, has been really critical. But this is a huge undertaking, and it's been all about collaboration. Literally, my full-time job is nothing but relationship-building right now.

Brian: What kind of advice would you give another brand that has been doing some content marketing and is looking to expand? How did you build your team in a way that was effective and didn't get in too deep, too fast?

Amanda: I'm approaching my 10-year anniversary with the Cleveland Clinic, so this didn't happen overnight. We started small. My team was three people when I got here, and it's not been about a lot of additional FTEs until this past year.

Most of it was just reorganizing and aligning teams to be working more closely together. Editorial became a centralized team. How we approach growth and traffic-driving became a centralized team, so that things become more coordinated and aligned, and you're not constantly competing or bumping heads on strategy.

A huge key to success has been constant, consistent communication up, good, bad, and ugly. It's about how incremental results have occurred. I didn't just go in five years after we started with some big presentation. It was routine, regular updates. And even still in the middle of this big project, every single week, I'm sending out an update to key stakeholders on what's going on and where we are with numbers.

And sometimes they're great and sometimes not, but everybody knows where we are. And it really does keep people grounded in what's going on. And again, when you come asking for support and help, they know the story already, and you're not playing this big game of catch-up. It's just this incremental journey with consistent communication.

Brian: What's the makeup of your team? How many people do you have doing strategy? How many editors?

Amanda: Our team is structured into three big buckets: editorial, content growth, and then product and operations. Editorial is straightforward. Those people we want writing all day long, and we try to make our process such that that's really their focus. They're not distracted by a lot of other things. That said, some of those team members also are involved in video script writing. They might be involved in the podcasts, because that podcast interview might turn into a series of *Health Essentials* articles. That's the hope. Again, efficiency is the name of the game, so we involve the writers in everything that's going to enable them to create the most relevant content possible.

The content growth function is all the levers we have to pull to drive traffic. So that team is SEO, social media, email, podcasts, video, and voice because those are a little bit smaller, and mostly around repurposing. So content that we're doing for other things they're then leveraging to try to get maximum exposure or to utilize them across those different channels in different ways.

I don't run our media production studio; that's a whole different thing. The video that my team does is primarily for our own purposes. Either it's health library content, it's for social media, or it's the podcast in video form. It's, again, more of an efficiency play of the things that my team is already doing that we need video components for. Most of that work is outsourced with a partner that we've had in place for quite a while.

And then with voice, we're repurposing a lot of content. So that team takes the editorial daily tips and is reformatting them and putting them into the right systems to enable a lot of what we're doing there. With podcasts themselves, we have our anchor show, the *Health Essentials* podcast, which is produced the most often. My team completely manages that process. We work with our clinical teams to schedule the experts, and we produce it.

There are other shows that some of the service lines do on their own. They will work with our media production studio and produce them, but my team then manages the entire web presence including all the app implementation. We are doing 17 shows now. We're trying to juggle it all.

And on the email side of it, we do a lot of different newsletters. We're working in Marketo. We're working in Dynamics. [Marketo and Dynamics are both software programs.] That team is small and mighty, but really trying to just orchestrate the whole series of emails and make sure that we're doing everything legally and with best practices and staying on top of lists and everything like that.

And then the third arm of my team is the product and operations team, which really helps keep everything moving. We have a handful of people that we call content architects, who are working with people from the other functions to build the pages, making sure we're creating the right experience to display that content, and using all the features and functionality and components that we have at our fingertips to build a great experience for the user, depending on what that intent is, and what we're trying to do.

We have project managers on that team who are helping facilitate this work, keeping track of everything, putting everything into our WordPress system, and making sure everybody's got the reports they need. That team also interacts a lot with our actual development team. I have a colleague who runs the development side, but our operations team will tell them, "This is what we need next. These are the components we don't have that we could use to do this." There's a lot of collaboration on that front too.

Brian: How much of your effort goes into creating new content and how much into optimizing existing content?

Amanda: It ebbs and flows a bit. It might be 60/40 or 70/30 depending on the day or what's in front of us, but we definitely put a lot of resources behind optimizing existing content. Most of the stuff that we publish is evergreen. Medicine doesn't change that much. There might need to be updates and tweaks as things evolve, but for the most part, the diseases and conditions we treat are pretty much the same.

We make sure that our content is ranking well, is accurate, and is updated. We have everything reviewed every two years, no matter what, because medicine and treatments evolve, and we need it to be trusted and accurate. At the same time, when that much of your traffic is coming from organic search, it's also understanding what's behind that—how much are people searching for a particular topic? And is this article the best it can be? And if the answer is no, then we have work to do. And we keep doing that work.

With *Health Essentials*, articles that we wrote 10 years ago are definitely not the same as what we're writing today, with how our style has evolved, the length of them, and all the capabilities and team members that we now have, they're different. Just because a topic was covered 10 years ago doesn't mean we can't go back, redo it, overhaul it, and make it great. We need to use what we have available to us today for that same topic. We do a ton of optimization and updating.

Brian: You talk about treating your content marketing as a product. Do you still stick to that?

Amanda: Absolutely. Content marketing is not some fad and is not a project. These are products. People subscribe to a product from you. They engage with your content with expectations of you. And product development, and the way you think about traditional marketing from that perspective in terms of the price to engage with you, the packaging of the content, the promotion, and the placement, it all applies.

When you think about it that way, and you think about those elements, it changes your mindset completely. This is no longer just another blog post. This is how you deliver a client or a customer something they're sacrificing time, an email address, or something else for. They're purchasing it from you, and you have an obligation to deliver value and do something great.

CASE STUDY: SALESFORCE

Jessica Bergmann has transformed the structure of content marketing at Salesforce, creating a centralized content structure that allows the company to deliver consistent value to its customers. Jessica is vice president of content and customer marketing at Salesforce.

INTERVIEW WITH JESSICA BERGMANN

Brian: How did you change your organizational structure to help support the companywide focus on content marketing?

Jessica: The most important organizational change we made was to make content marketing a strategic function in marketing, with an equal seat at the integrated planning table with product marketing, campaigns, and creative teams.

This organizing principle is what really changed outcomes for us. And it's endured, even as some parts of the team have shifted from a centralized to a distributed model.

To do this, we introduced two new roles—content strategist and editorial lead—and added these roles to each of our brand, persona, and industries teams. Content strategists on each team are responsible for content plans that address audience needs and orchestrate the experience across our owned and earned channels. Editorial leads manage the editorial calendar and ensure a consistent voice and tone for a given audience.

This helps us bridge what audiences are looking for and how we achieve our business objectives. Content teams wake up every day to think "audience-first" and how we earn the right to market to the audience while offering every next step to learn more about our products and services. And they do this in partnership with product marketers, creative, and campaigns teams focused on how to educate about our products, tell our brand story, and hit ACV (annual contract value) targets.

Another crucial part of our organizational structure is a centralized content operations team. Our mighty team of four manages a central content operations tool for all global teams, managing real-time editorial calendars, workflows, tagging and taxonomy, and a global measurement dashboard. They've onboarded hundreds of team members around the globe, and work hard every day to stop the slew of new spreadsheets and separate folder systems that prevent teams from working together. And approaching things consistently.

When your teams know how content will be measured, what exists, when it's coming, and how they can plug into a bigger effort, that is when you see the change.

And while there's never a perfect organization, there are a few lessons we have learned along the way.

You need the support of your most senior marketing leadership to make content marketing a priority and a strategic function. It was a massive change management exercise and still is. Our CMO recognized we needed to make this change, and without CMO support, I'd say it's nearly impossible to make it happen.

You also can't create a companywide content strategy and playbook and expect all teams to adopt it. You do need to hire for content marketing expertise and teams trained to put this strategy into action.

We first operated as a small center of excellence and consulted teams that influence or produce various forms of content. We gave them the frameworks, tools, and templates and empowered them to run. We spent a lot of time teaching teams how to fish, and then they would say, "Just tell me what to produce." Or "What's the bill of materials?" They wanted a checklist or a container to fill.

Truly great content requires an understanding of "What are we solving for and why now? Who's the audience? What can we uniquely offer when there are so many content sources out there?" And a lot of those teams didn't want to go through that process. They just wanted to create something and move on.

This is why we've found success with content marketers acting as a strategic function in each team, supported by global content operations. It's been our momentum for success and what allowed us to create big strategic and innovative efforts like Salesforce+ and the award-winning "Leading Through Change."

Brian: Do those content strategists and editorial leads report up to a central team, or do they report to their individual groups?

Jessica: When we kicked off what we called the #contentrevolution a few years back, we had all of the strategists and editorial leads report into a centralized team, but they were also embedded into the day-to-day planning of their respective brand, persona, or industry teams. Many of the strategists even joked about having a dual personality since they felt like a part of two teams.

In an effort to move faster during the pandemic, we made the switch to a more distributed model and moved the content strategists and editorial teams directly into their operating units for clouds and industries. The brand content strategy team remains central and supports our biggest brand initiatives globally, also acting as a center of excellence for the operating units. Our social, editorial/blog, customer marketing, and content operations teams are also centralized, in addition to a new video marketing function. This newly formed video marketing team supports YouTube and our digital streaming service for business, Salesforce+. These centralized teams manage our channels and owned media properties and work with strategists and editorial leads, as well as contributors across the company.

Brian: You have some really big projects and initiatives—Dreamforce, Vantage Point, and Salesforce+. How do you coordinate and maintain consistency with so many things and especially things that require so many touchpoints across so many different people?

Jessica: Well, you've hit on the key challenge for our team. Especially at an organization of 80,000 employees that moves incredibly fast. The only way to manage all these initiatives and moving parts is for teams to work with central systems and from a central strategy. You must have that. If everyone's working in different systems and has a different understanding of the truth, you can't deliver magic. So our investment in content strategy and operations and tight partnerships with cross-functional teams at the company is how we deliver content across so many touchpoints and audiences.

We regularly look at our priorities as a marketing organization and team using a V2MOM (vision, values, methods, obstacles, and measures) process. This is how innovation and big investments in content are made. When our marketing organization commits to big bets like Dreamforce, Salesforce+, and our recent #TeamEarth campaign, we put the full power of the company behind it.

We also write a team-level V2MOM to determine our resources and commitments to these big bets and our owned media channels and products.

This past year, we invested more in media products that allow us to build a meaningful first-party relationship with our audiences. That includes Salesforce+, the first digital streaming service for business; *The 360*, our blog and newsletter all about uniting your teams around the customer; *Vantage Point*, our first complimentary print publication targeted at an executive audience; and Trailhead, our free online learning platform.

All these efforts are outlined in our V2MOM—with clear measures of success—and then reviewed and socialized with our leadership and partner teams. From this, we establish the right working groups, meetings, Slack channels, and reviews.

This prioritization process—together with a very talented team—is how we manage Dreamforce, media products, big brand campaign launches, and new partnerships with the Olympics and Formula 1 in a single year.

We also use a content performance dashboard so anyone in the company can see how content is performing. We gave everyone access to content performance metrics, so teams are accountable and have a consistent view on what works and what doesn't, rather than cherry-picking vanity metrics to hold up as success.

We measure content performance by three factors: Did you bring in the right audiences? Did you keep them engaged? And did you move them to a next step?

Each content asset is scored on traffic, engagement, and progression using an algorithm. And we make it actionable with red, yellow, or green color indicators to show if the asset is below or above benchmarks for a particular content type.

This helps guide teams on what they need to optimize, promote, or cut. And it teaches us what works when we invest in optimization.

There is no doubt teams behave the way they're measured, so this content dashboard has helped us influence the right behaviors and more consistent content quality across teams.

Brian: You talk about the four Cs of content marketing—content, creative, campaigns, and customer 360. How do you use those to help align your teams?

Jessica: First coming from the B2C space, I saw how integrated teams planned together to deliver the best experience across channels to generate interest that leads to purchase. But in B2B companies, success is measured by getting contact information so sales can follow up. That leads to individual teams planning for 90-day windows and putting a contact form in front of everything so their team gets attribution. It also leads to "awareness" content that is locked up tighter than Fort Knox.

By planning together with the 4Cs, we can develop long-range efforts that reach the 95 percent of buyers not yet ready to buy, and the next steps that clearly explain how our products and services help them reach their goals. Together.

We can also better calibrate where we put our paid spend to support all parts of the journey. We now consider thought leadership, search, and timely editorial in relation to big campaign pushes and events. And getting someone to subscribe means success. This means we're in their inbox and consideration set when they're ready to buy.

It took time for the four Cs to find a groove and agree on who is responsible and who is the final approver. And a few empathy sessions to teach other teams how we work and why change is necessary to improve our content performance results. But we now operate as an integrated team and always check to make sure someone from the 4Cs is represented in all our planning sessions and key reviews or decisions. Our audience experience and work are better for it.

Brian: What advice would you have for content marketers working in large organizations who are much earlier in their content marketing journey?

Jessica: No matter your level or where you are in your content marketing journey, you have to be part of the early planning and define the right measures of success with your leaders. If you don't, you will be downstream from a lot of ideas, "meh" content, and opinions that will make success difficult.

I've been the very first content marketing hire. I've also been brought into teams that know they need to "do content marketing" but don't want to change the way they operate in order to do it.

It's a losing battle if you are given subpar content and processes and asked to "clean it up."

So start with "What does success look like?" and "How will we know if it's worked?"

If you're having a hard time getting a seat at the table, show them examples. This is what success can look like for us. This is what great content feels like, and this is how it can change our performance metrics. Show your strategy through mockups or existing work and paint a vision they can taste and feel.

My last piece of advice is this: *Focus on the one thing that will have the biggest impact and one quick win.* Show them early momentum while you make progress toward bigger, more meaningful goals.

This should get you a seat at the table and a path to success.

CASE STUDY: SWEET FARM

Content marketing doesn't have to happen in blogs or podcasts or produced digital media. Live streaming and virtual meetings have taken off in the past few years, partially due to Covid.

Sweet Farm started in Half Moon Bay, California, in 2015. It was initially founded as an animal rescue. It slowly evolved into a sustainable vegetable farm, as well, that started giving corporate tours and education. And then Covid hit and almost ended everything. Nate Salpeter is the cofounder of Sweet Farm, as well as a consultant and investor.

INTERVIEW WITH NATE SALPETER

Brian: Tell me about Sweet Farm, how it got started, and your original vision.

Nate: My wife, Anna Sweet, and I cofounded Sweet Farm back in 2015, but the story begins before that. She and I lived in Seattle. We were getting more and more involved with where our food was coming from, and we were educating ourselves. And the more we learned, the more we did not like it.

We started growing our own food on our rooftop in downtown Seattle. We had already been looking at parcels of land up in Seattle to start the Sweet Farm project when my wife got a job offer outside San Francisco. We went from downtown Seattle to just south of Half Moon Bay along the Pacific coastal highway. She grew up on a small farm in upstate New York; I just had exposure to farming through visiting my grandparents on a four-acre farm that just had piles of rocks. But we love learning and love surrounding ourselves with people who are really experts in their field.

We wanted to create an organization that was dedicated to helping others live a more compassionate and sustainable life. It began as a farm animal rescue. That was the first program that we started. Of course, we had to build out facilities to do that. Our first year was the first few rescues, getting the facilities in place.

But quickly, we realized that you can't talk about the food system without really addressing it as a system. So that meant expanding it to growing fruits and starting a vegetable program. We started this vegetable program and started to get people coming out who wanted to get their hands in the soil.

When Covid hit, all of a sudden, all of our programs screeched to a halt. Right? You can no longer interact. We had to figure out how to do two things. One is, how do we continue to educate, and continue to execute those programs? And the other is, how do we continue to bring in the revenue that is needed to support all these programs?

On March 25, 2020, we had an emergency board meeting, trying to figure out what we were going to do. And one of our board members, Jon Azoff, said, "Hey, you know, I'm stuck in all these meetings all day. I would totally pay you guys 100 bucks just to show up to, like, our coffee break. Just like 10 minutes. You just tell us a little bit about the animals, and it'd be great. Like it'd be fun."

We put that up online that night, right after the board meeting. My wife, Anna, put it up online, took out just a few dollars ad on Facebook, and the very next day, we got a booking, a random booking. I went out into the field, I had my phone, and it was just supposed to be 10 minutes. It turned into this 30-minute thing. And everyone was laughing and asking amazing questions. And I came back from the field, and I said, "That was incredible. Everyone enjoyed it. People were laughing and smiling."

It was clear that this is a great much-needed break for folks. It was different. The next day, we had three bookings. By the third or fourth day, one of our friends said, "You've got to call it, like, a 'Goat-2-Meeting,' right?"

We started using "Goat-2-Meeting." Within the first week, we were booking a week out. You fast-forward three weeks, we were already in Business Insider. Since then, it exploded through channels of everything from the news outlets to the podcast circuit. We were on NPR. We were in *Fast Money* and *All Things Considered*. We were a trivia question on *Wait Wait . . . Don't Tell Me*. It was just like a wild, wild ride.

Since then, we've done somewhere around 8,700 of those virtual engagements. It grew so quickly, that there was no way that we could handle all those calls. We worked with other incredible organizations doing very important work in the sanctuary space. At the peak, we're doing about 300 to 350 of these virtual tours a day.

It generated somewhere around 1½ million in revenue for the program, and a lot of that was paid out to our partners as well. It helped them stay financially afloat during the pandemic. And for us, it's all program expenses for the education programs. What was nice about the program, in addition to the financial piece, was the way we were approaching education.

For most of these people, from all over the world, this may be their first look into the issues in the food system. Here are a bunch of people at work, they're taking a coffee break, and they're not looking for doom and gloom. They're looking for something light and refreshing that will put a smile on their face. And it turns out, you can do education in that way, as long as you are very conscientious about how you layer in your messaging. You can still be informative without causing people to leave a coffee break depressed.

And it's not just the education. You must inspire people to take action. If you don't do that, then the impact gets limited right there. For a lot of these groups, it was very simple, right? They have corporate offices with coffee stations, or they have cafeterias at their companies or at schools where we can get the teachers and the kids and the parents to request that they try different plant-based creamers. And we were very honest with them. I don't like every type of creamer. For me, one type tastes funny, but other people love that one.

Brian: Can you talk a little about the impact Goat-2-Meeting has had on your business as far as opportunities, partnerships, or collaborations?

Nate: It opened up a lot. It gave us exposure to companies that we wouldn't have otherwise been exposed to. We have partnerships in place with WCG Clinical, for instance. They did 93 percent of the world's Covid-19 vaccine trials. They're a sponsor of one of our animals. We do monthly seminars talking about food, technology, ag technology, how to compost at your house, and we do all these virtual events. We build the curriculum based on what those groups are interested in and what the company goals are. Those kinds of partnerships came out of the Goat-2-Meeting program, just because they saw what we're doing and our passion for the mission.

LogMeIn is the creator of GoToMeeting. They reached out, and we weren't sure if we were going to get sued or something, and turns out it was their marketing team, and they were just over the moon. And so they sponsored us for a year. At this point, we're kind of free agents. So, you know, if there are other companies out there, who knows? But, yeah, it was just pretty wild.

EPIC THOUGHTS

- For content marketing to work, find out what success looks like directly from your executives.

- Systems matter. When everyone uses the same systems and is looking at the same numbers, progress happens. Rogue spreadsheets and reports generally undermine the system.

- Progress takes time. Cleveland Clinic became a content marketing powerhouse over a 10-year period. Be patient.

EPIC RESOURCES

- *Jerry McGuire*, directed by Cameron Crowe (1996, Tristar Pictures/Sony Pictures Entertainment).

- Amanda Todorovich, interview by Brian Piper, June 15, 2022.

- Jessica Bergmann, interview by Brian Piper, June 11, 2022.

- Nate Salpeter, interview by Brian Piper, June 16, 2022.

PART II

Defining Your Content Niche and Strategy

CHAPTER 6

The Six Principles of Epic Content Marketing

BY BRIAN PIPER

Empty your cup so that it may be filled;
become devoid to gain totality.

BRUCE LEE

We asked several industry experts how they defined "epic content marketing" and got the following answers:

Marketing that is so great, that people will pay for it.

—JAY BAER, CONVINCE AND CONVERT

It's not about the content—it's about the commitment to the process. It's very much like training to be a champion in any sport. Some (dare I say most) of your content will *not* be epic. Remember Prince left thousands of hours of content unpublished. The best creators in the world are epic, not because they find some niche or have something go viral, but because they commit to the long game and consistently give to their craft and their business. That's what helps you increase the chances that *some* of your content will end up epic.

—ROBERT ROSE, THE CONTENT ADVISORY

The great content is often visual, collaborative, and detailed. But to be truly epic, it needs to go beyond this. It needs to be differentiated in a bigger way. It may be so provocative that it moves a conversation forward. Or so engaging that a community springs up around it.

—ANDY CRESTODINA, ORBIT MEDIA STUDIOS, INC.

The Covid-19 pandemic has reminded us of the importance of being human. Whether a brand is B2C or B2B, the human element is more important than ever. Brands that make an emotional connection with their buyers have a better chance of cutting through all the clutter. Brands need to create a distinct personality so their buyers recognize their content.

—BERNIE BORGES, IQOR

It's all about the audience. Those who say that epic content marketing is about cutting-edge design, captivating visuals, or attention-grabbing headlines are looking at things from the wrong perspective.

How does your audience feel about your content? Does it answer a timely question, address a pressing challenge, or cause them to take action? Epic content marketing does these sorts of things and in a meaningful way.

—DENNIS SHIAO, ATTENTION RETENTION LLC

There's the three Es of content marketing that everything has to have in some combination: entertaining, educating, and engaging. When you are fully aligned with your brand, yourself, your history, who you are, and you are hitting all three Es and you're doing it well. That's how you get to epic content marketing.

—CHRISTOPHER PENN, TRUST INSIGHTS

There are two things that make content epic for me:

One is if the content changes the way I think or opens my mind to see things in a brand-new way.

Secondly, content is epic if it is produced at a higher level than any other content in the space around it.

—A. LEE JUDGE, CONTENT MONSTA

I think epic content falls primarily into two categories: content that makes you think, and content that makes you feel. Content that makes you think is focused on insights, not information. Create something that can't be found on Google. Feeling content derives from a sense of awe. To make people feel "awe," you need to touch an internal chord that is deep and unique. Humor is a third option, but I often find that people remember the humor but forget the product!

—MARK SCHAEFER, SCHAEFER MARKETING SOLUTIONS

I think the best content marketing strikes a chord with a customer. It doesn't need to necessarily "build a relationship" with individuals, but it needs to establish trust, expertise, and authority.

—CATHY MCPHILLIPS, MARKETING ARTIFICIAL INTELLIGENCE INSTITUTE

There's a lot of awesome content out there that is tons of fun to consume, but the truly epic content is the stuff that's not just enjoyable, but also strategically valuable. It supports broader business goals. Content for content's sake does little for the business, even if it's hilarious, heart-warming, or interesting. The special stuff checks both the "interesting" and "strategic" boxes.

— MELANIE DEZIEL, COFOUNDER AND VP OF MARKETING AT THE CONVOY

I think the one characteristic that makes content marketing epic is empathy. This is not only because it takes time to dig in and really understand your audience, but because it means delivering more emotion-driven content that builds a deeper relationship.

—CARLA JOHNSON, RE:THINK LABS

Before we dive into what makes content marketing work, let's look at why your current content may not work for or benefit the business.

- **It's all about you.** Remember, customers don't care about you; they care about themselves and their problems. We often forget that point when we describe how wonderful our widget is (that no one cares about). The more you talk about yourself and your products, the less that content is spread and engaged with.
- **You are afraid to fail.** Taking chances with your content and experimenting a bit reveals the possibilities for your content marketing and uncovers new and valuable customer stories. And

remember back to Robert's chapter (Chapter 4) on the business case? Failing may actually be *not* creating a process for content marketing.

- **You are setting the bar too low.** Your content marketing should be the very best in your industry—better than all your competitors' content marketing and better than that of the media and publishers in your space. How can you be the trusted expert in your industry if it is not?

- **You are not sourcing correctly.** Most brands outsource some portion of the content marketing process. Don't be afraid to find internal content champions and outside journalists, writers, and content agencies to help you tell your story.

- **You are communicating in silos.** Are you telling different stories in PR, corporate communications, social media, email marketing, and other media? Do all departments follow a consistent corporate storyline? Epic content marketing means that your company is telling a consistent story.

- **You don't seek out discomfort.** Seth Godin states in his book *Linchpin* that if you don't consistently step out of your comfort area, you are doomed to the status quo. Do something completely unexpected with your content from time to time.

- **There is no call to action.** Every piece of content should have a call to action. If it doesn't, at least recognize it as such and understand the real purpose behind why you developed the content.

- **You create a backup plan.** There is only try and reiterate. Forget a backup plan. A backup plan (for example, pay-per-click or sponsorship) is admitting to failure before you begin.

- **There is no content owner.** Someone in your organization (possibly you) must take ownership of the content marketing plan.

- **There is no C-level buy-in.** Organizations without C-level buy-in are 300 percent more likely to fail at content marketing than are companies with executive buy-in (according to Content Marketing Institute research). But then remember that most chief experience officers *want* to do content marketing.

- **You are not immersed in your industry.** Everywhere your customers are, you need to be (whether it be online, in print, or in person).

- **You are not serving a defined niche enough.** You need to be the leading expert in the world in your niche. Pick a content area that is both meaningful to your business and attainable.
- **You are too slow.** As much as I hate to say it, speed beats perfection in most cases. Figure out a streamlined process for your storytelling.
- **Distribution of content is inconsistent.** Your content marketing is a promise to your customers. Think about the morning paper (if you receive it): when it doesn't come on time, how upset are you? You need to have the same mindset with your content marketing. Distribute content consistently and *on time*. Develop your content marketing editorial calendar (see Chapter 12).
- **There is not enough thinking with search in mind.** Most likely, the largest portion of your website traffic comes from search engines. If you create pieces of your content with search in mind, you stay focused on the problem and how customers communicate that problem. You also get found!
- **You're not looking at your data to optimize your existing content.** You may have content that is on the verge of showing up on the search engines for terms that people are searching a lot. If you're not looking at your data, you'll never uncover those opportunities (see Chapter 21).

THE SIX PRINCIPLES OF EPIC CONTENT MARKETING

Perhaps you now think that there is no longer a need for sales-related content. That's far from the truth. The problem is that customers only need sales-related content at a very particular moment in the sales process. If you are honest about the content you have, your organization has plenty of feature- and benefit-related content. What you need are stories that engage your customers . . . and that move them to take action.

Now, before the principles of epic content marketing are reviewed, remember that the goal with content is to "move" the customers in some way. We marketers need to positively affect them, engage them, and do whatever we must to help stay involved in their lives and their conversations. The following are the six principles of epic content marketing. Follow them closely.

- **Fill a need.** Your content should answer some unmet need or question for your customer. It should be useful in some way to the customer, over and above what you can offer as a product or service.
- **Be consistent.** The great hallmark of a successful publisher is consistency. Whether you subscribe to a monthly magazine or daily email newsletter, the content needs to be delivered always on time and as expected. This is where so many companies fall down. Whatever you commit to in your content marketing, you must consistently deliver.
- **Be human.** The benefit of not being a journalistic entity is that you have nothing to hold you back from being, well, you. Find what your voice is, and share it. If your company's story is all about humor, share that. If it's a bit sarcastic, that's OK too.
- **Have a point of view.** This is not encyclopedia content. You are not giving a history report. Don't be afraid to take sides on matters that can position you and your company as an expert.
- **Avoid "sales speak."** The more you talk about yourself, the less people will value your content. Don't use jargon and avoid technical terms, unless those are the terms your audience uses.
- **Be best of breed.** Although you might not be able to reach it at the very beginning, the goal for your content ultimately is to be the best of breed. This means that, for your content niche, what you are distributing is the very best of what is found and is available. If you expect your customers to spend time with your content, you must deliver them amazing value.

EPIC CONTENT MARKETING IN ACTION

Think about the content sources that you rely on every day. What makes them so special? Do they provide information that you can't find anywhere else? Are they consistently delivered around the same day and time? Is there a particular point of view that you appreciate? Do they help you live a better life or grow in your career?

There are a number of content sources that I have "subscribed" to that have become part of my life:

- *Morning Brew* newsletter. Frequency: daily.
- *The Hustle* newsletter. Frequency: daily.

- *The Tilt* newsletter. Frequency: every Tuesday and Friday.
- *Total Annarchy* newsletter. Frequency: fortnightly.

As a business, your goal is to become part of the content fabric for your customers. If you do, selling to them becomes relatively easy.

THE EPIC CONTENT MARKETING PROCESS

Now that you understand what truly epic content is made of, it's your job to develop an organizational process for content marketing. As you'll see in the next few chapters, this process starts with the following:

- Identifying the goal or objective
- Defining the audience
- Understanding how the audience buys
- Choosing your content niche
- Developing your content marketing mission statement

This may seem like a lot for just a part of your marketing program (actually, it's not), but this is exactly what leading media companies do when they launch a magazine, newsletter, or television show. Since you are a publisher too, you need these steps as well. So many small and large companies start to develop content without a clear plan in place. I'm hoping this doesn't happen to you.

THE REST OF THIS BOOK

This first part of this book was designed to give you a solid foundation for what content marketing is and where the possibilities lie. The remainder of this book will focus on how you can find your story, how you can better understand the process of developing epic content, and how you can transform your organization or your content entrepreneur business into a content marketing factory that attracts and retains more of the right kind of customers.

Are you ready? Let's go!

EPIC THOUGHTS

- If you want to be successful in content marketing, your goal should be to develop and distribute the absolute best information in your industry. If not, why should your customers care?

- What are the informational sources on which you rely? Why do you engage in them? What makes them special? Can you be on that list for your customers?

CHAPTER 7

Content Is the Asset; Subscription Is the Goal

BY JOE PULIZZI

Champions keep playing until they get it right.
BILLIE JEAN KING

My favorite Michael Jordan/Nike commercial came out toward the end of his career. It's a 30-second spot of Jordan getting out of his car, walking past photographers, and going out a door. There's no flash and no game-winning shot. It's just Michael . . . and then you hear his voice.

"I've missed more than 9,000 shots in my career. I've lost almost 300 games. Twenty-six times, I've been trusted to take the game-winning shot and missed. I've failed over and over and over again in my life. And that is why I succeed."

The one thing that most people take from this commercial is that you have to try in order to succeed. But I think the meaning is so much deeper than that when applied to marketing and content goals.

ON SETTING GOALS

Success is easier to define for athletes (sorry, athletes). *There is usually a very distinct goal that an athlete is shooting for*: a championship, a gold medal, a specific time goal, or simply a game win. Michael Jordan always stated that his goal was to be the best basketball player to ever play the game. He measured that goal by leading the Chicago Bulls in winning the National Basketball Association championship six times, leading the league in scoring 10 times (more than anyone else in NBA history), and winning five Most Valuable Player awards.

For us mere mortals, business owners, and marketing managers, this is where we must start: we must have at least one tangible goal.

Michael Jordan knows when he's failed because he knows what his goal is. If a person doesn't have a goal, there cannot be failure. I believe that is why so many people don't set goals—they don't want to set themselves up for any failure in life. In some cases, the same is true for marketers.

Finding content goals that ultimately drive your business can be an excruciating process. *It takes passion, determination, and some soul searching to truly determine what kind of content you need to create that will have an immediate impact on your customer.*

Is there one overarching number, measure, or goal, like the number of championships won, that can drive our business?

THE BUSINESS GOALS OF CONTENT MARKETING

With content marketing, there are a number of possible business goals you can have. The following paragraphs show some of them, which make up key goals behind the content marketing buying funnel (see Figure 7.1).

FIGURE 7.1 The content funnel becomes the content hourglass when you add in the goals after sale. (*Source: Managing Content Marketing*)

BRAND AWARENESS OR REINFORCEMENT

Almost always, the first thing that comes to mind when you look at content marketing is brand awareness. The goal may be that you are just trying to find a more effective way than advertising to create awareness for your product or service. This is the long-tail strategy. Content marketing is a great vehicle for that, as it's organic and authentic and a great way for you to start driving engagement with your brand.

LEAD CONVERSION AND NURTURING

How you define a lead will vary, but from a content marketing perspective lead conversion is where you have encouraged others, through the exchange of engaging content, to give up enough information about themselves that you now have permission to "market" to them. This information exchange can include signing up for a "demo," registering for an event, subscribing to your e-newsletter, or gaining access to your resource center. Once you have the prospect's permission, you can use content to help move them through the buying cycle.

CUSTOMER CONVERSION

In many cases, you already have a lot of content for customer conversion. We marketers have traditionally focused on this area—the "proof points" to the sale. Examples include case studies you send to your prospects that illustrate how you've solved the problem before or a "testimonials" section on your client page. Ultimately, this is the content you've created as a marketer to illustrate to the hot prospect why your solution is better or will uniquely meet their needs.

CUSTOMER SERVICE

Content marketing can really earn its "subscribe" stripes with customer service. How well are you using content to create value or reinforce the customer's decision *after* the sale? This endeavor goes well beyond having a user manual, a documented process for success, and a "frequently asked questions" (FAQs) section on your website. These are the best practices for how to use your product or service. How can customers get the *most* out of your product or service? What are the successful, innovative ways that you've seen your product or service get extended into other solutions?

CUSTOMER LOYALTY AND RETENTION

Just as you have a planned lead nurturing process to turn prospects into customers, you also need a planned customer retention strategy. If your ultimate goal is to turn customers into passionate subscribers who share your stories, this area needs major attention. Options may be a customer e-newsletter or possibly a user event or webinar series.

CUSTOMER UPSELL

Marketing doesn't stop at the "checkout" button any longer. If you're particularly good at using content to service the customer in a subscribe model, you also have the opportunity to be effective at creating ongoing engagement for the other products and services you offer. Why stop communicating with prospects once they become customers? Instead communicate with them more frequently (certainly not in a creepy way), and engage them with additional value. Customer upsell and customer retention goals can work hand in hand.

PASSIONATE SUBSCRIBERS

If you can successfully move customers to this stage, you have really accomplished something. Content—and especially content generated by satisfied customers—can be one of the most powerful ways to reach any business goal. This is when content marketing starts to work for you exponentially.

So which of these goals makes sense for your content marketing? Maybe it's only an inbound marketing initiative and you're just trying to help drive more leads into the sales and marketing process. Maybe you're trying to create a program that increases awareness, drives down the cost of organic traffic to your website, and increases your position with search engines. Maybe you are working to improve your customer retention rate. Take a moment now to get your mental juices flowing. Write down your content marketing goal, and put it up somewhere so that you see it every day.

SUBSCRIPTION

Great ideas often receive violent opposition from mediocre minds.

—ALBERT EINSTEIN

Ann Handley, author of *Everybody Writes* (now in its second edition), is an amazing writer. When her fortnightly newsletter, *Total Annarchy*, launched in 2018, it went out to just over 2,000 emails. Three years and 100 newsletters later, its readership has increased to well over 40,000 readers.

Jimmy Donaldson started posting videos to YouTube in 2012 when he was 13 years old. Ten years later, his channel, @MrBeast, has more than 100 million subscribers, and he is one of the highest-paid YouTubers. He is the creator of MrBeast Burger and the Ocean Cleanup and has an estimated net worth of nearly $100 million.

General Electric has built an audience of more than 100,000 subscribers to its *GE Brief* newsletter and drives more than 3.7 million monthly visits to its GE Reports online media portal, which features content on emerging technology.

Ann Handley is a keynote speaker, author, and content expert. Jimmy Donaldson is a creator and content entrepreneur. GE is one of the largest companies in the world. Even though the businesses couldn't be any more different from one another, subscription is key.

CONTENT AS AN ASSET

Do most marketing professionals view content marketing as an asset?

The answer is no—almost across the board. Marketers view spending on content marketing as an expense. *This has to change.* We said this in the first edition, and we still see it over and over with marketers.

First, a question: What is an asset?

According to Investopedia, an asset is "a resource with economic value that . . . [a] corporation . . . owns or controls with the expectation that it will provide future benefit." An asset, like a house or a stock investment, is a purchase that can increase in value over time.

Traditionally, marketing spend has been viewed as an expense. Take advertising: advertisers create the ad and distribute it over a fixed time, and then it's over. The hope is that expense has transferred into some brand value or direct sales exchange, but the event itself is over.

Content marketing is different; it needs to be viewed and treated differently.

ACQUIRING THE ASSET OF CONTENT

Whatever your goals—whether direct sales, lead generation, search engine optimization, or social media presence—you are spending money on content acquisition and distribution. For that reason alone, you need to think differently about acquiring content assets.

You are not acquiring content expenses. You are acquiring an asset!

THINKING LIKE A PUBLISHER

We are all publishers, and that means thinking differently about content and its importance to your organization.

When you invest in a video, a podcast, or a white paper, those pieces of content create value in a couple of significant ways.

One, *the finished content is used over a long period of time; it has a shelf life.* The content you create has value long after the investment is paid off (fitting the definition of an asset; see Figure 7.2). An example is content created for search engine optimization. One blog post can deliver returns for years after production.

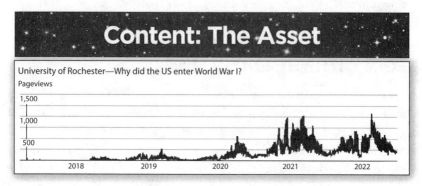

FIGURE 7.2 Content may not have immediate traffic, but it's value may grow over time as organic potential increases. (*Source: University of Rochester*)

Two, *content can be and should be reimagined and repurposed.* You may start by investing in a video, but at the end of the year, that single video may result in 10 videos, 5 blog posts, 2 podcasts, and 30 sales tools fit for different levels of the buying cycle.

When you think like a publisher, everything you develop for publishing purposes is an asset. Having that mentality means that you need to think about all the resources that create and distribute that content differently. It's not about a marketing campaign; it's about creating long-term engagement with customers through epic content.

HOW DOES THINKING ABOUT CONTENT AS AN ASSET HELP?

Thinking in these terms will help you in a couple of ways.

If you treat content as an asset, people in your organization will *stop treating content as that "soft, fluffy thing" that they can take or leave.* In every meeting or conversation you have, use the word "asset." Live it. That effort will start to rub off, and content will gain importance in the company.

By thinking this way, you will more actively *market the asset.* I heard a story recently about a company that invested $30,000 in a white paper and received only a handful of downloads. That's a marketing problem, not a content problem. Would you plan to sell your house but not tell anyone about it?

A lot of organizations do just that with their content: they produce the content but then don't let customers and prospects know it's available through basic paid and organic marketing (see Part IV of this book for more on marketing your stories). Make sure you don't make that mistake.

We need to elevate the practice of content marketing.

BEGIN WITH THE END IN MIND

At The Tilt, our business goals include brand awareness, thought leadership, and lead generation, as most businesses do. But everything The Tilt does starts with the subscriber. When you start looking at how you can build subscribers in different channels, here are a few facts regarding email versus social that you should consider:

- The typical social media user engages with an average of 7.5 different accounts (Hootsuite).
- Individuals average 1.75 email accounts (Prosperity Media).
- Americans spend less than 35 minutes on any one social channel (eMarketer).
- Americans average 300 minutes each day checking email (Small Business Trends).
- The average click-through rate (CTR) of the top three social channels is 1.11 percent (Status Brew).
- The average CTR for email across all industries is 10.29 percent (Constant Contact).

The data from The Tilt's survey of content entrepreneurs shows that email is a high-value vehicle, with as many as 85 percent of entrepreneurs sending email newsletters.

These statistics show the value of email subscribers over social media followers when it comes to reaching your business goals.

THE DIGITAL FOOTPRINT

Owned subscription sources (for example, print and email) are still primary, because content originators (aka publishers) can actually own the data from those channels (called first-party data). Secondary subscription sources, such as Twitter followers or YouTube subscribers, are important as well, but since that data is owned and the rules are controlled by other companies (and not by the originators of the content), you can't place as high an emphasis on those.

You are your own media company. As a media company, you need to focus on your subscription channels in order to deliver on your marketing goals. And the only thing that keeps those subscription channels growing and vibrant is consistent amounts of epic content.

Here are some tips to drive subscription:

- **Make content-for-content offers.** As readers are engaging in your content, be sure you have a clear offer that takes your content to the next level. This means offering a valued e-book, research report, or white paper in exchange for subscribing to your email list.
- **Use pop-ups.** As much as I loathe pop-ups or pop-overs as a reader, I *love* them as a content marketer. They work.
- **Focus.** So many companies want to throw 100 offers in front of their readers. Don't confuse the issue. If your goal is subscription, that should be your main (and only) call to action.

Once you focus on subscription as your goal, *make it a priority to find out what makes a subscriber different from a nonsubscriber.* Once you find that thing that makes a subscriber truly unique, you'll be able to plan relevant content, provide value to your subscriber, and start to build loyalty. Then everything will start coming together for your content marketing program.

EPIC THOUGHTS

- As a content marketer, don't create content for content's sake; do it because you want your business to grow. Focusing on your objectives is key.

- Stop thinking about your marketing as an expense. Invest in assets that will continually grow the business over the long term. If you look at marketing more like renewable energy, it makes all the difference in your planning.

EPIC RESOURCES

- Ann Handley, "How to Newsletter," accessed June 16, 2022, https://annhandley.com/ah/wp-content/uploads/2021/11/ah_100news.pdf.

- MrBeast, "@MrBeast," accessed June 16, 2022, https://www.youtube.com/user/mrbeast6000.

- General Electric, "GE Reports," accessed June 1, 2022, https://www.ge.com/news/.

- The Tilt, "8 Stats Show Email Subscribers Worth a Lot More Than Social Media Followers," accessed June 18, 2022, https://www.thetilt.com/audience/email-subscribers-worth-more.

- Hootsuite, "Digital 2022 Global Overview Report," accessed June 24, 2022, https://hootsuite.widen.net/s/gqprmtzq6g/digital-2022-global-overview-report.

- Prosperity Media, "How Many Emails Are Sent per Day in 2022?," accessed June 18, 2022, https://prosperitymedia.com.au/how-many-emails-are-sent-per-day-in-2021/.

- eMarketer, "Average Time Spent per Day by US Users on Social Media Platforms," accessed June 18, 2022, https://www.emarketer.com/chart/244117/average-time-spent-per-day-by-us-users-on-social-media-platforms-2017-2022-minutes.

- Small Business Trends, "Hey Marketers, Americans Still Spend 5 Hours a Day on Email," accessed June 18, 2022, https://smallbiztrends.com/2019/09/email-usage-statistics.html.

- Status Brew, "2021 Social Media Benchmarks Facebook | Instagram | Twitter," accessed June 18, 2022, https://statusbrew.com/insights/2021-social-media-benchmarks-facebook-instagram-twitter/.

- Constant Contact, "What Is the Average Click-Through-Rate for Email?," accessed June 18, 2022, https://www.constantcontact.com/blog/average-click-through-rate-for-email/.

CHAPTER 8

The Audience Persona

BY JOE PULIZZI

> Never underestimate the intelligence
> of the audience.
> ARMANDO IANNUCCI

Repeat this sentence: "I am not the target for my content." This thought is critical as you read this chapter. Business owners and marketers tend to bend their content to their thinking. Don't fall into this trap.

If you are thinking and acting like a media company and publisher, everything you do with your content marketing will begin and end with your audience. If you do not understand the wants and needs of your audience, there is no way you can be successful with your content.

Most of the time, marketers think that their content audiences are the same as their buying audiences. For example, John Deere distributes *The Furrow* magazine to farmers. These farmers are the same people that buy John Deere equipment. But in your situation, your direct-buying audience may not be the same as the audience for your content.

Let's use a university as an example. It has many audiences: some are buyers, some are influencers, and some are stakeholders. The first, most likely audience is the students. But there are also parents, who help support and fund the students. And there are alumni. And don't forget the teachers. And what about the local, state, and federal governments? Depending on the goal of your content program, you could target dozens of different audiences.

So before you start any content program, you need to have a clear understanding of who the audience is and ultimately what you want that audience to do.

WHY ARE AUDIENCE PERSONAS IMPORTANT?

An audience persona is a helpful tool to use as part of your content marketing plan. It's the "who" you are talking to and with.

When content is developed for your content marketing program, it is the persona that gives context. At any one time, you may have employees, freelance writers, agencies, and even outside bloggers creating content for you. *The persona keeps everyone on the same page with who is being talked to and why the communication matters for the business.*

AUDIENCE PERSONAS IN ACTION

Whether you're creating the persona as a B2B customer for a large brand (see Figure 8.1) or a B2C (business-to-consumer) customer, you will notice that these personas focus on the buying decision and the factors that go into the users making their final purchase choice.

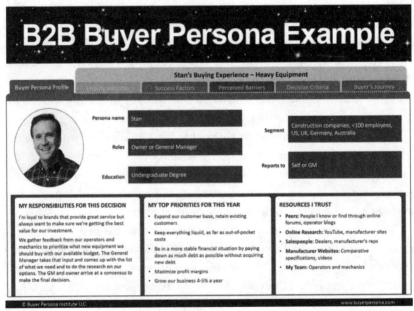

FIGURE 8.1 A sample B2B buyer persona from BPI (*Reprinted by permission of Buyer Persona Institute*)

MULTIPLE PERSONAS

Adele Revella, founder of the Buyer Persona Institute (BPI) and author of *Buyer Personas*, says, "You should never have more personas than you have capacity to go to market." This means, don't create 100+ personas if you don't have the resources to build different messages, content, and go-to-market strategies for all those personas. She says: "The goal is never buyer personas. The goal is better go-to-market strategies."

Hank Barnes of Gartner believes that businesses should create an enterprise persona. This persona is a detailed profile of the ideal customer. He comments, "I am 100% convinced that if vendors spend a fraction of the time they put into buyer personas on building an enterprise persona, they'd get an incredible payback."

PUT YOUR JOURNALIST HAT ON

What do you need to know about your persona? The easiest way to find out is by asking the following questions.

1. Who is it? How does this person live an average day?
2. What's the person's need? This is not "Why does the person need our product or service?" but "What are the person's informational needs and pain points as it relates to the stories we will tell?" It is also important to consider when, where, and how the person would want to receive that information.
3. Why does this person care about us? Remember, the persona most likely doesn't care about your products or services, so it's the information you provide that will make that person care or will garner the person's attention. The information should also showcase your ability to credibly deliver to the person's satisfaction.

Your audience persona doesn't have to be perfect, but it needs to be detailed enough so that your content creators have a clear understanding of whom they are engaging.

COMMON MISTAKES WHEN CREATING PERSONAS

Adele defines the persona as "a composite picture of the real people who buy, or might buy, products like the ones you market, based on what you've learned in direct interviews with real buyers."

The following are Adele's five key persona mistakes and how to fix each one.

MISTAKE NUMBER 1: MAKING UP STUFF ABOUT BUYERS

Marketers typically gather facts about buyers by talking to a sales representative, meeting with a product expert, or conducting online research.

It shouldn't be surprising that these sources don't have the information that marketers really need. Sales reps will readily admit that buyers mislead or even lie about how they compare and choose one solution over another. Moreover, even product experts are unlikely to be buyer experts, since they interact mostly with current customers as well as a select few big prospects. And mining online data leads to personas that are little more than job descriptions with high-level pain points.

If content marketing is going to benefit from persona development, it needs to uncover specific insights unknown to your competitors or anyone inside your company. This information is so valuable that you would never post it on your website. However, it will tell you, with surprising accuracy, exactly what you need to do to deliver content that persuades buyers to choose you.

How to fix this mistake. The only way to gather clear, unexpected insights about how your buyers make decisions is *to have a conversation with them.* Make it a goal to conduct in-depth interviews with recent buyers of the type of products and services that you offer. Ask buyers to walk you through their decision, starting with the moment they decided to solve this problem. Each in-depth conversation should take 30 or 40 minutes, but the time it will save you in planning, writing, and revising content will be immeasurable.

MISTAKE NUMBER 2: GETTING SIDETRACKED BY IRRELEVANT TRIVIA

Jim Kraus is the president of the Buyer Persona Institute. Jim says the key to not getting sidetracked is to remember that the persona is not about an individual; it's about the buying decision. BPI focuses on two buying decisions (or personas): the economic buyer (typically C-level buyers who make the decision to make a certain type of investment and sign off on the final purchase recommendation) and the buying committee (those involved in the actual purchase decision, including identifying potential alternatives, evaluating them, and making final recommendations).

Marketers sometimes make the mistake of gathering buyer information that doesn't really help them deliver more effective content or campaigns. If your marketing team is debating whether your buyer persona is a man or a woman, or if you are bogged down finding just the right stock image of your persona, then you are focusing on the wrong things. Unless you're a B2C marketer, the buyer's gender, marital status, and hobbies are rarely relevant.

How to fix this mistake. You may decide to include other data in your buyer personas, but content marketers really need only these "Five Rings of Buying Insight":

1. **Priority initiatives.** What are the three to five problems to which your buyer persona dedicates time, budget, and political capital?
2. **Success factors.** What are the tangible or intangible outcomes that the buyer associates with success, such as "grow revenue by X" or a promotion?
3. **Perceived barriers.** What factors can prompt the buyer to question whether your company and its solution can help with achieving their success factors? This is when you begin to uncover the specific reasons certain companies "drop out of the running" and others move on to the final selection stage and become the eventual winner.
4. **Decision criteria.** What aspects of each product will the buyer assess in evaluating the alternative solutions available? To be useful, the decision criteria should include insights from both a buyer who chose a competitor and one who decided not to buy a solution at all.
5. **Buying process.** What personas, processes, and information sources are used in exploring and selecting a solution that can overcome the perceived barriers and achieve the buyer's success factors?

These five insights, when gathered directly from buyer interviews, will tell you how to reach undecided buyers with content that addresses their key decision-making process points. Using the buyer persona profile and these five insights (go to EpicContentMarketing.com's bonus resources page to access this template) will help you organize your findings from your calls so that everyone on your team has access to these critical insights.

MISTAKE NUMBER 3: DEVELOPING TOO MANY BUYER PERSONAS

This mistake happens when marketers layer buyer personas onto their existing market segments, frequently defined by demographics such as industry or company size. Many people think they should create a new buyer persona for each of the relevant job titles in each of these segments. Not so.

One company I worked with initially planned to build 24 different buyer personas. Ambitious? Yes. Necessary? No. When the company started interviewing the buyers, it was able to pare that list down to 11. Because its marketers are continually conducting new buyer interviews and gaining new insights, the company expects to consolidate that list even further. Remember to only create a persona if you are actively creating content for that group of people.

How to fix this mistake. When you have captured the Five Rings of Buying Insight about buyers, you will see that differences in job titles, company size, and industry do not necessarily relate to differences in your insights. For content marketing and most other marketing decisions, you only need a separate persona when there is a significant difference in several of those findings.

For example, you may find that buyers of your RFID (radio frequency identification) technology in both the hospitality and consumer products industries have nearly identical priority initiatives (a mandate to be more competitive) and perceived barriers (an incremental approach is needed). If you have a strong story to communicate on each of these points, one persona may be the best way to ensure effective messaging and content marketing.

MISTAKE NUMBER 4: CONDUCTING SCRIPTED QUESTION-AND-ANSWER INTERVIEWS WITH BUYERS

Using a telephone script or online survey to learn about your buyers won't reveal anything you don't already know—inevitably, your buyer's first answer to any question is something obvious, high level, and not particularly useful. The structure imposed by surveys and scripts leads to nice charts, but it fails to reveal the new insights that you need.

How to fix this mistake. It takes a bit of practice, but you can learn how to have the unscripted, agenda-driven conversations that will lead recent buyers to tell you, in incredible detail, exactly how they weighed their options and compared your solutions with your competitors' offerings.

The key to success is asking probing questions based on your buyers' answers. For example, if buyers tell you they chose you because your solution is easy to use, you might ask follow-up questions to understand why the solution needed to be so. Or you might ask about what training the buyers expect to attend before the solution is considered to be "easy" in their minds. Another follow-up question might seek perspectives on the resources the buyers will consult, or steps they will take, to compare your solution's ease of use with their other options.

When you avoid these first four mistakes, your buyers' needs will be the focus of your marketing strategies and tactics. You'll become so attuned to your buyers' perspective that you will consistently impress them, confidently delivering content that answers their questions and persuades them to choose you.

MISTAKE NUMBER 5: THINKING THE PERSONA IS THE END GAME

The persona is just a tool to help you understand what it is that your buyer actually needs. You also need to have a solid understanding of what it is that your business offers. When you find the intersection of those two areas, that is the North Star you need to focus on and build your strategy around (see Figure 8.2).

FIGURE 8.2 The intersection of buyer needs and your business offerings

Having a persona is a great tool to help you craft your message. But if you don't take the final step to align the persona with your sales enablement strategies, and then ensure that you distribute the strategy directives, along with the persona, to your team, you'll be wasting your efforts. This "activation" of your persona by connecting it to the strategy is the critical step in having an effective tool to help you reach your goals.

SETTING UP LISTENING POSTS

I started in the publishing industry in February 2000 at Penton Media. I learned what great storytelling was all about from my mentor, Jim McDermott. Jim constantly talked about the importance of "listening posts." Listening posts are all about getting as much feedback from a variety of sources as possible so you can find the truth.

Setting up listening posts is critical for all editors, journalists, reporters, and storytellers to make sure they truly know what is going on in the industry. For you, listening posts are critical so that you have accurate audience personas and truly understand the "pain" they are going through on a daily basis. All of us need listening posts to truly discover our customers' needs. The following are all means of getting feedback from customers—in effect, functioning as listening posts.

1. **One-on-one conversations.** As in Adele Revella's key point, nothing can replace talking to your customers or audience directly.
2. **Keyword searches.** You can use tools such as Google Trends and Google Alerts to track what customers are searching for and where they are hanging out on the web.
3. **Web analytics.** Whether you use Google Analytics or another provider such as Adobe Analytics, diving into your web analytics is key. Finding out what content your customers are engaging in (and what they aren't) can make all the difference to your success.
4. **Social media listening.** Whether through LinkedIn groups or Twitter hashtags and keywords, you can easily find out what your customers are sharing, talking about, and struggling with in their lives and jobs.
5. **Customer surveys.** Survey tools like SurveyMonkey can easily be deployed to gather key insights into your customers' informational needs.

EPIC THOUGHTS

- As you grow as a content marketer, you'll have many, perhaps dozens or more, on your team creating content. Audience personas get all contributors on the same page.

- Almost certainly, you have multiple personas that purchase your products or services. It can get complicated. Start with the most important persona for your content plan.

EPIC RESOURCES

- Gartner, "The Enterprise Persona Provides the Context for (Pretty Much) Everything," accessed June 18, 2022, https://blogs.gartner .com/hank-barnes/2021/07/13/the-enterprise-persona-provides -the-context-for-pretty-much-everything/?_ga=2.164139199 .1415479479.1655591591-1263784611.1654095246.

- Buyer Persona Institute, "Buyer Persona Example," accessed July 9, 2022, https://buyerpersona.com/buyer-persona-example.

- SEMrush, "5 Buyer Persona Examples That Go Beyond the Basics," accessed July 9, 2022, https://www.semrush.com/blog/ buyer-persona-examples-beyond-basics/.

CHAPTER 9

Defining the Engagement Cycle

BY BRIAN PIPER

*They always say time changes things,
but you actually have to change them yourself.*
ANDY WARHOL

Creating an engagement cycle for your content is incredibly difficult. Most smaller businesses never even try to tackle it at all. But it's important . . . very important.

DOES ANYONE CARE ABOUT YOUR SALES PROCESS?

Simply put, the engagement cycle is a combination of your internal sales process and your definition of the customer's buying cycle. If your goal is to (try to) deliver the right content at the right time for your customers and subscribers, you need to understand how both work together in harmony. Without a defined engagement cycle, you are just creating lots of content and hoping for the best.

Just as in real life when you meet someone, determining what you want to say to a persona is a combination of two things: content (which is a function of your point of view) and context (you have to determine the correct time and place to start the right conversation).

The traditional way of advertising is to take your point of view and blast out the message to (it is hoped) a target group for your product or service. The theory goes that if you blast loud enough, long enough, and in the general direction of your personas, eventually you will reach some of them.

While advertising still works, there is always a lot of waste—it may not be done at the right time, in the right place, with the right content, and so on. The buying process has changed. The consumers now control the engagement with you; they control when and if they want to receive your message. It's up to you to have a relevant conversation with them from the very first time you meet.

But the reality is that you can't be prepared to have *every* conversation about your product or service at any time. No matter how many resources your organization may have, it's almost impossible to prepare for every scenario where you will be talking with a customer or prospect.

Additionally, when consumers have access to information at every moment, the customer buying process can be chaotic and nonlinear. In the past, when there were very few sources for consumers to get buying information, a business could predict, with some certainty, how a customer learned about the need for a product. That gave businesses a lot of control over how they marketed their products.

This is why, historically, marketers developed a sales process (or funnel), so that we might put some order to this chaos and have a common language in our business for the categories of sales opportunities. Depending on your business, you may categorize your consumers as "visitors," "leads," "prospects," or "readers"—and, ultimately, "customers" or "members."

If your organization is like most, even if you don't have a formal sales process, to some degree you try to deliver a relevant message to the customer during the sales process. For example, if you're selling widgets online, you may always try to cross-sell and upsell *after* the users have put items into their shopping carts. If you're selling big-ticket items, your salespeople probably have a well-defined funnel through which they pass leads (leads, prospects, qualified, and so on), and they give out case studies and testimonials after they've become "qualified."

But today businesses and content entrepreneurs are trying not only to create a "customer" but also to create subscribers who want to engage in the companies' content. Your ultimate goal is to create a true community that is filled with superfans. And while it's important for you to internally map your content to your sales process, you must remember that whether it's your shopping cart experience, a traditional lead-nurturing sales funnel, or conversion of customers into evangelists that love to talk about your company, this sales process is an internal and artificial process that you superimpose on the customers' buying experience.

Remember: *Your buyers don't care one bit about your sales process.* The sales funnel does not capture the emotional and realistic decision points that the buyers go through during their "buying process." And in fact, the goal or call to action may *not* be to have the "customers" purchase anything at all. Instead it may be to have them "refer a new customer" or "share their story."

THE ENGAGEMENT CYCLE

To deliver the best content at the right time, you need a better, more granular process. You need to combine your internal sales process with your customer's "buying" process and develop something new . . . something we call the "engagement cycle."

An engagement cycle is a defined process that your audiences go through as you help them engage with your brand. The engagement cycle is not perfect, but it can help with the development of compelling content at certain stages of the buying process that either aids the prospect in buying or assists the customer in spreading your content. In short, you need to be working hard to deliver the right conversations at the right time.

Let's look at each of the processes separately before we layer them together.

MAP YOUR AUDIENCE PERSONAS TO YOUR SALES PROCESS

The sales process is how you watch the consumer proceed through your sales and marketing efforts. Your funnel might be very well organized—as in the case of enterprise B2B marketing or considered purchases in B2C sales (for example, a car or house). In these cases, there are very defined and tight conversion layers where each stage is defined by the consumer behavior (lead, prospect, qualified, and so on).

However, if you run an online retail or brick-and-mortar shop, you might have looser or more generalized sales processes. One process might involve the following progression: visitor, to browser, to shopper, to buyer; interestingly, these stages might happen within seconds. Or if you're a publisher, the funnel might be visitor to subscriber. Many publishers just have a goal of creating a subscriber, whom they then use to monetize through advertising or upselling. Regardless of the time involved or the name for it, the sales cycle is how we content marketers identify those customers who:

- Know nothing about us
- Then know something about us
- Then are interested in what we have to offer
- Then compare us with other solutions
- Then do what we want them to do

For example, if you are a small business software company targeting IT decision makers, you have a fairly simple sales funnel process, which involves the following:

- **Contacts.** These are people whom you've contacted or with whom you have some level of introduction.
- **Leads.** These are people you've identified who have an active interest in your solution.
- **Qualified opportunities.** You have qualified leads having interest and a budget and from whom a purchase of some kind is likely.
- **Finalists.** These are qualified opportunities with people who have pared down their list to one or two options and who have your company in the mix.
- **Verbal agreement.** You are the chosen solution and in the negotiation process.

Your sales funnel may be more (or less) complex than that, or it may be completely different. But regardless of its complexity, you should have *some* kind of funnel for your business that tries to make sense of buying patterns.

THE CONTENT SEGMENTATION GRID

Simply put, the content segmentation grid is a mash-up of your sales process and the content you have that moves customers through that process. Why is this grid so important?

I'm sure you've seen companies, possibly competitors, create lots of content and throw it anywhere they possibly can. While this can work and has worked in the past, it's not much different from "spray-and-pray" advertising.

Developing a content segmentation grid minimizes the possibility that your content doesn't work and also provides you with clear opportunities to capture feedback and make improvements.

Now to build the content segmentation grid. You'll do this along two axes. The first axis is the personas, and the second is the sales funnel.

Once you have your grid, start filling in the cells with your existing or new content items (you can choose from among the types in Chapter 14). Going back to the software example, your content segmentation grid might look something like Figure 9.1.

Content Segmentation Grid

	SALES	CONTACTS	LEADS		QUALIFIED		FINALIST	VERBAL
PERSONAS	Ben Marketing Manager	White Paper 1 White Paper 2	Blog Subscription		Online Assessment	Webinar	Case Study 1 Case Study 2	
	Haley CMO	White Paper 3		Magazine		Online Assessment		

FIGURE 9.1   The content segmentation grid in action

One thing you may notice in this example is that most of the content marketing is focused at the top of the funnel. This is almost universally common, so don't worry if this is true for you as well. A content marketing strategy generally starts by focusing on awareness and education, which is almost always at the top of the funnel.

One benefit of this exercise is that it often reveals that the content marketing is either very light or very heavy on one stage or one persona. The middle of the content segmentation grid, often called the "messy middle," is usually where one needs to develop fresh content to fill in the gaps.

Once you are armed with your content segmentation grid, you are ready to take the next step, which is to layer in each audience persona's buying process.

MAP YOUR PERSONAS TO THEIR BUYING CYCLE

The buying process is how your customers buy from you or, once they've bought, what you want them to do next. What's their process? For your product or service, it might vary by product—or by persona—but what you want to do is map out how your customers buy from you. Figure 9.2 shows the customer's buying cycle for the IT software example.

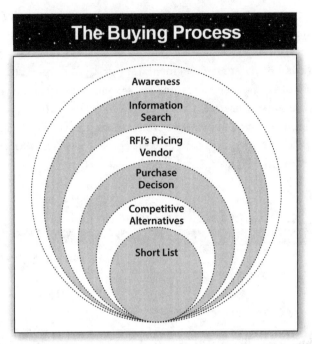

FIGURE 9.2 The buying process orbit (*Source: Managing Content Marketing*)

The buying cycle is represented as an orbit because it's usually not a linear process. In fact, during the buying process, consumers often jump in and out of orbits as they move closer in. But as consumers move closer to the center of gravity, the focus on what they want becomes more pronounced, and what they're looking at becomes more limited as they go through each phase. So, for example, with the IT software solution, each phase looks as follows:

- **Awareness.** Consumers are trying to figure out what options exist.
- **Information search.** Now the consumers are searching for information and finding solutions for their problems; this may be the first time you get a phone call.
- **Request for information (RFI) on pricing or vendor.** You have been identified. Ask yourself: "What makes us better? What is our pricing for this solution?"
- **Purchase decision.** This is not always the last step. People often go through researching a solution to their needs and then decide to *not* make a purchase. But those who do decide to make a purchase will go back to vendors and do a final comparison.

- **Competitive alternatives.** The online searches begin. Have you ever gotten a call from consumers who seem to be late in their process? This is where they are. This is the feature comparison stage. In many cases, consumers may be surprised by what's missing (or what's there) and may go all the way back to the awareness stage.
- **Short list.** At this stage the solutions are looked at very closely, and then a contract for the sale is presented.

Again, this is not perfect, but mapping this out is an invaluable exercise.

CREATE THE CUSTOMER/CONTENT SEGMENTATION GRID

Now that the sales process has been outlined and laid out side by side with the buying process, you can better understand the engagement cycle by mashing these together with your content assets.

As you see in Figure 9.3, the sales funnel is mapped with contacts turning into leads, then being qualified, and then going to finalist (or short list). But then, under that, the buying process, awareness/education, and so forth are mapped.

Content Segmentation Grid with Buying Cycle

SALES	CONTACTS	LEADS		QUALIFIED		FINALIST	VERBAL
Buying Cycle	Awareness and Education	Information Search Vendor	RFI Vendor Information	Make the Purchase Decison	Alternative Searches	Short List of Vendors	Agreement
Ben Marketing Manager	White Paper 1 White Paper 2	Blog Subscription		Online Assessment	Webinar	Case Study 1 Case Study 2	
Haley CMO	White Paper 3		Magazine		Online Assessment		

FIGURE 9.3 The content segmentation grid combined with the buying process

Notice that there's overlap between the sales funnel and the buying process. There are generally more conversion layers—or decision points—through the buying process than in the sales funnel. But this gives you a way to start to get a common vocabulary and a common way to map out a content marketing strategy.

You may find, for example, that there's a lot of content developed for leads in the "Awareness & Education" stage, but not a lot of content for leads in the "Information Search Vendor" stage. This tells you that you may want to spend additional time developing content that not only educates the audience to the benefits of your type of solution but also positions your company as a provider of it.

Don't get overwhelmed with this process; it's not a requirement to go to this extent. And you certainly don't have to develop content segmentation grids for every product, process, or audience persona. You may only do it for the process to which your new content marketing initiative is directed. Or perhaps you only need to do it to help move customers to evangelists that love you and will actively share everything about you and your company.

In the end, creating an engagement cycle and mapping that with your personas to create a complete content segmentation grid is a powerful way to see where there are gaps in your story.

EPIC THOUGHTS

- Your sales process (internal) has nothing to do with how your customers buy (external).

- The easiest course is to populate your content grid with lots of content at the top of the funnel. This is a completely natural impulse, but the opportunities may lie in the "messy middle," where customers need a little push to get close to that buying decision.

- Don't get stuck on this part of the process. If you feel you aren't ready, move on to Chapters 10 and 11, which deal with the content niche and the content marketing mission. Honestly, most companies don't map their content to the buying process (which is why there is such an opportunity here).

EPIC RESOURCE

- Robert Rose and Joe Pulizzi, *Managing Content Marketing*, CMI Books, 2011.

CHAPTER 10

Becoming the Leading Source for Your Customers

BY JOE PULIZZI

We are all experts in our own little niches.

ALEX TREBEK

When you're getting started with content marketing, here's the first question you should ask: On what topic can you be the leading informational expert in the world?

Brands don't take their content seriously enough. Sure, they create content in dozens of channels for multiple marketing objectives. But is your organization's *mindset* focused on being the leading provider of information for your customers? If not, why isn't that your priority?

Your customers and prospects can get their information from anywhere to make buying decisions. Why shouldn't that information come from you? Shouldn't that at least be the goal?

GETTING UNCOMFORTABLE WITH YOUR NICHE

One of my favorite parts of *The 10X Rule* by Grant Cardone is on *setting uncomfortable goals:* "Those who succeed were—at one point or another in their lives—willing to put themselves in situations that were uncomfortable, whereas the unsuccessful seek comfort from all their decisions."

The same goes for your content marketing goals. Your ultimate objectives—those big hairy audacious goals (BHAGs)—should make you cringe at least a little bit.

I disagree with marketing experts and consultants who say it's not necessary to be the leading information provider for your industry.

Yes, it is a bit audacious to go out on a limb and clearly state that your content marketing should be an irreplaceable resource for your customers . . . that you are indeed driving where the market is going from an information standpoint (like a media company). That said, be audacious!

If you are not striving to be the go-to number one resource for your industry niche, *you are settling for the comfortable*, whatever that means to you in goal-setting terms.

WHAT IF YOUR CONTENT WAS GONE?

Let's say someone rounded up all your marketing and placed it in a box, as if it never existed. Would anyone miss it? Would you leave a gap in the marketplace?

If the answer to this is no, *then you've got a problem.*

You should have customers and prospects needing—no, longing for—your content. It ought to become part of their lives and their jobs.

Makes you a bit uncomfortable, right? Darn straight.

What will you and your content marketing team have to do to reach that goal? What unique, audacious content creation, distribution, and syndication will you have to get involved in to truly be the leading resource?

This is your turf. Don't stand there and let your informational competitors steal time away from your customers.

THE TRUSTED EXPERT

If you truly have a product or story that is worthy of being talked about (if you don't, you have bigger problems than content marketing), then *becoming the trusted expert in your industry is central to you selling more on a consistent basis.*

Today it's harder and harder to buy attention. You have to earn it. Earn it today, tomorrow, and five years from now by delivering the most impactful information your customers could ever ask for. Set the uncomfortable goals that will take your business to the next level.

THINKING BIG, GOING SMALL

Let's say you run a small pet supplies store in the local community. You think your content niche is pet supplies. You're wrong!

Think about this for a second: Is it possible to be the leading expert in the niche area of pet supplies? Probably not. Companies such as Petco and PetSmart put millions behind that concept.

That means even though you want to think big with your goals, your actual content niche needs to be small. How small? As small as possible.

Let's go back to the pet store example. By looking at the key audience personas, you've noticed that the most questions, as well as your highest-margin products, are around aging pet owners who like to travel with their pets. Bingo! While you can't be the leading expert in just pet supplies, you can be the leading expert in the pet supplies needed by elderly pet owners who travel around the country with their pets.

But let's break this down even more by using Google Trends. The trending for "traveling with pets" has been steadily going down over the past 15 years. This means that fewer people are searching for that exact topic. If you look at the rising searches data within Google Trends to see search terms that are performing ahead of the pack, you'll find that "service animals" and "emotional support animals" are breakout terms (see Figure 10.1).

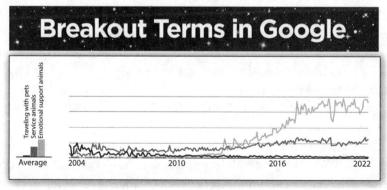

FIGURE 10.1 Which stock would you like to own: traveling with pets or emotional support animals? (*Source: Google Trends*)

While not an exact science, you can use search trends to identify content opportunities for your niche area.

HOW WE CHOSE CONTENT ENTREPRENEURS AS OUR CONTENT NICHE

I wrote *Content Inc.* in 2015 to detail the business model that we used to take Content Marketing Institute from zero to millions in five years. As we all know, Covid struck in early 2020 and changed so many things. It brought death and sickness and fear, and people lost their jobs and prospects.

I started getting more and more emails from friends asking about the *Content Inc.* model. As interest grew, book sales and podcast downloads started increasing. I saw a need. Specifically, that need was around the business of content. While there are people creating every kind of content on every feasible platform, most of those content creators don't understand how to set up their content business, build an audience that can be monetized, create real content systems that work, and understand what goes into an exit plan. And so we launched The Tilt in 2021 to cover those specific issues for those creators who truly wanted to be content entrepreneurs.

FRACTAL MARKETING

Your content niche can actually target an audience of one. A few years ago, Andrew ("Drew") Davis coined the term "fractal marketing" and used this technique in two amazing ways. He defined fractal marketing as continually splitting your customer into a smaller and smaller niche. His first example was how he used this technique to get a job at the Jim Henson Company (having limited experience and no connections) by writing a letter every month for three years. And the second was to engage with billionaire philanthropist Warren Buffett by writing a letter every day and creating a "Letters 2 Warren" Tumblr page, which resulted in confirmation that Mr. Buffett was reading his letters, led to an in-person discussion with Mr. Buffett in the green room of the *Today Show*, and eventually helped bring about changes in the newspaper industry.

Drew shows us that the smaller you go with your content niche, the higher the payoff in the long run. While you may never target an audience of one, the more you can narrow your audience persona, and thus your content niche covering that audience, the more successful you will be.

THE BEST PLACE TO START

Ardath Albee, the author of *eMarketing Strategies for the Complex Sale,* states that sometimes focusing on your best customers is the place to start with your content strategy. When she launched the company Einsoft, she didn't have the resources to target multiple buyers with multiple niches. So she decided to group her 10 best customers and look at the similarities among those customers. That became the audience persona, and the content niche was created focusing on that group (of just 10).

There is no silver bullet, but starting with a smaller, profitable group of customers is the best method for deciding which content niche you should explore as a business. Once you perfect a content strategy for that group, you can move on to other content niches targeting different audiences.

EPIC THOUGHTS

- The natural inclination is to go big with your content niche in order to cover more of your market. Avoid this urge. Go big with content marketing by going small with your niche.

- Focus your niche on the most valuable portion of your audience . . . and maybe even the few best customers you have.

EPIC RESOURCES

- Grant Cardone, *The 10X Rule*, Wiley, 2011.

- "traveling with pets," Google Trends, accessed June 20, 2022, https://trends.google.com/trends/explore?date=all&geo=US&q=traveling%20with%20pets.

- "'traveling with pets' [versus] 'service animals' [versus] 'emotional support animals,'" Google Trends, accessed June 20, 2022, https://trends.google.com/trends/explore?date=all&geo=US&q=traveling%20with%20pets,service%20animals,emotional%20support%20animal.

- Andrew Davis, *Brandscaping*, CMI Books, 2012.

- Andrew Davis, "Letters 2 Warren," Tumblr.com, accessed July 9, 2013, http://letters2warren.tumblr.com/.

- Ardath Albee, *eMarketing Strategies for the Complex Sale*, McGraw-Hill, 2009.

CHAPTER 11

The Content Marketing Mission Statement

BY JOE PULIZZI

All you need is one person to say yes to an idea.
JOY MANGANO

In the dining room of our house, there is a mission statement on the wall. I refer to it often. So do my two children (when they're home), now both at college.

The mission statement is our family purpose, our tilt. It's what we strive to be today and into the future. I believe that mission statement has been crucial to our family's success and happiness.

Here is what it says.

THE PULIZZI MISSION

As Pulizzis, we hold true the following with ongoing purpose and action:

We *thank God* every day for our blessings, even on days when we are challenged or face hardships.

We *always share* what we have with others and help out whenever we can to whoever is in need.

We *praise each other*, as we are each blessed by God with unique talents.

We *always finish* what we start, *always try* even though we may be afraid, and *always give* the activity of the moment our full attention.

Short version:

- Thank God.
- Always share.
- Say nice things.
- Give our best.

To be honest, I initially thought this was just a nice idea and a motto for our family to live by. Now, more than 20 years in the making, our mission statement has played a critical role in our lives. Why? Because there is never any gray area for our family goals. When the kids have questions about what they should and shouldn't do, my wife and I refer to the mission statement. Now, after years of this, my kids refer to the mission statement themselves—sometimes reluctantly.

And the best part? When visitors come into our house, the mission statement is noticed right away and almost always commented upon. It's one of those little things that make a difference.

THE CONTENT MARKETING MISSION STATEMENT

A mission statement is a company's reason for existence. It's why the organization does what it does.

Andy Crestodina from Orbit Media calls this the XYZ method. He explains, "Our company is where [audience X] finds [content Y] for [benefit Z]."

In almost every one of my keynote presentations, I cover the content marketing mission statement. It's critical to set the tone for the idea of content marketing . . . or any marketing, for that matter. Marketing professionals from small and large businesses get so fixated on channels such as blogs, TikTok, or Pinterest that they really have no clue of the underlying reason why they should use that channel in the first place. The why must come before the what. This seems obvious, but most marketers have no mission statement or core strategy behind the content they develop. Epic content marketing is impossible without a clear and formidable why.

Think of it this way: What if you were the leading trade magazine for your niche area? What if your goal was not to first sell products and services but to impact your readers with amazing information that changes their lives and careers?

WHY AMERICAN EXPRESS SUCCEEDS

American Express's website features its mission statement:

Become essential to our customers by providing differentiated products and services to help them achieve their aspirations.

Let's dissect this a bit. The mission statement includes:

- **The core audience target.** Current customers
- **What material will be delivered to the audience.** Differentiated products and services
- **The outcome for the audience.** Achieve their aspirations

The mission statement of American Express is incredibly simple and includes no words that can be misunderstood. This is an efficient corporate mission statement. Let's take this and construct a content marketing mission statement.

CONTENT MARKETING MISSION STATEMENTS IN ACTION

P&G (Procter & Gamble) has produced HomeMadeSimple.com for more than 20 years now. Millions of consumers have signed up at Home Made Simple to receive regular updates and tips to help them be more efficient in the home.

This is the content marketing mission statement for HomeMadeSimple .com:

> Whether it's a delicious recipe, an inspiring décor idea or a refreshing approach to organizing, we strive to help you [a mom] create a home that's truly your own. Everything we do here is designed to empower and inspire you to make your home even better, and most importantly, a place you love to be.

Home Made Simple's mission includes:

- **The core audience target.** On-the-go moms (P&G doesn't explicitly say this on its site for obvious reasons, but this is its audience.)
- **What material will be delivered to the audience?** Recipes, inspiring decorating ideas, and new approaches to organizing
- **The outcome for the audience.** Improvements to your home life

So for P&G, if the story idea doesn't fit into these three tenets, it's a nonstarter.

Why is the content marketing mission statement so critical for businesses and their content? Your team needs to come up with great content ideas all the time—for the blog, for your YouTube page, and for your newsletter. The way that you know whether story ideas are appropriate or not is to check each one against your content marketing mission statement.

If someone from P&G has a great idea targeted at dads and wants to put it on Home Made Simple, it won't get accepted; it's the wrong target audience. What if the story is about how to fix a tire? Nope, it doesn't fit with the promise of what you'll consistently deliver.

Here are other mission statements worth checking out:

- **LinkedIn.** "To connect the world's professionals to make them more productive and successful."
- **The Tilt.** "Providing education and training to help content creators build financially successful businesses."
- **Red Bull.** "Giving wings to people and ideas."
- **River Pools and Spas.** "Our mission is to use swimming pools as a means to bring joy to families, to provide the opportunity for financial peace to all team members, to improve the swimming pool industry, and to make a positive difference in our community and in the world."

- **Cradles to Crayons.** "Provides children from birth through age 12, living in homeless or low-income situations, with the essential items they need to thrive—at home, at school, and at play."

AUTHORITY TO PUBLISH

Have you ever seen an image on a company LinkedIn page or an article on a corporate blog that just doesn't fit? We all have. Companies that do this most likely don't have a content marketing mission statement as a filter.

As you develop your content marketing mission statement, be sure that the content around which you create stories is an area in which you truly have expertise. If you don't, then what's the point?

MISSION BEST PRACTICES

The informational needs of your customers and prospects must come first. Although there must be clear marketing objectives behind the mission statement, they don't need to be outlined in your mission statement. The HomeMadeSimple.com mission statement doesn't say anything about selling more Swiffer pads. To work, your mission statement has to be all about the pain points (in other words, what keeps your customers up at night?) of your readers and followers. If it isn't, it simply won't work.

WHAT DO YOU DO WITH IT?

Not only does the content marketing mission statement provide the basis for your content strategy moving forward; it's also instrumental to your entire content creation process. Here's what you need to do with your content marketing mission statement:

- **Post it.** Display the mission statement where it can be found easily by your audience. The best place to put it is anywhere you develop non-product-oriented content for your customers, such as your blog site, a Facebook page, or a main content site (such as an American Express OPEN Forum).
- **Spread it.** Make sure everyone involved in your content marketing process has the mission statement. Encourage others to print it out and pin it up on the wall. Give it to employees involved in the content creation process as well as any agency partners or freelancers you may

be using. So often, content creators in a company are not aware of the overall content mission. Make sure you don't let that happen.

- **Use it as a litmus test.** Use the mission statement to decide what content you will and won't create. Often a bad judgment in content creation can be fixed by running the content by the mission statement.

MATCHING WITH THE BUSINESS OBJECTIVE

Ultimately, it's all about marketing. It's about selling more products and services. If you are not changing behavior for the good of the business in some way, you are just producing content, not content marketing.

Let's reexamine the five company examples mentioned previously in terms of how their business objective should coincide with their mission statements:

- **LinkedIn.** The entire platform is built around networking and connecting professionals. The company's statement is focused on its particular users and the outcomes they can expect.
- **The Tilt.** The Tilt gives its content and information away for free. It invites content entrepreneurs into its online community where it provides free advice and networking.
- **Red Bull.** Red Bull is much more than just an energy drink company. It strives to give the consumers of its beverage (and its content) opportunities to push their ideas and dreams. These users are "top athletes, busy professionals, college students, and travelers on long journeys," according to the site.
- **River Pools and Spas.** River Pools is incredibly customer-focused, providing training, answering questions, and being transparent with all the work it does. It takes the same approach when it comes to its employees and franchise dealers, training them on its processes and techniques while focusing on customer satisfaction.
- **Cradles to Crayons.** This organization collects, packages, and distributes donated items to local children at various locations across the country.

Sometimes your content marketing mission statement is fully aligned with what you sell (as is the case with The Tilt). Other times the content you develop may be broader than your products and services (as is the case with

Red Bull). The important thing is to be aware of your mission statement and know what kind of products or services need to be sold at the end of the day. Knowing is half the battle, and if your audience isn't showing the right kind of behaviors in the long run, that may mean the content alignment and your products or services are just too far from each other.

This takes us back to one of the original questions: On what topic can you be the leading information expert in the world? But this time let's add a short statement at the end: on what topic can you be the leading information expert in the world *that truly matters to your customers and your business?*

EPIC THOUGHTS

- For your content marketing mission statement to work, you need to clearly define three things specific to your content creation: (1) the core audience target, (2) what you will deliver to the audience, and (3) the major audience takeaway.

- Once your mission statement is created, distribute it to every content creator on your team (both inside and outside the company).

- Epic content marketing, in most cases, means telling a different story each time, not the same story repeatedly, but incrementally better each time. Is your mission statement innovative or just a retread of someone else's story?

EPIC RESOURCES

- "Mission statement" definition, accessed June 20, 2022, http://en.wikipedia.org/wiki/Mission_statement.

- American Express, "Vision and Mission," accessed June 20, 2022, https://www.americanexpress.com/in/company/mission.html.

- Home Made Simple, accessed June 20, 2022, http://homemadesimple.com.

- LinkedIn, "About LinkedIn," accessed June 20, 2022, https://about.linkedin.com/.

- The Tilt, "About Us," accessed June 20, 2022, https://www.thetilt.com/about-us.

- Red Bull, "Red Bull Energy Drink," accessed June 20, 2022, https://www.redbull.com/us-en/energydrink.

- River Pools and Spas, "Fiberglass Pools Is Our Business, but Delighting Customers Is Our Passion.," accessed June 20, 2022, https://www.riverpoolsandspas.com/about-river-pools.

- Cradles to Crayons, "Our Mission and Model," accessed June 20, 2022, https://www.cradlestocrayons.org/what-we-do/our-mission-and-model/.

- Simon Sinek, *Start with Why: How Great Leaders Inspire Everyone to Take Action,* Portfolio Trade, 2011.

PART III

Managing the Content Process

CHAPTER 12

Building Your Editorial Calendar

BY JOE PULIZZI

*Be an amateur. Not everything you do
has to be good, especially at first.*
ANN HANDLEY

Over the past 23 years of my publishing career, I've noticed a couple of things about editorial calendars:

- First, they are utterly critical for any content marketing program to be successful.
- Second, most businesses don't use them.

New social media platforms are sexy. So are new marketing ideas. Calendars, for most of us, are . . . not so sexy.

Let's be honest: even though content marketing has existed in various forms for hundreds of years, most marketers are short-term, campaign-driven types—similar to the people you might see on *Mad Men*—who tend to shower their campaigns with the latest social media tools.

But that's not content marketing. Content marketing is not a short-term campaign; it's a long-term strategy to attract, convert, and retain customers.

You can't have a long-term content strategy without the tools to manage it. And one of the most effective tools you can use is the editorial calendar. So let's take a look at how this works.

THE THREE COMPONENTS OF AN EDITORIAL CALENDAR

Traditional marketing departments used to gear up around the latest product push. But more and more marketing resources are starting to look like publishing operations, similar to what you'd see from *Inc.* magazine or *Entertainment Weekly.*

Because content marketing is a long-term strategy and often involves multiple content producers, customers, and outside influencers, keeping track of all the stories and formats (online or offline) can be tricky . . . and problematic.

Note: Though in the following paragraphs I describe how I use spreadsheets and documents to create a calendar, there are many online tools that can work to help you create your customized editorial calendar. Start with simple tools such as Google Sheets combined with the WordPress Editorial Calendar plug-in. (If WordPress is your content management system, this is available for you to use.) As your business progresses, consider moving up to a paid software-as-a-service offering, such as Kapost, monday.com, HubSpot, Trello, CoSchedule, Airtable, and Asana (to name just a few).

COMPONENT 1: UNDERSTANDING WHAT AN EDITORIAL CALENDAR IS AND IS NOT

The editorial calendar is much more than just a calendar with content assigned to dates. A good editorial calendar maps content production to the audience personas (whom we want to sell to), the engagement cycle (delivering appropriate content based on where the prospect is in the buying process), and the various media channels.

Beyond dates and headlines, your editorial calendar should include the following things:

- **A prioritized list of what you are publishing based on the content strategy you've developed.** This may contain existing content that will be redesigned or repackaged, content that will come from partners, or content yet to be developed. It's your inventory.

- **Assigned content producer(s) and/or editors responsible for the content.** Here you name the people responsible for producing the content. If you have multiple editors, identify them as well.
- **The channel(s) for the content.** This is where you list the formats and channels targeted for the content. For example, you may have a blog post that is part of an e-book series that you are publishing on LinkedIn. In this case, you may want to also deliver pieces through multiple distribution outlets such as your email newsletter or social sites like Twitter or Instagram.
- **Metadata.** These are "tags" you assign to keep track of what you're working on and what role it plays in your content strategy. The number of tags you want to include is up to you. You'll probably want to have tags for important aspects of the content such as "target persona" or "engagement cycle" so that you can make sure you're balancing your editorial content with your overall goals. You may also want to include columns (or tags) for things like content type (for example, white paper, video, or email) or even search engine optimization keywords.
- **Dates for both creation and publishing.** These include the dates that the content is due to the editor, along with target dates for publishing. As you become more sophisticated, you may want to include the refresh date (a triggered date to update the content when needed).
- **Workflow steps.** If you work for a larger organization, you may want to add workflow steps, including legal, fact-checking, proofreading, or other elements that will affect your content creation and management process.

As you begin to assemble the elements in your editorial calendar, remember that the calendar is a management tool.

Include only the elements you need to manage your process. For example, if you write one blog post a week and two email messages a month to support your small business, there's no reason to overcomplicate your editorial calendar. Keep it as simple as you can. Figure 12.1 shows what a basic editorial calendar looks like.

Sample Editorial Calendar

	Author	Topic	Status	Call to Action	Main Keyword	Category	Next Update
Week of May 21							
Monday, May 21							
Tuesday, May 22							
Wednesday, May 23							
Thursday, May 24							
Friday, May 25							
Week of May 28							
Monday, May 28							
Tuesday, May 29							
Wednesday, May 30							
Thursday, May 31							
Friday, June 1							
Week of June 4							
Monday, June 4							
Tuesday, June 5							
Wednesday, June 6							
Thursday, June 7							
Friday, June 8							
Week of June 11							
Monday, June 11							
Tuesday, June 12							
Wednesday, June 13							
Thursday, June 14							
Friday, June 15							
Week of June 18							
Monday, June 18							
Tuesday, June 19							
Wednesday, June 20							
Thursday, June 21							
Friday, June 22							

FIGURE 12.1   A basic look for an editorial calendar

COMPONENT 2: ORGANIZING THE CALENDAR

Set your calendar document up in the way that works best for you.

For the sake of simplicity, let's assume that you'll have one spreadsheet for the year—and that each tab will be one month. Across the columns you might have:

- Content headline
- Content type
- The audience persona you're writing this piece for
- The person who will write or create the content
- Date due
- The person who will edit the content
- Channels—where does this get published?
- "Metadata" tags
- Publish date
- Status (perhaps indicated by green, yellow, or red)
- Any notes
- Key metrics (for example, comments posted, page views, and downloads) (I recommend keeping your key metrics on a separate sheet, however.)
- Call to action (the primary action or behavior you've asked for)

Finally, as separate documents—or even tabs within your editorial calendar—you may want to include "brainstorming" elements (for example, ideas that are under consideration or new stories that come up during the process). If you are using a tool like Kapost, DivvyHQ, or Trello, it will keep a log of all your ongoing ideas as well as your active content assets.

In the end, your editorial calendar will become the most frequently used tool in your process. And whether it's a combination of documents, a single spreadsheet, an online production tool, or just a monthly email that you send to your team, the key is that it works for you. In the end, whatever helps smooth out your process and keep you and your content team on track is the best editorial calendar format.

COMPONENT 3: DEVELOPING THE EDITORIAL STYLE GUIDE

Obviously, when any of us talks about a calendar, the first thing that person thinks of is a guide for planning what content gets created and when.

But your calendar has another important function. It's the basis for developing an editorial style guide as a tool for your content creators, editors, and producers. (Yes, even if those people are all you.)

This style guide can also develop into a social conversation style guide (in other words, a social media policy), providing guidelines for how people respond and converse.

As more people start "telling the story" of your brand, be sure that they have the right tools and training to properly communicate your brand's voice. You also need to police or monitor them to make sure they are keeping to that voice.

And even if you're flying solo right now, keeping your editorial voice consistent will keep your content more professional and trustworthy. And it makes it much easier if you ever need to bring other writers in.

As with the continuing story, it's easy to let the tone, quality, and style slip bit by bit until the story is way off track. This is where your editorial style guide comes into play.

Here are some key things to include:

- **The overall tone and voice of your content marketing.** Who are you? What do you convey in your content?
- **The length of pieces developed.** What the average (or minimum/maximum) should be.

- **Branding guidelines.** How to refer to the company, product lines, individuals, and so on.

For grammar, style, and word usage, you can also choose to conform to guides such as the *Associated Press Stylebook* and *The Chicago Manual of Style*. UX Writing Hub, which we've cited in the Epic Resources, offers a variety of style guides.

EPIC THOUGHTS

- Ultimately, your editorial calendar is your most powerful tool as a content marketer. If you don't plan for epic content, it doesn't happen.

- There are many technology tools out there, but use what's easiest for you.

- Your editorial guide is not just for text. You should use it for video and audio content as well.

EPIC RESOURCES

- Plugin Directory, WordPress.org, "Editorial Calendar," accessed June 23, 2022, http://wordpress.org/extend/plugins/editorial -calendar/.

- *Chicago Manual of Style*, 17th ed., University of Chicago Press, 2017.

- *The Associated Press Stylebook*, 56th ed., Basic Books, 2022.

- UX Writing Hub, "Top 16 Content Style Guides 2022 (and How to Use Them)," accessed July 11, 2022, https://uxwritinghub.com/ content-style-guides/.

CHAPTER 13

Managing the Content Creation Process

BY JOE PULIZZI

There is nothing so useless as doing efficiently that which should not be done at all.

PETER DRUCKER

When the first edition of this book came out, there were very few companies that had a content marketing team or processes. Now there are numerous organizations that have been creating and refining content marketing teams, roles, tasks, and governance. There are also hundreds of blog posts and examples of how to structure and build your content team.

To do content marketing successfully, you need to have the following five things:

- People to do it
- Roles and responsibilities for those people to fill
- A schedule by which the tasks are fulfilled
- Rules and guidelines
- Knowledge of what we are measuring and why

The most difficult of these may be finding the roles within the company to drive the process. If that's the case for you, the paragraphs that follow will tell you how.

ASSEMBLING A TEAM WITH SPECIFIC ROLES AND RESPONSIBILITIES

Given the size of your organization, you may have one person—or many— responsible for your content marketing initiative; in general, however, no matter how many people take responsibility for the function, the following roles are needed.

Note: The following are roles within the organization, not necessarily position titles (although they could be).

THE MANAGER OR CHIEF CONTENT OFFICER

At least one person in your organization should own the content initiative. More recently, organizations call this a chief content officer, or CCO. (In a small business, the owner or partner or even a general marketing person may be the one performing this function.) In some organizations, we've seen the VP of content marketing, content strategist, or content marketing director take on this role.

This is the "chief storyteller" role for your content effort; the person performing this role is responsible for executing the goals that you set out to accomplish. *When content marketing fails, it's usually not because of a lack of high-quality content; it's because of a drop in execution*

That is why this manager may be your most important asset, even though this person may not be creating any of the content. The CCO must ensure excellence in every content marketing tactic, including:

- Content/editorial
- Design/art/photography/video/audio
- Web resources for content
- Integration of marketing and the content, including social media
- Project budgeting
- Contract negotiation with freelancers
- Audience development
- Research and measurement

In organizations where there is no budget for a dedicated CCO, this role may be filled by the director or vice president of marketing. Many brands have a manager inside the company who oversees internal content production as well as the production of content by an outside agency. Although brands can outsource a wide variety of content production through vendors, *it's important to keep the CCO inside the organization.*

MANAGING EDITOR(S)

The editors have a critical role in the content marketing process and are probably the most sought after by brands today. As more brands develop content, employees are being asked to blog and write on behalf of their companies. Unfortunately, the writing style of employees who have never created content before often leaves much to be desired. That's where the managing editor comes in. This role, sometimes outsourced and sometimes part of the CCO's responsibility, manages the editorial functions of the content marketing effort. These editors are your day-to-day content execution people. They help internal employees develop and write content, podcasts, and videos, and they assist external people in aligning their content creation with the company's organizational goals.

Managing editors work with the employees on the following:

- Content production
- Content scheduling
- Keyword selection for search engine optimization (SEO)
- Search engine optimization of posts
- Style corrections
- Tagging and images
- Podcast and video creation

Sometimes the managing editors are there to teach so the employees can do more on their own. They also may act as coaches, encouraging the managers, executive team, or even external creators to produce content against the schedule.

CONTENT CREATORS

Content creators produce content that will ultimately help tell the story. This role typically overlaps with that of the managing editors, who are also producing content, but the role of content creator also may simply be performed by a subject-matter expert within the organization. For example, typical content producers include anyone in the C-suite, the head of research and development, the product manager, the customer service director, or a hired consultant or outside influencer. In many cases, this role is outsourced when there is a lack, or gap, in resources to produce the content. It's important to note that this person does not need to be a writer (although it's helpful if the person is). In general, this person is there to be the "face" or "voice" of the authentic organization. Content creators may be interviewed for content; they may produce a long, rambling email that is transformed into a cogent blog post; or they could be featured on a podcast or video segment.

CONTENT PRODUCERS

Content producers format or create the ultimate package in which the content is presented (that is, they make the content "pretty"). Chances are this role already exists in your organization to some degree; it is handled either in-house or by an agency.

CHIEF LISTENING OFFICER

The role of the chief listening officer (CLO) is to function like an air traffic controller for social media and your other content channels. CLOs are there to listen to the groups, maintain the conversation, and route to (and/or notify) the appropriate team members who can engage in conversation (customer service, sales, marketing, and so on). For the content marketing process, this function serves as the centerpiece of your "listening posts." You establish listening posts so you can continue to get a "feed" of information; you can then always be ready to react and adapt as your subscribers react and change.

So often today, companies have CLOs for social media response purposes but don't leverage these roles for purposes of content marketing feedback. The hope is that your content creates several reactions in the community. The CLO can then route important feedback to the CCO, so that the chief storyteller can modify the plan on an ongoing basis.

WHAT TO LOOK FOR IN FREELANCERS

Whether you represent an experienced digital publishing machine or a novice brand looking for the benefits of content marketing, you most likely need freelance creators to help tell your story. You may find that you need help developing ongoing content—or that you need additional content producers to keep up with the velocity.

How do you go about finding good external content contributors (sometimes called "stringers")? Should you look for a good writer or podcaster and teach them your business? Or should you hire someone who knows your industry and teach them to write or make videos? The following are a few tips to consider:

- **Expertise is helpful, but lack of it is not a deal killer.** Given the choice between a good creator who has a personality that closely matches that of your organization (but who is short on industry expertise) and an industry veteran who knows how to create content but is someone you can't stand to be in the same room with—*go with the personality.* Chemistry and personality are things that are entirely hard to change; research is a skill that can be taught—passion isn't. If you and your freelance content producer don't have good chemistry together, the relationship will go nowhere fast. And while it might be a strategic advantage to bring in an industry "rock star" to get your content some attention (and there are great reasons to do this occasionally), unless there's a great personality fit, be very careful that you don't wrap your story into the star's and get lost in the middle.

- **Hire right—vloggers, journalists, podcasters, oh my!** Because you've spent so much time on your strategy and your process, you should be very aware of what kind of creator you're looking for. Understand that copywriters work very differently and have very different sensibilities than journalists do. Documentary creators and podcasters approach content from different perspectives. If you're looking for someone to write blog posts for you, a copywriter is probably not your best bet. If you're looking for someone to beef up your persuasive call to action for all the great white papers you're putting together, then a great copywriter may be exactly what you need.

- **Develop the right business relationship.** Understand the elements of your business relationship and make them clear. For example, will there be one content item per week—and your creator will be paid a monthly fee? If so, how will you handle months that have $4\frac{1}{2}$ weeks? Will there be an extra post or podcast episode that week? Spell out the invoicing and payment terms. Given the size of your organization, you need to make clear the invoicing and payment terms—or understand what the creator needs. Also, be clear on expectations.

At this point, you should know your velocity and how long and how detailed the content needs to be. There should be no surprises such as finding blog posts that are only 300 words when they're supposed to be 1,000 . . . or expecting a 5-minute tutorial and instead getting a 30-second quick tip . . . or discovering that content themes have gone wildly off-topic.

Here are some of the things you'll need to communicate to your freelance creators:

- What content they will produce, and where it falls on the editorial calendar (Be very specific when drafts are due.)
- The goals for their specific contributions (especially if it's a custom-branded piece versus a piece for your publication)
- What expertise or other third-party information they will need access to (Will they be interviewing internal people, bringing in external information, or reworking your existing material?)
- Your budget (per piece, hourly, retainer, or barter)
- The number of revisions for each piece

Over the past 10 years, new models of performance have taken shape in the digital content world. Many publishers are using the pay-for-performance model, where a smaller base fee is paid for the raw content, but the creator is paid a bonus for content performance (based on both sharing metrics and search engine placement). Tools such as Skyword, Percolate, and Contently make this possible. Content creators are very aware of this type of model, but setting clear expectations is a critical first step.

BUDGETING FACTORS

In the past, freelance writers used to get paid $1 per word. This still remains true for high-quality and unique content, like research reports and white papers. For standard blog content the average is around 12 cents per word according to copy.ai.

Word of warning: You usually get what you pay for. You may find success in the retainer model—that is, working with a freelancer on several content assets over a period of time and then paying a monthly fee for the work. This arrangement is usually appreciated by both sides. The business can budget more easily with a set number, and the freelancer doesn't have to count words or hit a specific time requirement in a video. After all, a piece of content should only be as long as it needs to be, so why set a limit? (A range should be just fine.)

BEFORE DIVING IN, TEST

With the number of creators in the workforce, there is no need to start a long-term relationship at first. Test out a few pieces of content and see how they work. Ask yourself: Is the person's style to your expectations? Does the person deliver on time? Is the person actively sharing the content via their own social network? (This could be very important.)

Once the creator has met your expectations in these areas, then set out on a long-term deal. I've seen too many marketers and publishers get their rock star freelancers, only to kill the deal a few months later with neither party happy. Test it out first so you don't waste your time.

A CODE OF ETHICS

Wherever there is talk of content marketing, there is talk of transparency, ethics, and the credibility of branded content. One content network and publishing platform, Contently, did some excellent work in this area back in 2012, and it is just as relevant and even more important today.

I asked Shane Snow, Contently's CEO, about the code of ethics he developed. Here's a bit of background from Shane:

> We started Contently because we wanted to help talented, professional journalists survive as freelancers and build careers doing what they loved. As our business grew into providing tools and talent for content marketers, we saw the need to educate our clients and journalists on the ethical expectations they should have as they do business together.
>
> Brands don't have decades of publishing experience, and thus they often aren't familiar with the accepted standards of ethical publishing. Journalists can be uneasy about taking on clients who don't understand those standards. We talked to editors at major newspapers like the *New York Times* and ethicists from the Society of Professional Journalists in order to understand whether editors would hire journalists who'd previously worked for brands (the answer is yes, so long as they're transparent about it), and to establish the different responsibilities that we felt should go along with creating content for brands versus traditional, constitutionally protected media publishers.

And thus the Content Marketing Code of Ethics was born. Here it is, in its entirety, reprinted with permission.

CONTENT MARKETING'S CODE OF ETHICS

Content marketing should seek to adhere to stricter standards of reporting than traditional journalism, due to its different legal position and increased commercial motivations. Content marketers should take care to disclose the sponsorship and intent of their work while abiding by the following practices:

- Adhere to journalism's core values of honesty, integrity, accountability, and responsibility.
- Acknowledge facts that may compromise the integrity of a story or opinion.
- Minimize potential harm to sources or subjects of stories.
- Expose truth as fully as possible.
- Always credit sources of content or ideas, never plagiarizing or repurposing stories or prose, whether one's own or another's, whether written content, photography, or other media, whether the original source is known or not.
- Fulfill promises made to contributors and sources in the course of reporting.
- Ensure that the reader understands the source, sponsor, and intent of the content
- Disclose all potential conflicts of interest or appearance of conflict.

MANAGING INFORMATION AS IF IT WERE A PRODUCT

Although each brand we've worked with executes the content marketing process differently, there seems to be one key differentiator between those organizations that are successfully changing behavior through content and those that aren't: *information as a product.*

Whether you sell products or services, the new rules of marketing require that, along with everything else you sell, the process of delivering consistently valuable information must be considered throughout the organization as, yes, a product.

What does this mean? When people from an organization look at its content marketing as a product, they inherently create a number of initiatives and processes around that product, including:

- Up-front business planning
- Product testing
- Research and development
- Product success measures (marketing return on investment)
- Customer feedback channels
- Quality control
- Product evolution planning

Successful companies such as Procter & Gamble, IBM, and SAS have all approached their content in a similar fashion.

WHY APPROACH INFORMATION AS A PRODUCT?

The answer to that question is simple: organizations today have no choice but to place that kind of importance and processes behind their content initiatives. Customers today are in complete control; they filter out any message that does not benefit them in some way. Since that is the case, organizations must first build a solid relationship with customers using valuable, relevant information—then, and only then, will organizations be able to sell the other products and services that grow the top line.

THIS IS HAPPENING MORE AND MORE

This trend has been happening for more than 10 years, and we see it all around us with big brands. It's very common to see titles like "chief content officer," and businesses have been hiring full-time journalists for years to write their content. Traditional businesses are purchasing media companies every day (such as HubSpot's purchase of *The Hustle*) or are building out media empires (as Red Bull Media House and Arrow Electronics have done).

WHAT YOU NEED TO DO

Any company that is serious about growing top-line revenues, while at the same time being concerned about how to market in the future, needs to make the "information-as-a-product" concept a priority.

Small organizations with limited budgets should start seeking out expert journalists and storytellers to begin overseeing their content program.

Midsize to large organizations may want to look into hiring an agency that understands that storytelling, and not paid media channels, is the key to future growth.

THREE TAKEAWAYS

In order to be successful, you need a marketing culture that includes both a strong marketing and publishing core and a keen understanding of how consistent editorial content can maintain or change customer behavior. Here are three things you should always keep in mind when establishing and maintaining a content marketing culture:

1. **Start to think about your content packages as a series (like a television show).** Set up the pilot as a test, and then, if it's successful, roll ahead with the series.

2. **Train all product managers in the basics of content marketing.** The power of the story revolves not in the product; instead it depends on the true needs and pain points of the target audience. The product manager must have a thorough awareness of this. Most product managers never think about this aspect, and the opportunities are wasted.

3. **Establish a pilot team.** Content marketing is not a difficult concept, but it means thinking differently about how to communicate with both customers and employees. A full marketing makeover takes time, especially in a larger brand (see the Cleveland Clinic case study in Chapter 5). Find the storytellers in your marketing department and set up a "skunk works" operation (that is, one that functions independently from the company's main R&D operation) as your testing ground. Focus on achieving an objective or two instead of getting them all—in effect, hitting a single or two instead of a home run. Once you have reached some objectives with this group and success is clear, then you can push it through the entire organization.

ON WORKING WITH CONTENT MARKETING AGENCIES

There are numerous content marketing agencies these days. In the search for "content gold," providers of marketing services have been "heading west," as more brands continue their move toward creating owned media programs and establishing content marketing dominance.

THE FIGHT FOR CONTENT

The battle royale to establish or increase budgets for content development and distribution is being fought by both the usual suspects and the uninitiated in the content marketing industry, including:

- Pure content marketing agencies
- Advertising agencies that have a newfound appreciation for branded storytelling outside of media placement
- Traditional media companies that have either editorial teams or full content divisions dedicated to working on editorial and branded content projects
- Public relations organizations that are starting to focus less on placement and more on owned channels
- Direct marketing agencies that are moving from "offer-focused" to "engagement-focused" content
- Search engine optimization companies that are shelving the SEO business in response to Google algorithm updates that change search rankings to focus on quality content creation from credible websites
- Social media agencies that are realizing that it's not the channel but what goes into the channel that counts
- Web content and user experience agencies that are moving away from solely technical website production, audits, and analysis to advise on multichannel content
- Digital agencies that are pairing interactive services with consistent content production
- Research organizations showcasing industry experts and thought leaders for strategic content and consulting assignments
- Content entrepreneurs that have solidified a niche and offer services for hire

These agencies and more are battling for content marketing dollars from brands. Some have legitimate budgets, and others are working with a pile of Monopoly money trying to figure out the secret to social media success.

Whatever your feeling is on who owns the rightful mantle of "content marketing agency" really doesn't matter. The truth is that thousands of agencies formerly touting any one or a number of the aforementioned banners are now trying to "ride the wave" to content marketing salvation.

REALITY BITES

After years of consulting and working with businesses asking for content help, from strategy to blog posts, visual content, content distribution, integration, hiring, research, and everything else under the sun, here's what we've learned: *there is good help out there, but it's hard to tell the partners from the posers.*

In the following paragraphs, you'll find some truths about content marketing agencies, and how smart brands should view the outsourced marketing services provider of the present.

> A lot of people in our industry haven't had very diverse experiences. So they don't have enough dots to connect, and they end up with very linear solutions without a broad perspective on the problem. The broader one's understanding of the human experience, the better design we will have.
>
> —STEVE JOBS

- **Most content marketing agencies don't market with content.** I hear it all the time: the "shoemaker's shoes" conundrum; that is, most content agencies rarely make time to practice epic content marketing, saving it all, apparently, for their customers. Agencies of all kinds have a long history of producing advertising and marketing programs for clients while forgetting to market themselves. No clearer examples of this exist than with content marketing.

  Marketing services organizations are notorious for focusing on sales-led marketing programs, where cold calls and sales relationships rule. Whether a lack of resources or a lack of patience is cited as the reason, agencies that offer content marketing services very rarely produce epic content that attracts and helps retain their own customer base.

The lesson for brands: Before you hire a content marketing agency, ask to see the work it has performed—on its own behalf. Take a deep dive into all its content. Is the content truly great, or is it "me-too" blog content that you can find anywhere?

- **Most search engine optimization agencies don't understand content marketing.** Search engine optimization is an incredibly important tactic. As search engines get smarter, it's almost impossible to game the system. Today getting found through search engines has more to do with amazing online storytelling than most anything else.

I had a conversation with an SEO executive team, and team members were seriously contemplating taking the entire company in a new direction—to content marketing. Why? Their reasoning was (besides the fact that pure SEO budgets were drying up) that the value they used to provide to customers (which used to be immense) simply wasn't there anymore.

Hundreds, if not thousands, of SEO agencies are in the same position. I've seen a few make this transition incredibly well. Others have simply put the "content marketing" moniker on their SEO content production service and called it content marketing. Yes, they've added such services as infographics creation, video production, and blog content creation, but content production is only one small part of the content marketing process. Strategic planning aspects of mission statement creation, audience persona gathering, internal content integration, and measurement outside of content consumption metrics are often absent.

The lesson for brands: A holistic content marketing strategy includes up-front planning and multiple goals, which in turn must bring in nondigital channels (such as print and in-person vehicles). SEO is just one very small part that covers a few marketing objectives. Make sure your content marketing strategy goes beyond top-of-the-funnel considerations.

- **Most agencies are less concerned about strategy than they are about execution.** Want to hear a dirty little secret that content agencies subscribe to? *Give away the strategy to get the execution.*

I was guilty of this many times while I was at Penton Media. I would give away whatever strategic insight I needed to win the content project. It was the ultimate "value add." Why? Planning lasts just a short time, while execution can last forever. The thinking was that giving up the planning guidance for free could result in a content project contract (such as producing a serial blog, custom magazine, or video series) that may last for years or more.

Like it or not, strategy and planning usually have been viewed not as a useful service to customers but as a closing strategy to get the execution business. This also has meant that most of the internal talent has gone to execution, not strategy.

And today? This is exactly the reason why so many businesses are struggling to find solid strategic partners for content planning, while content execution increasingly is becoming a commodity.

And the worst part? I've never seen a content planning document from an agency that recommended having less content or (God forbid) stopping the content program altogether (which is sometimes the correct remedy).

The lesson for brands: Regardless of whether you hired agencies to just do content execution, you must ask them for a sample of an executable content marketing strategy as well. You at least need to see if they understand the strategic argument for—and more importantly, against—content creation. There may be a time for producing less content, but without strategic guidance, the answer will always be more (and this is just shortsighted).

- **Most agencies still see content marketing as a campaign.** As you've learned throughout this book, content marketing is not a campaign—it's an approach, a philosophy, and a business strategy.

  Similarly, a viral video—and its resultant success or failure—is not content marketing. A campaign is not content marketing. A campaign can be the result of a content marketing approach, but in and of itself, it is not content marketing. In other words, releasing the long form of a 30-second advertisement is not a content marketing approach; it's just a clever form of advertising.

  Most agencies aren't built for consistent, long-form content creation and distribution. They're built for speed, for great creative that makes an immediate impact (one hopes). Compare this with what it takes to create content marketing efforts such as Procter & Gamble's Home Made Simple: day-in, day-out content planning, production, and evolution over a long period of time, with the goal of attracting and retaining customers.

The lesson for brands: Be wary of any agency pitching you a "campaign" over a "program." There is one thing that's certain with any campaign: it has an end date. Not so with content marketing.

A REVIEW

Even though content marketing is almost 200 years old, we are in the middle of a revolution. Total consumer control, combined with an absence of technology barriers for brands, has resulted in a content marketing renaissance. At the same time, it has forced marketing service providers to alter their business models, and their sales speak, to include editorial-based content creation.

While, overall, this is good for the industry, it has created confusion about what true content marketing is—and what the practice of content marketing can look like for both agencies and brands.

If you feel you need to work with an outside partner to help you manage your content marketing process (which is completely fine), make sure you heed the warning mentioned previously and choose a content marketing agency that will truly help you attract and retain customers through epic content creation and distribution.

EPIC THOUGHTS

- No matter what you call it, your company's story—your content strategy—has to be tended by someone in your organization. If you don't assign someone to do this, be prepared for duplication and confusion.

- Start looking to add to your organization those marketers who understand how to tell a story. Those with journalism backgrounds should be a priority.

EPIC RESOURCES

- "Contently's Code of Ethics for Journalism and Content Marketing," Contently.com, accessed June 23, 2022, http://contently.com/blog/2012/08/01/ethics/.

- Skyword, accessed June 23, 2022, http://skyword.com.

CHAPTER 14

Content Types

BY JOE PULIZZI

Do not follow where the path may lead.
Go instead where there is no path and leave a trail.

MURIEL STRODE

This chapter is all about content, or media, types. These are not channels (such as LinkedIn or your website), although some, like blogs, can mean both a content type and a channel. Regardless, as you run through these content types, think of the types of content that will make the most sense based on your marketing objectives.

There's a lot to cover. We'll discuss blogs, newsletters, white papers, articles, e-books, webinars/webcasts, videos, custom print magazines, print newsletters, digital magazines, podcasts, executive roundtables, industry ranking systems, printed books, audiobooks, online events, comic books, road shows, online games, infographics, online research projects, and discussion forums.

BLOG

WHAT A BLOG IS

Shorthand for "weblog," the blog offers an easy way to present brief chunks of frequently refreshed web content. Backed with easy-to-use technologies for syndication (for example, RSS) and commenting, blogs are often the centers of social media solar systems that can incorporate sophisticated SEO strategies and community-building campaigns.

Blogs can be text (and image) content, but there are also video blogs, or vlogs. In Chapter 16, we'll review leveraging a blog as your main content platform.

THREE KEY PLAY POINTS

1. **Encourage conversations.** Even "bad" comments can be an opportunity for developing good customer relations.
2. **Be a good "netizen."** Participate on other blogs as well as your own. Develop a top 15 hit list where you need to be "hanging out" (more on this in Chapter 19).
3. **Loosen up.** Authenticity trumps perfection when connecting with readers.

QUESTIONS TO ASK BEFORE YOU BLOG

One of the most frequent questions I receive while traveling is about blogging. The questions revolve around *how to get started, what to talk about,* and even *what software to use.*

What I ask people in response usually startles them, prompting them to think about what they want to say rather than how they can impact the reader. Here are a few questions I ask:

- Who will be the primary readers/viewers (subscribers) of your blog?
- What do you want to tell them? (What's your story?)
- Do you understand the key informational needs of the people in your audience? What are their pain points?
- Are you hanging out online where your customers are? Do you or can you make a target hit list of blogs or sites that your customers frequent online?
- Are you leaving comments that add to the online conversation on the blogs you cover?
- Do you have a firm grasp on the types of keywords to focus on that your customers are searching for? (Check out Google's Keyword Tool online.)
- Do you follow those keywords using Google Alerts or watch their usage on Twitter? (Do so to find the influencers in your market.)

- Can you commit to blogging/vlogging at least two times per week? (Content consistency is key.)
- What is your ultimate goal in starting a blog? One year after you start blogging, how will the business be different?
- How will the execution process work within your company, and how will you market the blog?
- How will you integrate the blog with the rest of your marketing? How can the blog make everything else you are doing better?

These are the general starter questions for both businesses and individuals. It might be a bit overwhelming for first timers, but knowing the answers is necessary.

Ann Handley says, "Here's a handy, memorable formula that captures the sweet spot of your quality content . . . Utility x Inspiration x Empathy = Quality Content." Most blogs out there don't make it.

The worst thing you can do as a business is to start a consistent dialogue with your customers and then stop. It's better not to do anything at all than to stop cold turkey.

Remember, blogging is just a tool. That said, it can be a very powerful tool to communicate valuable, compelling content on a consistent basis. If you are ready to get started, here are 10 steps to successful blogging.

10 BLOGGING TIPS TO REMEMBER

1. **Use killer titles.** Your blog title is like the cover of a magazine. There is one purpose for a magazine cover: to get you to open the magazine. The same holds true for a blog post. The greatest blog post in the world might not be read unless you have a compelling title.

   OptinMonster has a free Headline Analyzer tool that you can use to test out different headlines and get recommendations on what you can do to improve it.

   Headline Tips

   - Think about the problem (see tip number 2).
   - Focus on important keywords for your business (use Google's Keyword Tool for help with this).
   - Numbers rule. With titles, be very specific. For example, instead of saying "Ways to Increase Your Stock Return," say "9 Ways to Make More Money with Small-Cap Stocks."

2. **Focus on the problem.** This is where you always should start. *What are the pain points of your target consumer? What keeps them up at night?*

   If your blog focuses 100 percent of the time on what keeps your customers and prospects up at night, you most likely will be successful.

3. **Be aware that there is no correct length.** Blogs are best for the consumer when they are short, instructive, and to the point. Search engines prefer longer-form content, so a longer piece can help with your rankings—but only if it's quality content that people will read. Produce content of the length that is required to provide the users with the answers to their questions.

   Short Tips for Writing

   - Keep sentences short.
   - Use bullets.
   - Keep paragraphs short.
   - Get rid of unnecessary words.
   - Edit, edit, edit.

4. **Think first about the call to action.** Each blog post should have some sort of call to action. Here are calls to action you can—and should—put on your website*:

   - Download our white paper.
   - Join us on Twitter (or Facebook, LinkedIn, YouTube, or whatever).
   - Ask us a question.
   - Download our e-book.
   - Sign up for our free webinar.
   - Request our toolkit.
   - Sign up for our newsletter.
   - Request a demo.

     Remember, *much of your blog traffic will probably never come back.* Show your readers additional, relevant content offers, such as a valuable niche newsletter, so you can continue to communicate with them. Getting opt-in email names should be one of your top blogging goals (to grow the database).

---

*I am grateful to Debbie Weil for providing the list items.

5. **Think "content packages."** This book initially started out as a series of blog posts. As I continued to develop blog posts, I started to think about how they could evolve into a book.

   Continually think about how you can take blog posts and repackage them into something more substantial. Plan for this ahead of time instead of repackaging after the fact. It will save you immense amounts of time and resources by planning up front.

   One blogging idea could be 10 pieces of content. Think about that for a second.

6. **Spread the love: do guest blogging.** Target the top 15 bloggers in your industry and offer to do relevant guest posts on their blogs. Never turn down an opportunity for a guest post.

7. **Promote key influencers with lists.** Everyone loves lists, especially the people on the list.
   - Create a niche list.
   - Be sure it's easily shareable (including a widget).
   - Do a blog post or video about the list.
   - Let those featured on the list know about it.
   - Do a press release about the list.
   - Repeat, repeat, repeat.

8. **Measure, measure, measure.** Here are a number of blog metrics you can measure as part of your blog (all these metrics can be accessed through Google Analytics or another analytics program). Choose the ones that make the most sense with your overall content marketing and blogging goals. Make sure that you and your team know what the goal of the blog is and that everyone sees the statistics. Measure the following:
   - Visits and unique visitors
   - Page views
   - Time on site
   - Sign-ups to your newsletter
   - Search rankings
   - Inbound links to your blog

9. **Do an influencer question-and-answer session.** Most industry heavy hitters will do a podcast interview or Q&A, if you ask. They will probably also share it with their network when it's finished.

10. **Outsource.** According to SEMrush research, almost 50 percent of companies of all sizes outsource their content marketing.

Most businesses outsource a portion of their content marketing. Find a great writer to help you. Find a content agency or content team to take your blogging/strategy to the next level.

Some companies have a difficult time telling engaging stories. Enlist help; it's available.

NEWSLETTER

WHAT A NEWSLETTER IS

Formerly referred to as an e-newsletter, a newsletter is a permission-based means of regular communication with current and future customers, usually distributed monthly, weekly, or daily. Newsletters can include complete articles or brief descriptions with links to articles on your website.

THREE KEY PLAY POINTS

1. Don't spam your newsletter. Get permission and offer opt-out links at the bottom of every newsletter you send out.
2. It can be a good vehicle for promoting other content: webinars, e-books, white papers, live events, and so on.
3. The best newsletters include something that you can't find anywhere else. The old days of linking to your blog or archive content just doesn't work as well as it used to.

10 WAYS TO OPTIMIZE YOUR NEWSLETTER LANDING PAGE*

In our social media world, email assets are more important than ever before. As content marketers, it is critical that we develop audiences and build channels, with a primary emphasis on email in conjunction with social channels such as Facebook and Twitter. Why? Theoretically (and legally) the customer names that sign up to our social channels do not belong to us (they belong to Facebook and Twitter). Your email database, on the other hand, is a significant business asset.

When we created TheTilt.com, we decided to make our entire home page the sign-up for our newsletter. We knew that capturing our online users and getting their contact information was the most important strategy for us, even at the risk of losing someone here or there.

---

*Thanks to Jeanne Jennings for her input on this section.

Here are 10 steps you can take now to optimize your newsletter landing page to get more customers and prospects to sign up for your content:

1. **Spell out the benefits.** On the landing page, clearly list why someone should sign up for your newsletter.

2. **Show them a picture.** Show readers a sample picture of what they will be receiving. (What does the email newsletter look like?)

3. **Link to a sample.** Link to a sample newsletter, and have that sample open in a "daughter window" (that is, don't take them away from the landing page).

4. **Bring the sign-up above the fold.** If prospects must scroll down to get to your sign-up area, there is a problem. The sign-up needs to be above the fold.

5. **Have no more than five to seven fields.** The fewer fields, the more likely prospects will be to sign up. Only ask for the fields you truly need. For The Tilt, we use one . . . your best email address.

6. **Be sure to have a clear link to a privacy statement (below the fold).** Although very few (if any) people will ever click on it, be sure to have a privacy statement available that has been checked by your legal team.

7. **Tell customers what you will and won't do with their information.** At the bottom of the page, be very clear about how you will use the customers' information they'll be giving to you.

8. **Include a button that says "subscribe" or "sign up" (not "submit").** Words like "submit" and phrases like "click here" don't accurately spell out the positive action you want prospects to take. Use "subscribe" or "sign up."

9. **Get rid of needless distractions.** The landing page for your newsletter has one goal: to get people to sign up for the newsletter. Get rid of all the distractions that may take them away from the sign-up page, such as the general navigation, third-party advertising, house ads, or other calls to action.

10. **Be sure to include testimonials and awards.** Put at least one good testimonial about what a user thinks about your newsletter. Get permission to use that person's name and title. Have you won any awards? List those as credibility points as well.

Remember, you want a simple form that shows at least as much value as the information that people are giving you (you are trading your content for their names). Don't overcomplicate the process.

As always, *test your changes.* The behavior of buyers is not consistent across industries, so be sure to test what works for you and what doesn't.

WHITE PAPER

WHAT A WHITE PAPER IS

The "granddaddy" of content, white papers are topical reports, typically 8 to 12 pages long, on issues that require a lot of explanation. Also known as conference papers, research reports, or technical briefs, they are perfect for demonstrating thought leadership on issues vital to your buyers. *Note:* Consider the people in your audience and how they engage in content. It is possible your "white paper" should become a series of videos.

THREE KEY PLAY POINTS

1. A white paper can generate leads and/or subscriptions.
2. It positions the company as a thought leader.
3. It's applicable to print, electronic PDF, and digital magazine formats.

ARTICLE

WHAT AN ARTICLE IS

A flexible medium, in both length and format, an article opens opportunities for companies to address issues, trends, concerns, and topics of immediate interest to their intended audiences. An ongoing article publishing campaign, complemented with a roster of speaking engagements, has been the traditional tool for establishing thought leadership in numerous industries.

THREE KEY PLAY POINTS

1. **Once isn't enough.** Plan on a series of articles to create impact.
2. **Look for opportunities** to place your articles in print media, on the web, and on your website as well as on others in need of great content.
3. **Always think from the editor's point of view.** Your article must conform to the publication's requirements (length and tone, for example) and be of immediate interest to its readers.

THE DIFFERENCE BETWEEN ARTICLES AND BLOGS

Marketers always ask about the difference between articles and blogs. Blogs have a clear point of view—a personality. Articles have no point of view but are informational treasure troves. Think of FAQ articles or an informational series of articles on your website.

Tip: When customer service answers a key customer question via email, think about putting it in your article repository.

E-BOOK

WHAT AN E-BOOK IS

Think of an e-book as a white paper on steroids: a report, generally 12 to 40 pages or more in length, that presents complex information in a visually attractive, reader-friendly format. The content is both informative and entertaining; the tone, collegial; the format, "chunky" rather than linear, to facilitate skimming and scanning.

THREE KEY PLAY POINTS

1. **Develop your distribution strategy early.** How will you get your e-book into readers' hands?
2. **Think visually.** Make liberal use of bullets, callouts, sidebars, graphs, and so on.
3. **Conclude with a solid call to action.** What should readers do next? For that matter, include some call to action or link on every page. Why not?

WEBINAR/WEBCAST

WHAT A WEBINAR/WEBCAST IS

Take your presentation and put it online: that's the essence of the webinar (slides and audio) or webcast (slides, audio, and video). Visually, the content is delivered slide by slide in the online equivalent of a live presentation. The audio component can be delivered via telephone or computer. Remember, you can do this live or on-demand.

THREE KEY PLAY POINTS

1. **Webinars make an excellent call to action** for follow-up offers to other forms of content, such as e-books, white papers, newsletters, and so on.
2. **You benefit twice:** first, from the live event; then from the people who download the archived event. In a six-month period, generally, 80 percent of those people who register for a webinar will attend either the live or archived version.
3. **A successful webinar requires** an aggressive promotions strategy, typically via your website, blog, newsletter, and other media or social media channels.

VIDEO

WHAT VIDEO IS

Almost 92 percent of internet users report watching some type of video content each week. Video is the fastest-growing and most-consumed content format. Social videos get 12 times more shares than text and images combined. The incredible growth of TikTok has supercharged short-form video, and all the other players are jumping on board and creating their own versions. TikTok, YouTube Shorts, and Instagram Reels can all be considerations for your video series.

Everyone with a smartphone is a content consumer and potential content creator. And it's easy to take a picture, record a video, capture some audio, and post it for the world to see . . . in seconds. That said, make a plan.

THREE KEY PLAY POINTS

1. **Think beyond the "talking head" approach.** Inexpensive editing tools such as iMovie or Final Cut make it easy to assemble professional-looking video content. Most social platforms include integrated tools for editing.
2. **Instead of taking a one-shot approach,** consider a video series that builds interest, and an audience, over time. The most successful YouTubers distribute videos consistently over a long period of time.
3. **Don't sweat "perfection."** Many of the most successful online videos have production values that would scandalize traditional media

broadcasters. Actually, the most important part of the video is the audio, so focus your tools on the audio equipment first.

CUSTOM PRINT MAGAZINE

WHAT A CUSTOM PRINT MAGAZINE IS

All brands are now publishers. The custom print magazine takes this approach quite literally, offering the familiar magazine format with a new twist: it's sponsored, produced, and issued by one company or brand.

THREE KEY PLAY POINTS

1. Be prepared to spend at least $40,000 for even a small initial distribution.
2. The most effective frequency is quarterly or more often.
3. It can be an excellent way to bypass gatekeepers.

PRINT NEWSLETTER

WHAT A PRINT NEWSLETTER IS

Whether it's merely a double-sided sheet or a 16-page document, a print newsletter offers attention-grabbing content meant for rapid consumption. As a tactic, consider it for customer retention, and remember that the average length runs between 4 and 12 pages.

THREE KEY PLAY POINTS

1. **Print newsletters are terrific** for an on-the-go audience, including business travelers and commuters.
2. **Production quality matters.** The way your content is presented is as important as the content itself.
3. **Make sure you know** your audience's precise information needs before you commit to an editorial platform.

THE OPPORTUNITIES IN PRINT

I was on the phone recently talking to a customer about different options in print. He was interested in the discussion because he felt his company needed to do more *nontraditional marketing*.

Just think about that for a second: print is *nontraditional* marketing. That's where we are today. Social media, streaming, influencer programs . . . that's all very traditional. Because of that, brands should be looking at print as an opportunity right now to get and keep attention

THE *NEWSWEEK* MOVE

Newsweek, Entertainment Weekly, and *InStyle* have ceased publication in print format.

When I have conversations with marketers and publishers about these kinds of moves, I always hear the notion that "print is dead." Well, I'm here to tell you that there has never been a bigger opportunity for brands in the print channel than right now.

While I would not want to be in the broad-based, horizontal print game, highly niche, highly targeted publications are flourishing as a marketing tool.

SIX REASONS TO RETHINK PRINT

Here are a few reasons why there might be an amazing opportunity in the print channel:

1. **It grabs attention.** Have you noticed how many fewer magazines and print newsletters you are getting in the mail these days? I don't know about you, but I definitely pay more attention to my print mail. There's just less mail, so more attention is paid to each piece. Opportunity? The decisions that magazines like *Newsweek* are making leave a clear opportunity for content marketers to fill the gap.

2. **It focuses on customer retention.** Sixty-four percent of B2B marketers create original content for customer retention and loyalty goals. Historically, the reason custom print magazines and newsletters were developed by brands was for customer retention purposes.

3. **There are no audience development costs (for you).** Publishers expend huge amounts of time and money qualifying subscribers. Many times, publishers need to invest multiple dollars per subscriber per year for auditing purposes. (They send direct mail, they call . . . they call again . . . so that the magazine can say that its subscribers have requested the magazine. This is true for controlled [free] trade magazines.)

   So let's say a traditional publisher's cost per subscriber per year is $2 and its distribution is 100,000. That's $200,000 per year for audience development.

That's a cost that marketers don't have to worry about. If marketers want to distribute a magazine to their customers, they just use their customer mailing lists. That's a big advantage.

4. **What's old is new again.** Social media, online content, and apps are all part of the marketing mix today. Still, what excites marketers and media buyers is what *is not* being done (think "nontraditional"). They want to do something different and something new. It's hard to believe, but the print channel is new again and is seeing a rebirth. Could we possibly be seeing a golden age in print, as we are seeing in television?

5. **Customers still need to know what questions to ask.** I love the internet because buyers can find answers to almost anything. But where does someone go to think about what questions they should be asking? I talked to a publisher recently who said this: "The web is where we go to get answers, but print is where we go to ask questions."

   The print vehicle is still the best medium on the planet for thinking outside the box and asking yourself tough questions based on what you read; it's "lean back" versus "lean forward." If you want to challenge your customers (as *Harvard Business Review* does), print is a viable option.

6. **Print still excites people.** I talked to a journalist who said it's harder and harder to get people to agree to an interview for an online story. But mention that it will be a printed feature and executives rearrange their schedule. The printed word is still perceived as more credible to many people than anything on the web. It goes to the old adage, "If someone invested enough to print and mail it, it must be important."

DIGITAL MAGAZINE

WHAT A DIGITAL MAGAZINE IS

A hybrid between the traditional magazine and a souped-up PDF, a digital magazine offers self-contained, visually compelling periodical content that doesn't require special software to open and read. Issues are generally distributed by email via brand websites.

THREE KEY PLAY POINTS

1. Although many digital magazines are distributed in a container (such as Nxtbook or Issuu), some publishers distribute their digital magazine in a WordPress blog format.
2. Digital magazines are great for integrating print content with a web presence.
3. Consider adding video and podcasts to your magazine content.

PODCAST

WHAT A PODCAST IS

A podcast is simply an audio file you can listen to on a computer or phone. Podcasts are generally 5 to 60 minutes long, but there are many longer popular podcasts as well. The podcast audience has been growing quickly, and more than 40 percent of all internet users are listening to podcasts (according to Edison Research).

THREE KEY PLAY POINTS

1. Define a podcast theme, and stick to it.
2. Establish a regular release schedule: weekly, biweekly, monthly, and so on. Be consistent.
3. Integrate podcast content with your blog to gain listener insights. Consider using transcripts as blog posts.

EXECUTIVE ROUNDTABLE

WHAT AN EXECUTIVE ROUNDTABLE IS

An executive roundtable is a gathering of industry executives who are experts in their field and who have enough drawing power to pull in your prospects. Through brief presentations and interactions among roundtable participants, you have the opportunity once again to position yourself as a thought leader.

THREE KEY PLAY POINTS

1. Look for executives whose personalities are as appealing as their ideas.

2. Consider asking the roundtable executives for guest blog posts that complement their live topic ideas.
3. Turn the resulting discussion into a summary report you can offer as a white paper or e-book. Leverage video, audio, and transcripts to keep the content flowing long after the actual roundtable has taken place.

INDUSTRY RANKING SYSTEM

WHAT AN INDUSTRY RANKING SYSTEM IS

People love lists. An industry ranking system gives readers a preassembled "best-of" list that ranks available options in a given topic area—and subsequently ranks high with search engines. A list, whatever its contents, positions its assemblers as industry experts and gives their prospects a helpful reference tool.

THREE KEY PLAY POINTS

1. Rankings can be determined by some objective and measurable means or by subjective criteria.
2. Make liberal use of links to the listed resources.
3. Announce updates to the ranking system via blogs, Twitter, press releases, and so on.

PRINTED BOOK

WHAT A PRINTED BOOK IS

Even in the revolutionary age of Web3, a full-length book still carries an aura of authority. Whether self-published or created via a traditional publishing house, the book is the "big" content piece that often leads to press exposure, speaking invitations, and privileged status as *the* expert.

THREE KEY PLAY POINTS

1. Books are a major investment of time, so plan carefully! If you have a blog, think about how your blog posts can serve as chapters for your book.
2. Get your PR people on board fast to leverage the media potential.

3. Integrate influencers into your book for better social media distribution opportunities. If you've noticed, we include more than 100 content marketing influencers in this book.

WHY YOUR BRAND SHOULD WRITE A BOOK

Frankly, if you are going to position yourself and/or your company as the leading expert in your niche, you need a book. No, not an e-book distributed solely online. You need a "makes-a-big-thud-when-dropped-on-a-desk" book that is produced from dead trees.

I'm astonished and saddened that more organizations aren't looking seriously at developing a book. There is no better way to show true thought leadership than a printed book. A close second is this: it may be the best customer giveaway ever created. And third, once the book has been developed, you have an amazing resource from which to develop ancillary content, such as blog posts (excerpts), e-books, SlideShare packages, white papers, and much, much more.

EIGHT TIPS FOR MAKING YOUR BOOK HAPPEN

Creating a book that makes an impact on your industry and business is anything but easy. That said, here are some tips I've picked up along the way that can make a difference in getting the book off the ground.

1. **Do a deep-dive content audit.** You may already have a treasure trove of material that can be repurposed, or at the very least you have content that can be collected to form the initial workings of some key chapters. Be sure you do the work up front to see what you have to start with.

2. **Mine the blog.** For all my books, much of the material came from existing blog posts, just reworked. If you have been blogging for at least six months, you might already have half a book.

3. **Consider co-creation.** Do you have key, noncompetitive partners that target the same prospects and customers as you do? If so, consider reaching out to those partners about working with you on the book concept. Also, once you start promoting, you have multiple networks to reach out to.

4. **Get it funded.** *Get Content Get Customers* was self-published before McGraw-Hill purchased the rights. Much of the up-front investment came from selling bulk shipments to partner companies. If you don't like that route, find a sponsor that really wants to get your

message out there, and have that person or organization support it through either distribution or monetary funding.

5. **Determine your mission.** Be very clear about what you want your readers to get out of the book. Write your thoughts down, and keep that information posted on your wall as you work on the book. So many companies focus on what they are trying to say instead of pinpointing the focus on the pain points of the reader.

6. **Include the influencers.** If possible, include key examples from industry influencers, as well as partners, if it's good content. The more people you can include in your stories, the more opportunities for outside sharing.

7. **Consider a ghostwriter.** Believe it or not, many of the books from the authors you love have been written by someone else. The best ghostwriters out there start at about $50,000 and then go up from there. If you simply can't make the internal time or don't have the resources to get the writing done, consider using one.

8. **Stop somewhere and realize that perfection is unattainable.** At some point, you must draw a line in the sand and publish the book. As soon as you finish it, there will be some new research, some new story, or some new perspective that you should have covered. Don't worry about it; just use it for your next book.

Remember that there are many options for publishing your book, from a traditional publisher (such as this book's publisher McGraw Hill Education) to self-service opportunities, such Lulu Press and Amazon, to options somewhere in between, such as Scribe Media.

AUDIOBOOK

WHAT AN AUDIOBOOK IS

An audiobook consists of book-length content you listen to rather than read. When sponsored by a brand, it's a great way to capture the attention of podcast-downloading listeners.

THREE KEY PLAY POINTS

1. Vocal talent has to be as strong as the written content.
2. Get people to sample the content by giving away portions or chapters for free.

3. Record the audiobook yourself. If you have a relatively pleasant voice, with a small spend on a good microphone, you can record the book yourself. Also, people like hearing the author talking.

In order to build anticipation for my first novel, *The Will to Die*, I decided to launch each audiobook chapter for free as a podcast. This resulted in building an initial fanbase for the suspense/thriller. Four months later, when I launched the print and full audiobook version, we landed the number one spot in four Amazon bestseller categories. Much of this was because of the initial audience-building through audio.

ONLINE EVENT

WHY VIRTUAL?

The Covid pandemic has changed many things in our society. One of the big changes is that people got used to doing everything online: virtual meetings, virtual interviews, and virtual conferences. It's often easier to get people to attend a virtual event than an in-person event. It can, however, be much more difficult to make them stay.

THREE KEY PLAY POINTS

1. Most virtual events use the "conference" metaphor as the navigation model for the site.
2. Just as live conferences sell exhibits, you can sell sponsorships at your virtual event.
3. Hybrid events (both live and virtual simultaneously) are challenging to pull off. Simply put, targeting two audiences at the same time with an amazing experience is almost impossible. We recommend doing one or the other for best results.

COMIC BOOK

WHAT A COMIC BOOK IS

Here's what a comic book is *not*: it's not a gimmick just for kids. By reinforcing text with vivid pictures, comic books communicate in a fun, fast, and memorable way to readers of all ages.

THREE KEY PLAY POINTS

1. For instructional content, comics may be one of the very best tactics available.
2. Memorable comic books can certainly generate buzz.
3. As an alternative to a comic book, consider an online comic strip that appears every week.

ROAD SHOW

WHAT A ROAD SHOW IS

A road show is a mini-conference or tour that is typically conducted by a single organization, although related companies that don't compete will often participate. Usually, individual events last for a day or less and are conducted in cities where there is a high concentration of prospective customers.

THREE KEY PLAY POINTS

1. Concentrate on the takeaway. What will participants get by attending?
2. Coordination of event planning and promotions is crucial; both have to roll out on schedule.
3. You may need to train internal talent to maximize their effectiveness as speakers and presenters.

PUBLIC SPEAKING TIPS THAT ROCK

Over the past 20 years, I've made thousands of presentations, both in-person and online.

I've also had to sit through a *large number* of presentations by other individuals over that time. Not that I'm perfect by any means, but I honestly don't wish that on anyone.

After my blog and my books, public speaking events have probably done more to grow the business than anything else I've done. Frankly, there are not enough businesses that take presenting in public as a serious driver of revenue. As a business owner or a marketing professional, you need to cultivate evangelists within the company who can spread the content mission of your organization.

The following are some of my presentation speaking tips that I try to integrate into every presentation I do (in no particular order). I hope they are helpful to you.

- **Put your Twitter name on every slide.** Even at the least social media–savvy events, there are always multiple people tweeting. Putting your Twitter handle at the beginning of the slide deck usually doesn't do the trick. (What if someone comes into the room late?) Since I've added my Twitter handle to every slide, tweet mentions have more than doubled. What a great way to expand the reach of your message!
- **Be prepared with tweetable messages.** I learned from my friend Jay Baer to come prepared with tweetable sayings. It's best practice to put them on the slide and repeat them at least twice for maximum impact.
- **Promote your speech using the event hashtag.** The day before and the morning of your presentation, be sure to let people know you are speaking, what you are speaking on, and what time the event is. Be sure to use the event Twitter hashtag (such as #cexevent, the hashtag for the Creator Economy Expo). I can't tell you how many more people I get to my speeches who were undecided about which session to attend.
- **Never have more than 20 words on a slide.** If people have to read your slide, you'll lose them. Use headlines and text to cue your stories and pictures to amplify your point. My goal is to someday take the advice of Seth Godin and have all my slides with no words, just pictures.
- **If you use words, make them at least 30-point type size or larger.** If you do have text on a slide, make sure it's actually readable. Thirty points is the smallest I would go.
- **Don't stand behind the podium.** A podium places an unnecessary barrier between you and your audience. Talk *with* the people in your audience, not *at* them.
- **It's OK to walk around.** You're a human, and you have legs: use them. Find a few spots on the stage where you can walk back and forth. Hold your spot for five seconds, and then move to the next spot. Every time you start on a new topic, move.
- **Get a speaking wardrobe.** In order to be remembered, you need to use everything at your disposal. A wardrobe is key. Find something that people will remember. I personally always wear the color orange for every presentation. I haven't done a presentation in 15 years without an orange shirt. People expect it and always comment on it.

- **Smile a lot.** It's contagious. Always start the presentation with a big smile, and set cues for yourself to smile at least every five minutes. The more people smile, the more positive they will be in general (and with your reviews). It also helps keep people awake.
- **Use short links as calls to action.** In every slide presentation, I include several short links for people to get additional information about something I'm discussing. I've had well over 5,000 people download one of my presentations directly from one of my sessions. I use bit.ly links to track the content.
- **Give away something for participation.** I almost always give a signed copy of my book away to reward participation. It helps with questions later and always gets you talking with someone after the presentation (when you deliver the book). When you get to the Web3 chapters (Chapters 27 and 28), you'll learn how you can give away creator coins, nonfungible tokens, and Proof of Attendance Protocols to attendees. That encourages more questions and opportunities to network. This tactic has delivered many new customers over the years.
- **Have one main call to action for the presentation.** You want the attendees to do something, right? Don't give them too many options. Give them one thing you really want them to do from each presentation, and include a coupon code or short link to track it.
- **Use lists.** Most of my speaking and presentation titles include numbers in the titles: "8 Content Marketing Tips to Initiate Now," "6 Keys That Separate Good to Great Content Marketing," and so on. Numbers keep people focused on where you are in the presentation.
- **Switch the flow and tell a story every few minutes.** Your audience can only pay attention for so long. Every few minutes, stop the flow of your presentation by pausing and telling a story somewhat related to your point. People will remember the stories the most, which will keep them engaged and help drive your overall mission for the speech.
- **Take heed from Aristotle.** When I first started teaching public speaking, I always used Aristotle's advice on speeches: tell them what you are going to tell them (the intro), tell them (the body), and then tell them what you just told them (the conclusion). Much of public speaking and getting things to stick is repetition. This type of setup does the trick.

ONLINE GAME

WHAT AN ONLINE GAME IS

An online game is an electronic game like any other except it's branded—by you. An example of a recent successful game is Wordle. The *New York Times* purchased the game from the developer, who had created it for his wife and some friends. On March 31, 2022, the *Times* reported that the acquisition of Wordle had brought "tens of millions" of new players to the site and app.

THREE KEY PLAY POINTS

1. Games should work without burdensome software downloads.
2. They must run across multiple browser types and operating system platforms.
3. Game experience should reinforce a favorable experience of the brand.

INFOGRAPHIC

WHAT AN INFOGRAPHIC IS

As the name suggests, an infographic represents information or data visually, in a chart, graph, or other forms of illustration. But the power of an infographic goes beyond its immediate visual appeal; unlike a mere list, an infographic can expose the relationships among disparate pieces of information, delivering insight, not just raw data.

THREE KEY PLAY POINTS

1. Everyone's confusion can become your opportunity—where can you deliver value by providing clarity?
2. Think metaphorically to find a guiding image or idea that frames your information.
3. Make your resulting infographic easy to share online for maximum reach and distribution.

ONLINE RESEARCH PROJECT

WHAT AN ONLINE RESEARCH PROJECT IS

An online research project is a vehicle for gathering information and then presenting the information you gathered as a resource for your audience.

The first step is to poll your customers, visitors, or colleagues with paid or free online survey tools from providers such as SurveyMonkey.

THREE KEY PLAY POINTS

1. What do C-suite executives want to know most? What other C-suite execs are thinking. Anything you learn will be eagerly devoured by other execs.
2. Potential survey audiences include blog readers, Twitter followers, LinkedIn and Facebook colleagues, conference attendees, and newsletter readers.
3. Keep 'em short! Any more than 10 questions (and that's pushing it) and you'll lose participants.

The next step is to use the information to produce a report that will be useful to your audience.

At The Tilt, our annual "Creator Economy Benchmark Report" lands us more coverage, subscribers, and leads than anything else we do. To make this an "industry" report, we partner with other organizations, leveraging their subscriber lists. We also partner with an outside research company to make sure the report is truly "independent" in nature.

DISCUSSION FORUM

WHAT A DISCUSSION FORUM IS

A discussion forum is a simple "bulletin board" online site where customers and prospects can post thoughts and make comments on your products and services. Consider free services such as Discord or Telegram, or paid options such as Slack, Circle, or Mighty Networks.

THREE KEY PLAY POINTS

1. Make the interface simple; no one should struggle to participate.
2. Once it's up and running, the discussion forum can resolve many issues without imposing demands on your staff.
3. Treat forum participants as "insiders" entitled to breaking news about new products, new releases, and so on.

EPIC RESOURCES

- OptinMonster, "Headline Analyzer Tool by OptinMonster," accessed June 23, 2022, https://optinmonster.com/headline -analyzer/.

- SEMrush, "The State of Content Marketing 2022 Global Report," accessed June 23, 2022, https://www.semrush.com/state-of -content-marketing/.

- Hootsuite, "Digital 2022 Global Overview Report," accessed June 24, 2022, https://hootsuite.widen.net/s/gqprmtzq6g/digital -2022-global-overview-report.

- Small Biz Trends, "27 Video Marketing Statistics That Will Have You Hitting the Record Button," accessed June 24, 2022, https:// smallbiztrends.com/2016/10/video-marketing-statistics.html.

- Insider Intelligence, "Podcast Industry Report: Market Growth and Advertising Statistics in 2022," accessed July 9, 2022, https:// www.insiderintelligence.com/insights/the-podcast-industry -report-statistics.

CHAPTER 15

Finding Your Content Assets

BY BRIAN PIPER

Searching is half the fun: life is much more
manageable when thought of as a scavenger hunt
as opposed to a surprise party.

JIMMY BUFFETT

You've done it. You've developed why you need the content, created and vetted the audience personas, and identified the buying stages where this essential content will impact the business. As you start to dig into your content marketing channel and workflow strategy, you may realize that you simply don't have enough brand stories to meet the demands of the content marketing initiative.

In many content marketing programs, the core brand stories deal with transforming an employee's, customer's, or stakeholder's passion and expertise into one or multiple stories. How many times have you heard the following that stopped you in your tracks?

- Our [CEO, executive, or engineer] doesn't create content; in fact, no one in our organization creates content. (This one is almost certainly not true.)

- Our [CEO, executive, or engineer] can't write. (OK, maybe this one's true.)
- How are we going to get all this content created? I just don't have the resources or correct process. (This one is almost always true . . . to an extent.)

Now, before exploring some of the following ideas, you need to realize that almost *no company* has a shortage of raw materials for content marketing. What's usually missing is that the content is not in storytelling form or that a process has not been created to extract the information in a way that works with the content marketing plan.

THE VISUAL CONTENT AUDIT

Marketing executives are like most other people: they like to learn by example. Having them engage in the following test will help:

1. Gather all your marketing content, both print and electronic (make printouts), and place it on a conference table. Include brochures, newsletters, blog posts, reseller information, video stills, and so on.
2. Get your marketing executives in a room.
3. Ask them, "Is our content more about our customers' pain points or more about us and how great our products or services are?"
4. Then ask them, "Will people share and spread this information on social media? Will they talk to their colleagues about it? Will they search for it? Will they become so engaged in it that they will friend or follow you? Will they care if we stopped producing it?"

The purpose of the visual content audit is twofold. First, it starts a good discussion about what kind of content the company has been creating and whether it is helping or hurting the business. Second, it gives you a good sense of what content you'll need to develop to fit the gaps in your engagement cycle.

Note: You may just want to start with your content and marketing teams and not your executive teams.

THE CONTENT AUDIT

Before you can ever determine what kind of content you need, you first need to figure out what you have. In addition, you need to determine whether what you have is any good at all, or better yet, whether you have some raw content that is still incredibly valuable that you can leverage throughout your customers' buying cycle.

Alina Petrova of SEMrush breaks down the content inventory in two steps:

1. Collect your URLs.
2. Catalog your content into the following categories:
   a. Buyer's journey stage (awareness, consideration, decision)
   b. Content type (blog post, ebook, product description, landing page)
   c. Content format (text only, images/video present, with/without call to action)
   d. Number of words or video/audio time
   e. Date of publication or last modification
   f. Content hub (or cluster)
   g. Author (if you have multiple writers on your website)

This is your basic content inventory. Keep it safe, and refer to it often.

Why is this so critical? I've worked with dozens of companies that launched new ebooks and white papers and hired freelancers and editors, only to find out midway through the process that much of the content initiative had already been created. This simple content inventory will save you time and money.

THE PROCESS OF CONTENT ANALYSIS

To do a content analysis of your site, start with a content inventory to figure out what your web content currently looks like. The easiest way to do this is to use a simple spreadsheet that looks like Figure 15.1. You can download a more detailed content inventory worksheet at EpicContentMarketing.com.

Go through every single page on your website and record what you find using the format shown in Figure 15.1. If that's too daunting, start with the top 200 most-trafficked pages. Be sure to make careful notes and add more columns as needed. Keep in mind too that content is not only text but also video, photo images, audio, infographics, and everything else that lives on your website.

Content Analysis Spreadsheet

ID	PAGE NAME	DOCUMENT TYPE	LINK	KEYWORDS	META DESCRIPTION	INTERNAL LINKS	PURPOSE	NOTES
1.0.0	ABC Company	Home page	domain.com	Content marketing services, custom content	Content marketing, solutions for B2B brands	About 1.1.0, Services 1.3.0, Blog 1.5.0	Sell/market	Only 10% of pages here
1.1.0	About ABC	About Us page	domain.com/about	Content marketing solutions	We help you develop content that attracts and retains customers	Blog 1.5.0	Brand/PR	Staffing changes/needs updating
1.3.0	ABC Services Listing	Services page	domain.com/service	Content marketing strategy, social listening services	Our content marketing solutions are designed to help you create content that is compelling, relevant, and consistent	Home 1.00 Downloads 1.4.0	Sell/market	Pricing structure confusing

FIGURE 15.1 Sample content analysis spreadsheet

DEDICATED OVERSIGHT

Once you have performed your content inventory, you'll have all the information you need to manage your site accordingly.

Unfortunately, when your main focus is to consistently create content that engages your audience, it is an enormous task to go back and evaluate what was created in the past to ensure that it is still relevant to your audience.

It is very important to have high-quality content on your website, not only to optimize user experience but also to ensure that your brand is consistently held in high regard.

The last thing you want is for your credibility to be undermined simply because a user came across a broken link on your site. So whether it means hiring someone to perform content maintenance or having to take the time to do it yourself, make sure that your site receives dedicated oversight.

QUICK TAKEAWAY

Of all the things that impact user experience on your website, content is the most important factor. Make sure that it is always *updated, organized, and relevant.* Yes, it's a lot of hard work, and the more content you generate, the more content you will need to maintain. But the quality of your content is not something that you want to compromise.

EXTRACTING CONTENT FROM EMPLOYEES

Few CEOs love to write, but most like to talk. If it's a challenge to get your C-level executive to produce thought leadership content, capture the CEO's thoughts in a different format. Interview the CEO using Zoom and record the conversation.

Your managing editors can turn that into other content marketing pieces (for example, edited videos, blog posts, and white papers). Or if the content quality is good enough, you can use it in the unedited captured format. Or if the CEO can't really write but is willing to simply type an email, tell them to just write a long email to you, record voice notes, and use the phone notepad. Whatever works.

In other words, don't block the process by forcing the person into something they aren't comfortable with.

When you're at industry events, be sure to capture photos and videos. Mix and match them with pieces of content that you may or may not produce. Perhaps the video gets used in a customer interview.

Another possibility is just sitting down with the person. If there's a product manager who is shy or feels uncomfortable at the thought of having to write 500 words on a particular topic, interview them instead. Take the person to lunch and record the conversation. Again, reuse that content in multiple formats.

HELP EXECUTIVES TELL STORIES

When talking with executives about writing and creating content, you have to begin by simply teaching them what "writing" is. The act of writing is just transferring what's in your head to words. As the famed sportswriter Red Smith used to delicately put it, all you have to do is "sit down at a typewriter and open a vein."

Of course, the real magic in turning writing into a story or something else worth reading happens in the editing process. Relieve the members of your team of their worries by assuring them that the copy will be "polished up" during editing. Then get them rolling by offering the following tips:

- **Write it out.** Just write blind—get it out. Writers are usually surprised by how much structure and genuine goodness comes out by just opening up and not letting their mental "editor" get in the way. Tell your prospective contributors to just spend half an hour typing out their thoughts.
- **Storyboard it out.** If the people are having trouble getting anything going or opening up, tell them to just visualize what they want to say and write down key phrases or concepts onto sticky notes. They can even draw what they're thinking on sticky notes. This is an especially

great way to organize thoughts for a longer piece. (Mind mapping may help as well.)

CONTENT FUEL

Melanie Deziel wrote *The Content Fuel Framework*, which provides an incredible method to discover content opportunities. It is essentially a guide to creating a 10x10 matrix of focus areas (people, basics, details, history, process, curation, data, product, example, and opinion) and format options (writing, infographic, audio, video, live video, image gallery, timeline, quiz, tool, and map) and filling it in with ideas.

By the time you're done with the book, you have 100 content ideas addressing all different aspects of your funnel, your audience, and your channels.

EPIC THOUGHTS

- Before you create any new epic content, figure out first what you have to work with.

- Figure out a process to coordinate the content you have, and start thinking about when content will need to be updated. Assigning someone to this task will help.

- In any employee content program, don't start by forcing staffers into processes that leave them discouraged and unmotivated.

- Stuck on content thoughts? Try using a framework to fuel your ideas, and you'll be surprised how easy it is to come up with 100 different options across platforms and focus areas.

EPIC RESOURCES

- Alina Petrova, "The Step-by-Step Guide to Conducting a Content Audit in 2022," SEMrush, accessed February 9, 2022, https://www.semrush.com/blog/content-audit-for-content-marketing-strategy/.

- Melanie Deziel, *The Content Fuel Framework*, Storyfuel Press, 2020.

CHAPTER 16

The Content Platform

BY JOE PULIZZI

Expect the best. Prepare for the worst.
Capitalize on what comes.

ZIG ZIGLAR

Your content platform can be built in several different ways: as a website, blog, Twitter presence, YouTube or TikTok video, Twitch stream, print book, newsletter, and more. Although some may disagree, there is one true way to build your platform with content: by owning it.

Writer and coach Sonia Simone said it best: "Don't build on rented land." Yes, you can create a following on YouTube, Twitter, or TikTok, on someone else's blog, or as a guest writer on a popular media site, but you don't own or control anything on those channels; someone else does. Building your platform by focusing on, say, Facebook, is like building an amazing home on leased land. While it's nice to live in, the owner can stop by at any time and sell it right in front of your nose, and there is nothing you can do about it.

Just as with the important email subscriptions (names that you own) versus followers or fans (connections that someone else owns), the magnet that draws people to you on a daily or weekly basis needs to be owned by you. You need both content you own and content spread around other platforms, but the focus should be on a platform you can control.

THE MEDIA COMPANY EXAMPLE

Look at the greatest media companies in our history, whether it's the *Wall Street Journal* or the leading trade publication in your niche. Their platforms used to be strictly print newspapers or magazines. Today every media company's platform starts on the web. And that's where you will start.

Take a look at the newsletter *Morning Brew*. While the company is active on literally every social media channel, its most important channel (and the one that drives almost all its revenue) is its newsletter, where it has opt-in control of the data.

THE HUB-AND-SPOKE MODEL

Lee Odden, CEO of TopRank Online Marketing and author of *Optimize*, preaches about the value of the hub-and-spoke model (see Figure 16.1). The hub (your blog or website) becomes the center of your content marketing universe, and the spokes are places to syndicate your content. Here are some of Lee's suggestions:

- Create a social hub, preferably a blog, to which to drive social traffic.
- Develop distribution channels and communities off the hub.
- Spend time creating, optimizing, and promoting great content on the hub and growing networks in the spokes.

FIGURE 16.1 The hub-and-spoke model

When executed correctly, the exposure of content to communities empowered to publish creates editorial visibility and links back to your hub. In addition, outside links send traffic to your properties and increase search visibility.

WORDPRESS

WordPress, an open-source content management platform, is the most popular content management system (CMS) in the world. The WordPress code is free to use, but you need a WordPress developer to create a site for you.

I've used a lot of CMS platforms in my day. Today our entire Tilt Media organization runs on WordPress. Honestly, I don't care what type of platform you use, as long as you control access to it yourself. If your website is hosted by someone else (for example, Wix or Squarespace), you are missing out on an opportunity to own your platform. We'll talk a bit more about true ownership in the Web3 section (Chapters 27 and 28).

I say this often: "If your company does less than $50 million in revenue, you probably won't need any more than WordPress for your CMS." WordPress is used by Etsy, BBC America, and the Rolling Stones.

When choosing which CMS platform to use, be sure to select one that can be easily edited and maintained, includes simple publishing tools, and can be modified for a great user experience. (If you can't go in and modify your website or blog content right now, you have problems.) Besides WordPress, there are literally hundreds of other CMS possibilities for you to choose from (see http://en.wikipedia.org/wiki/List_of_content_management_systems).

MOVING UP THE HIERARCHY

As we discussed, your goal is to build content assets where you have the maximum amount of control. This is especially true for the types of subscribers you attract. While I believe that any fans, followers, or subscribers can be a good thing, they are not equal in value.

In *Content Inc.*, I go into detail about the "subscriber hierarchy." Our job as content marketers is to move up the hierarchy whenever we can. For example, Accidentally Wes Anderson (AWA) launched its platform on Instagram. But over the past four years, it has been moving that audience to its website and newsletter, which now has more than 50,000 subscribers. Of course,

Instagram is still its current home, but the website and newsletter will be its future.

As you analyze your digital footprint and begin to build your audience, your focus needs to be at the top of this hierarchy (see Figure 16.2). Simply put, it comes down to the amount of control you have with the platform and your communications with fans and subscribers.

SUBSCRIBER HIERARCHY

- Membership
- Email Newsletter
- Print Subscribers
- Podcast Subscribers
- Twitter Followers
- YouTube Subscribers
- LinkedIn Connections
- Instagram Followers
- Twitch Followers
- Pinterest Subscribers
- TikTok Fans
- Snapchat Followers
- Reddit Followers
- Facebook Fans

FIGURE 16.2 Our goal should be to continually move our subscribers up the hierarchy.

Note: Any of the platforms below "Podcast Subscribers" could be interchanged. Although the algorithms and current opportunities are different, the fact is that we can't control the data or content distribution on any social network or outside media platform.

Let's take a closer look at the different levels within the subscriber hierarchy.

- **Membership.** This includes ongoing online training or a private community group/discussion forum where you receive an email address for the service you provide. This type of subscriber is hard to beat.
- **Email newsletter subscribers.** You have a high amount of control. Extremely helpful and relevant emails will break through the clutter.

- **Print subscribers.** Subscribers generally trade vast amounts of personal information to receive a print magazine or newsletter. Communication is never instantaneous, and feedback is difficult. There are cost challenges due to print and postal charges.
- **Podcast subscribers.** You have full control over the delivery of audio content, but Apple Podcasts, Spotify, Overcast, and Stitcher do not give you access to who subscribes to your content.
- **Twitter followers.** You have full control over what you send to followers, but messages have a limited life span, so it may be challenging to reach an audience regularly. In addition, with the recent ownership changes at Twitter, this is a rented platform like any other. Proceed with caution.
- **YouTube subscribers.** You have some control over content, but YouTube can decide to hold some of your content back if subscribers aren't engaging enough with your content (called "subscriber burn").
- **LinkedIn connections.** You have full control over what you send to followers and connections, but the channel is very congested, so it may be challenging to break through with a consistent message. LinkedIn's algorithm will show what's getting engaged in, so content that doesn't perform might not be seen.
- **Instagram followers.** You have full control over your content, but Instagram's algorithm will only show engaging content (which again means your content may not be seen).
- **Twitch followers.** This is almost exclusively for the streaming of video games. Play the right game for a long period of time and you can win a following (the average stream time is three to four hours per session).
- **Pinterest subscribers.** You have full control over the delivery of content. Users will see your content if they choose to. There is no ultimate ownership over the platform.
- **TikTok fans.** Right now, TikTok owns the world's best algorithm. Quality content can perform well even if you don't have a large following.
- **Snapchat followers.** Users spend over 30 minutes a day on Snapchat and open the app over 25 times per day. If you target a younger audience, you might need to test it out.

- **Reddit followers.** The Reddit community is extremely loyal to the platform. Posting consistently helpful content builds a following. This is best as a secondary subscriber choice.
- **Facebook fans.** Facebook continually modifies its algorithm, which is out of your control. Fans may or may not see your content depending on this algorithm, although quality, helpful, and interesting content has the best chance of breaking through. Promotional content is almost always shut down by Facebook.

While you have more control with certain subscription options, Jeff Rohrs, author of *Audience,* is adamant that no company "owns" its audience. He explains: "The reason that the audience is in different places is that no audience is owned. Regardless of whether you're a major television network, pop star, or professional sports team with rabid fans, you simply do not own your audience. They can get up and leave—mentally or physically—at any time."

This is exactly the reason that amazingly helpful and relevant content is the only way to keep our audience connected to us, regardless of which subscription options you choose to leverage.

As a final note, the future of Web3 will play a role in this hierarchy. As we discuss in Chapters 27 and 28, *a "connect wallet"–type function could very well find its place at the top as blockchain technology continues to evolve. We are just not there . . . yet.*

EPIC THOUGHTS

- Build platforms on Facebook, LinkedIn, Twitter, and other places where your customers are hanging out. But focus first on the content platform you own. Don't build on rented land.

- Your platform may be either separate from your company's website or integrated. There is no one right way, so give it some thought and choose the path that makes the most sense to your customers.

EPIC RESOURCES

- Lee Odden, "Social Media & SEO at Search Congress Barcelona," *TopRank*, accessed June 23, 2022, http://www.toprankblog.com/2011/03/social-media-seo-search-congress-barcelona/.

- WordPress, http://wordpress.org/.

CHAPTER 17

The Content Channel Plan in Action

BY JOE PULIZZI

If one is lucky, a solitary fantasy can totally transform one million realities.

MAYA ANGELOU

Now that content marketing has been explained, the content niche and strategy have been delineated, and the specifics of content management and process have been worked out, it's time to examine content distribution.

Many content businesses start with channels (for example, Twitter and Instagram) instead of first focusing on what goes in those channels. If you start with channels, there is little possibility you'll be able to measure true impact without first developing the content strategy.

I've seen several channel plans, and almost all of them are confusing. For this part of the book, I want to make sure that you have a visual idea of how to develop and execute a content marketing plan. All the ingredients are in front of you: your goals, your niche, your audience, content types, and the assets you have. Now you need to mix these together to make something worth your customers' time.

Again, depending on how many personas and content strategies you actually have, you'll need more than one content plan, but let's start with one. To put a content plan in action, you need to bring back the following components:

- The channel
- The persona
- The content goal
- The primary content type
- The structure
- The tone
- Channel integration
- The desired action
- The editorial plan

THE CHANNEL

This is not the content type, but the core channel on which you are focusing for a content initiative. For this example, let's use the blog.

THE PERSONA

What audience are you targeting from your initial persona development? This is important because some channels are good for targeting certain personas and others are not. For example, our newsletter is the channel where we target active content entrepreneurs who are in the process of building their content business. Our blog is the channel we use to target content creators who may not have launched their own business yet or are creating content as a side hustle.

THE CONTENT GOAL

This is the point where you want to be clear about what your goals are for the content project. For example, after one of my speeches, I talked with a senior-level marketer for a leading gas station chain. They said that the company had thousands of "fans" on Facebook and wanted to know how they could use content to get more fans. I simply asked, "What is the purpose of you being on Facebook?" They didn't have an answer.

For each channel you use, *be specific about your purpose.* For The Tilt, even though we accomplish many objectives through our blog, such as brand awareness and customer retention, our main goal is to convince casual content creators that they can build a full-time, very successful content business by following our road map. Simply ask, "What does the audience need to get out of this piece of content?"

THE PRIMARY CONTENT TYPE

With a blog, the primary content type can be textual stories, videos, infographics, or a combination of those. At The Tilt, our primary content type is textual stories with a graphic image. We also do regular original research and feature content entrepreneurs and case studies.

THE STRUCTURE

The structure includes how the content type is built. Most companies use 1,000 words as a good, solid range for blog post length. Multiple headings should be used to capture attention, and if possible, use bulleted and numbered lists since they work well for web readers. In addition, multiple images should be used, and links should be scattered throughout to attribute sources.

These same structure recommendations are needed for other content types. If you're not sure where to start, use industry best practices. Videos for YouTube should be 7–15 minutes (the longer form is getting more traction), TikToks should be 9–20 seconds, and podcasts should be 30–40 minutes (depending on your show format). Obviously, these numbers will change based on your audience and niche, but if you don't have standards, you won't be able to make changes and measure the impact (more on this in Chapter 21).

THE TONE

What's the tone of your channel's content? Is it playful? Serious? Sarcastic?

When Sam Parr launched *The Hustle* newsletter, he knew that he wanted to deliver news to millennials and get straight to the point. The personal tone in the newsletter makes it feel like you're getting an email from a close friend.

Some other great examples of tone include the humorous tone used by brands like Old Spice or Geico in their ads, the empowering tone of Dove, or the strong and aggressive tone of Harley-Davidson.

CHANNEL INTEGRATION

Do you have an integration plan with other channels? If you use video, do you integrate that with YouTube by embedding the video into your blog? If you are promoting an e-book, do you leverage SlideShare as an embedded document?

For additional promotion, how are you using Instagram, Twitter, and other channels?

Hootsuite does an incredible job of leveraging its content across every possible platform. Hootsuite starts with its blog posts and then uses them to create Twitter threads, YouTube videos, social videos, Instagram stories, and on and on. Then it takes the new assets it created and adds those back to the original blog article so it contains the YouTube video, a prepackaged tweet that users can share, and other elements.

THE DESIRED ACTION

With as many channels as you already have working—and as your content marketing will inevitably overlap into your channels—metrics are what you want to track at this point. I use the term "metrics" here very specifically, as opposed to "key performance indicators" or "results" (see Chapter 20).

In this case, metrics are "goals" that will align with the stories you are telling. For The Tilt, we have very specific goals about subscription rates (currently our subscription goal is 500 net subscribers per month).

THE EDITORIAL PLAN

Remember the content marketing mission statement back in Chapter 11? We want to keep this top of mind as we develop compelling stories through the multitude of content types (see Chapter 14). Leverage your editorial calendar to make sure that the story creation process you are employing is consistently delivered to your audience persona.

So there you have it—the content channel plan in action. Keep in mind that you can create multiple channels. You're allowed to have more than one blog or multiple Instagram pages—and you don't have to launch them at the same time. For example, you may find that two different types of blogs are more appropriate than just one. Or you may want a separate podcast feed for an additional podcast series. There is no one right way to do things, so experiment, get feedback, and continue to evolve your channel plan.

The content strategy defines the channel strategy, not the other way around.

EPIC THOUGHTS

- Don't make the mistake that most organizations make and start with your channel first. By going through the proper steps for your content marketing strategy, you'll begin to see what channels make the most sense.

- Different channels require different types of storytelling. Stay away from "spray and pray," and develop a thoughtful, and differentiating, approach to each content channel.

EPIC RESOURCES

- Visme, "How Long Should a Video Be? Video Length Best Practices [2022]," accessed July 10, 2022, https://visme.co/blog/video-length/.

- Story Ninety-Four, "How Long Should a Podcast Be?," accessed July 10, 2022, https://www.storyninetyfour.com/blog/how-long-should-a-podcast-be.

PART IV

Making Content Work

CHAPTER 18

Rented Land for Content Marketing

BY BRIAN PIPER

*Always be a first-rate version of yourself,
instead of a second-rate version of somebody else.*
JUDY GARLAND

There are so many channels you can use to promote your content marketing. From social, to audio or video, to community channels. You can create epic content on any of these channels; just remember that whatever you create on outside platforms, you don't control. If you build a following on YouTube, you can't control the algorithm, and the data is owned by Alphabet. We'll look at a variety of channels in this chapter, but we'll start with social media.

According to the Hootsuite "Digital 2022 Global Overview Report," there are more than 4.62 billion social media users worldwide. These users are on 7.5 different social channels each month, on average, and spend around 2½ hours on these channels every day. The number of social media users has nearly tripled since the first edition of this book was published in 2013 (from 1.7 billion), and the time spent has almost doubled (from 1½ hours). Over the course of this chapter, we'll examine:

- Social networks such as Facebook, Twitter, and LinkedIn
- Video channels such as YouTube and TikTok

- Social audio channels such as Clubhouse and Twitter Spaces
- Photo-sharing sites such as Instagram and Pinterest
- Chat channels such as Discord and Slack
- Online communities such as Reddit and Quora
- Publishing channels such as Medium, Substack, and Patreon
- Messaging apps such as Facebook Messenger, WhatsApp, Telegram, and Snapchat

SOCIAL NETWORKS

Social media promotion is critical to online content marketing success today. No content marketing strategy is complete without a strong social media strategy. As Jay Baer says, "Content is fire and social media is gasoline." The most important thing to remember about social media is that it's about connecting with your users, not selling something to them. Even with all the scandal and division in social media over the past three to four years, there is no sign of slowed growth or popularity. A GlobalWebIndex report showed that one in every three minutes online is spent on social platforms.

FACEBOOK

With more than 2.9 billion monthly average users worldwide, it's most likely that your customers are hanging out there. With the 2021 transition of Facebook (the company, not the social platform) to Meta, it appears that the focus will be shifting to the virtual reality–based metaverse, but the current social channel is still the largest player in the current social space . . . at the time of this writing. Here are some tips for improving your presence and content presentation on Facebook:

- **You need more than just an interesting subject.** Even if your product category is interesting by its nature, execution is very important. Spend time posting well-edited photos and well-written copy. Volume certainly isn't everything on Facebook; consistent quality is much more significant.
- **It's good to be brief, but it's better to be good.** Short messages stand out on Facebook, but long messages work if they're compelling. Communicate your message succinctly unless you absolutely need the extra words.
- **Reels are real.** Reels are a new, short-form video format added to Facebook in 2021 to compete with TikTok. These appear in your

feed, in the Reels section, or on your Reels profile. You can also share your Facebook Reels to Instagram automatically.

- **Use Open Graph.** Open Graph Meta tags provide the ability for you to control how your website content appears when it's shared on Facebook. You can customize the title, description, URL, and even the image (even using an image that doesn't exist on the page). For images, remember, the optimal size is 1,200 X 627 and less than 5 MB. Use the Meta Sharing Debugger tool to see how a URL will look when shared on Facebook.
- **Pin it.** If you have a high-performing post or are promoting an event or offer, pin that post to the top of your page so it's the first thing your users see when they visit.
- **Use Facebook Live.** Streaming video on Facebook is a great way to engage with particular audiences. Pay attention to when your audience is most likely to be online (see Chapter 21), and stream during those times.

In short, create content that is useful, usable, visible, desirable, and engaging—the cornerstones of building a socially connected brand.

WHO USES FACEBOOK WELL?

With almost 2 million likes, Canva is engaging with its community effectively on Facebook. Here are a few reasons that Canva is successful at leveraging Facebook:

- Posts ask questions of users, leading to high levels of engagement.
- Users are asked to share their success stories using the tool. This content creates engagement and positive stories.
- The posts are highly visual and well designed.

TWITTER

Twitter has become the official broadcasting tool of the web. How do you make your story stand out on Twitter? Here are some tips to follow:

- **Post consistently.** Since Twitter feeds display chronologically, it's important to tweet regularly. Some brands tweet as many as 15 to 20 times a day, but best practices suggest you should try to get in at least 1 to 2 tweets a day.

- **Engage with influencers.** To be effective on Twitter, you should interact with other users. Retweet, comment, or at least react to other tweets, especially those of influencers in your space. Participate in Twitter Chats in your industry.
- **Make a thread.** Try using the longer-form Twitter threads to link several posts together. Twitter also launched Twitter Notes as we were writing this chapter, so it will be interesting to see what becomes of that.
- **Use the 4-1-1 rule.** For every one self-serving post, you should repost one relevant post and most importantly, share four pieces of relevant content written by others. Try to keep at least 80 percent of your posts valuable or entertaining.
- **Keep it visual.** Use images, animated gifs, or videos in your posts. Tweets with images received over 150 percent more retweets according to Buffer.
- **Tell a story through your tweets.** Present a consistent voice to tell the story of your industry and your brand. Each post should be compelling in its own right, but be sure to take a consistent voice into consideration.
- **Make use of hashtags.** Including one or two relevant hashtags with your tweet makes it simple for people to find your content. (For example, we at The Tilt use #CEXevent for our annual event.) Creating an original hashtag and linking it to a specific campaign is an even better use of the tactic.
- **Use it as a testing ground.** Tweet your original content, and keep tabs on which pieces of content get more shares. Use this information to direct your future content efforts.
- **Cover industry events.** Tweet live coverage of events that are significant for your audience to offer insights in real time. That way, your brand can act as the eyes and ears for individuals who can't make it to the event.

WHO USES TWITTER WELL?

With 500,000+ followers, the ASPCA has found a great social media niche for its nationwide brand. Why does this work so well for the ASPCA?

- The tweets provide content for a wide audience of animal lovers. They touch on everything from animal law to adoption.
- They are retweeted by a variety of news organizations and influencers.
- Um . . . a combination of both cute and emotionally charged pictures of cats and dogs (and other animals). Need we say more?

Note: Twitter is in a state of flux since being purchased by Elon Musk at the end of 2022. Use the tool if it adds value but remember that it is absolutely rented land.

LINKEDIN

LinkedIn is now much more than a repository for our business contacts . . . it's a full-fledged publishing platform. Here are some tips to make it work for you:

- **Spruce up your page.** Company pages offer a platform to share diverse types of content; yet some brands are notably absent from the professional network. Rope your page in, update the cover photo, add boilerplate information, and start sharing. For content entrepreneurs, make sure your page reflects your personal brand, and turn on creator mode for your profile. Add hashtags in your description for topics you cover.
- **Encourage staff members to stay plugged in.** People who work at your organization (especially executives) can connect their personal profiles to your brand, creating a new source of content that your audience can follow.
- **Use creator tools.** For content entrepreneurs, when you enable creator mode on your page, LinkedIn moves your Featured and Activity sections to the top of your page and gives you access to other features like newsletters and LinkedIn Live.
- **LinkedIn Live.** Use LinkedIn's new live video feature to connect with your followers and find new followers.
- **LinkedIn Newsletter.** There is an option to create a newsletter on LinkedIn for another way to connect with your audience on that platform. LinkedIn promotes the newsletter to all your followers, and if it drives engagement, LinkedIn will send it to second- or third-tier connections. It can be useful to build your audience, but be sure to direct readers back to your owned land where they can sign up for your email newsletter.
- **Think quality, not quantity.** LinkedIn users tend to be overwhelmed when brands and individuals overshare. Make sure you're only sharing the highest-quality content you create for your brand.
- **Leverage user-generated content with recommendations.** Bringing in a steady stream of recommendations from clients or customers provides a renewable source of user-generated content.

WHO USES LINKEDIN WELL?

With more than 26 million followers, Amazon gets high engagement on many of its posts, which often feature employee stories and social issues.

VIDEO CHANNELS

YOUTUBE

YouTube is the second largest search engine after Google, YouTube videos display within Google results, and consumption of online video is increasing substantially every year. Here are some effective tips:

- **Enable video embedding.** Make sure embedding is enabled, allowing other users to post your videos to their websites.
- **Mix professional and homegrown videos.** Just because you don't always have a professional videographer at your disposal doesn't mean you can't make great videos. Showcase homegrown videos alongside professional ones to help humanize your brand.
- **Show; don't tell.** Demonstrating your products or services in action is a much more effective way to create compelling videos than talking about what you do.
- **Use YouTube Shorts.** YouTube introduced its answer to TikTok, YouTube Shorts, in 2021. These are vertical videos that are less than 60 seconds in length, and they can help you drive viewers and subscribers to your longer content.
- **Think compilations, not long shots.** If you do create a long-form, give your audience little snippets of content that piece together a coherent narrative. Developing a video with a single shot (like a speaker presenting for five minutes) can easily fatigue your audience. Be sure to create a table of contents for your longer videos so users can skip to the portion that interests them.

WHO USES YOUTUBE WELL?

LEGO has more than 14 million subscribers, and some videos have more than that number of views. Here are some things LEGO does:

- LEGO runs campaigns to encourage subscribers to submit their own content, and then LEGO features the user-generated content.
- Many videos are episodic stories that draw the user into the next story.

MrBeast has 100 million subscribers, and some of his videos have more than 250 million views. He has also been posting videos on YouTube for almost 10 years. Here's what works for MrBeast:

- Quick videos that show, instead of just telling, have contributed to more than 26 million views.
- Videos range from professionally shot commercials to homegrown compilations.
- Most recently, MrBeast has invested millions into special shows surrounding pop culture movements such as Squid Games and "wearing a suit to see minions" as he evolves into one of the largest video media companies on the planet.

TIKTOK

TikTok launched in 2016 but didn't become available globally until 2018. It is a short-form video platform. At the time of this writing, TikTok has been downloaded more than 2.6 billion times. Here are some tips to make it work for you as a creator:

- **Be authentic.** TikTok viewers appreciate honesty and real people. Highly produced and crafted videos don't perform as well as less professionally produced content. Be sure embedding is enabled, allowing other users to post your videos to their websites.
- **Post often.** TikTok likes creators that post at least once a day. Even better if you can post three to four times a day. It seems like a lot, but remember, it doesn't have to be highly produced, just relevant to your viewers.
- **Find your niche.** The TikTok algorithm serves up related content by user interest. When you identify your followers, focus on creating content that they want to see.
- **Follow the trends.** Trends on TikTok can generate a lot of traffic. You want to be unique and add your personal take on things, but using a popular song.

WHO USES TIKTOK WELL?

In 2020, Miss Excel, Kat Norton, started posting TikTok videos giving tips on using Excel while she danced. Once she built a large following on TikTok (over 800,000 as of June 2022), she moved on to Instagram and then YouTube. She leveraged her following by creating online courses for Excel and other Microsoft products. She is earning six figures a day from her different offerings.

Note: At the time of publication, there was increased talk about TikTok possibly being banned in the United States. Use the tool if it adds value but remember that it is absolutely rented land.

SOCIAL MEDIA SENTIMENT AND LISTENING

While it's important to use the preceding methods to leverage social media, putting content out isn't enough. You also have to be ready to monitor your social channels and engage with the users in order to increase your social media sentiment. You need to know where your brand is being referenced across other Twitter channels. There are various tools and services that provide social media listening options that are very useful for any brand or content creator to have.

SOCIAL AUDIO

Social audio channels blew up during Covid. Users liked the fact that they could connect without having to turn their cameras on. Clubhouse was launched in April 2020. From January 2021 through May 31, 2021, it had 19 million installs. In the same period in 2022, it only had 3.8 million. Don't get me wrong; that's still a lot of installs, but the uptake has certainly cooled off.

Other platforms tried to follow along, with Twitter Spaces, Facebook Live Audio Rooms (which has been integrated into its live video product), LinkedIn Audio Events, and Spotify Live, but the rapid growth of these platforms has slowed. Here are some tips if you want to jump into these platforms:

- **Be natural.** Keep the conversation going by being relatable, and remember that it is a conversation with your listeners.
- **Engage with your listeners.** Bring other people up on stage to talk with you. Welcome people when they come into the room.
- **Collaborate.** Find someone else who can join you in your discussion and keep the narrative moving.
- **Participate.** Go into other groups and join in their conversations. See how other discussions are run, and pay attention to what works and what doesn't.
- **Consistency.** Keep regular times to gain a loyal audience.

WHO USES SOCIAL AUDIO WELL?
Isis Djata started listening to different rooms in Clubhouse and then started getting up on stage and sharing. She spent up to 15 hours a day on the platform, learning how it worked and what audiences were interested in talking about. She started offering moderator services for free, and once she learned how to do it well, she started charging for her services and was earning up to $60,000 a month.

PHOTO-SHARING SITES

INSTAGRAM

Instagram, owned by Meta (Facebook), is the web's dominant image-sharing site. Is image sharing part of your content marketing strategy? If so, here are some ideas:

- **Optimize your bio.** Be sure to put your calls to action in your bio.
- **Use hashtags.** Use branded and nonbranded hashtags at the end of your posts. You can use up to 30 hashtags on a regular post and up to 10 on an Instagram Story. The most popular posts have 11 hashtags.
- **Use everything.** Use Instagram Reels, Stories, and Guides. Use images, videos, and songs. Try out the shopping tools and carousels. See what combination keeps your users engaged. Once you find something that works, you can focus on doing just that.
- **Be social.** Participate in other accounts. Leave comments and reply to questions.

WHO USES INSTAGRAM WELL?
Kar Brulhart only has around 50,000 followers but managed to turn that into a six-figure income in her first year.

- Kar uses Reels to give tips to others on how to build their Instagram audience.
- Courses, digital downloads, coaching calls, and paid partnerships are some of the ways Kar monetizes her content.

PINTEREST

Pinterest is an extremely popular photo-sharing site, with more than 444 million active users in the third quarter of 2021, where you can actively manage your own photos and share images and videos from others. It's been extremely popular in the retail space to date. Interested in seeing if Pinterest can work for you? Here are some ideas that will help:

- **Decide if the platform fits your audience before jumping in.** As an interest-driven community, Pinterest is geared toward 18- to 34-year-old women with a household income over $100,000. If a good portion of your audience lands in this category, it's a good fit.
- **It's more than just images.** Videos are powerful (and pinnable). If you have a strong repertoire of video content, use Pinterest to drive traffic back to your website or YouTube channel.
- **Show your customers some love.** Strengthen relationships, highlight success stories, and drive more traffic by creating a board showing off the achievements of your customers. It's a great way to illustrate your work without much braggadocio.
- **Tag your topics.** Idea pins and video pins let you tag your content with relevant topics. Do this to help your content reach your potential audience.
- **Show your company personality.** Instead of a lone product image or a posed staff picture, show your product or team in action for an image with more personality. Action shots help the people in your audience imagine themselves as customers or clients.

WHO USES PINTEREST WELL?

With more than 15 million subscribers and 70+ boards, Joy Cho, @ohjoy, is a Pinterest superstar. Here are some ways she keeps herself at the top of boards:

- Her boards, featuring bright, colorful images with text, lead you into fun, personal carousels and videos.
- She talks directly to her users. She addresses questions they have and creates content they request.

CHAT CHANNELS

DISCORD

Discord is a free community-building platform that lets you use text, voice, and video to engage with your audience in different channels and threads. Initially used primarily by gamers, Discord has become one of the go-to platforms in the Web3 space for nonfungible token and creator coin projects. If you decide to use Discord, here are some helpful tips:

- **Be safe.** Turn off your DMs (direct messages). There are many scams and hacks that will try to use DMs in Discord to send you phishing links. Only accept DMs from people you have added as friends.
- **Be selective.** Join other communities, but don't try to keep up with everything. Pick a handful of communities where your audience is active, and focus on those. You can find yourself getting lost in conversations and threads that aren't relevant or useful.
- **Be active.** Stay active and engaged on your own Discord server. Make sure you have your security set up correctly, and monitor and engage in the conversations that are going on in your channels.

SLACK

Slack is a messaging app for organizations to connect and communicate. It provides an alternative to email and allows users to organize conversations by threads. To use Slack:

- **Set up reminders for yourself and others.** Slackbot is an assistant tool that gives you the ability to automate numerous operations, including sending reminders to yourself and others.

ONLINE COMMUNITIES

REDDIT

Reddit is a community platform that allows users to dive into in-depth conversations focused on their particular areas of interest. You have to be careful to not promote your business on Reddit, as users will call you out. *Digiday* even called Reddit one of the "trickiest platforms to crack." However, there are several brands that use it well to engage with consumers, create conversations, and post promoted content that may be of interest to the community. Nissan and *The Economist* host AMA (Ask Me Anything) threads where they answer community questions. Toyota sees good engagement by posting videos of races between its cars in the Formula 1 subreddit.

QUORA

Quora is a socially enabled question-and-answer site. Think of it as a forum open to the world, where experts from a variety of areas can "show their stuff." Just as for Reddit, direct marketing is not allowed, but brands can leverage the platform to engage and to provide information. By answering and posing questions, brands can establish themselves as experts and resources. Unacademy started answering as many questions as it could and has more than 70,000 followers on the platform.

PUBLISHING CHANNELS

There are many ways for brands and content entrepreneurs to use channels like Medium, Substack, and Patreon to distribute and monetize their content. Vlogger Tom Kuegler decided to use Medium as his main platform, collecting more than 50,000 followers in the process. Crypto publisher Bankless has developed a robust media company with its Substack newsletter as the centerpiece. For Patreon, RKG is a YouTube video series that offers memberships that provide early access to videos, behind-the-scenes photos, and an exclusive podcast.

SOCIAL MESSAGING APPS

Facebook Messenger, WhatsApp (which Meta also owns), Telegram, and Snapchat are all messaging apps that many brands and content entrepreneurs are using to connect and engage with their communities.

Adidas has been using WhatsApp to answer questions and promote items since 2015. In 2019 it created a program to let recreational teams "rent" local professional athletes for their upcoming games. The player would show up dressed in Adidas sportswear.

EPIC THOUGHTS

- You have many social channels to choose from. Yes, create an identity in each one, but decide which one to apply resources to. Consistency counts, so focus on what you can actually do on those platforms.

- Once you have a channel that works for you, try branching out and repurposing your content for another channel. See what happens after a month of consistent posting and decide if it's a platform worth pursuing.

EPIC RESOURCES

- Meta Sharing Debugger tool, accessed November 20, 2022, https://developers.facebook.com/tools/debug/.

- Canva, accessed July 11, 2022, https://www.canva.com/.

- ASPCA, accessed July 11, 2022, https://www.aspca.org/.

- Hootsuite, "Digital 2022 Global Overview Report," accessed June 24, 2022, https://hootsuite.widen.net/s/gqprmtzq6g/digital-2022-global-overview-report.

CHAPTER 19

Alternative Content Promotion Techniques

BY JOE PULIZZI

*What you do makes a difference,
and you have to decide what kind of difference
you want to make.*

JANE GOODALL

It's amazing how many marketers and businesses create their content, send out a few tweets about it, and then stop. As you develop any content, part of that plan needs to be how you are going to get that content into the hands of new and current customers—and how to market it. The marketing of your content is perhaps the most important part of the content marketing process. Why? As Gilad de Vries from Outbrain says, "If you create great content, but no one reads it, did you create great [epic] content?"

Content is created to be consumed. If it is not and it doesn't accomplish your objectives, start looking for a new role in the organization. Before you create any more epic content, *first* figure out how you are going to market it.

Like all things in content marketing, there is no wrong or right, including content promotion. Content marketers experiment, test, learn, and eventually find what works. This chapter is chock-full of content promotion tips and tricks.

SEARCH ENGINE OPTIMIZATION

Content and search engine optimization are inextricably linked; and although not new by any means, some companies don't put enough resources into this area (especially as search engines continue to change their algorithms). For the longest time, we believed that if we understood the basics of SEO and created epic, shareable content, that would be enough to get us found in the organic search rankings.

RUN AN SEO AUDIT

There are several steps and routines you can set up within your website content process to monitor and measure your search performance. As we'll discuss in Chapter 21, if you're not using data to monitor your content performance, you won't be able to effectively optimize it.

There are a variety of free and paid tools that can help you measure your search performance. The biggest players are MOZ, SEMrush, Ahrefs, and Majestic. There are a variety of other tools and AI and machine learning solutions (see Chapter 22) that may be much more effective for your specific needs, but the ones mentioned in the previous sentence are good go-to options.

If you have a lot of content (over 100 blog posts or more than 200 pages on your site) and it's your first time doing an SEO audit, it's well worth it to get a subscription to one of these services, at least for a month, to run your initial audit. If you have a smaller site or are just doing monthly monitoring, you can often get by with one of the free memberships that many of these tools offer.

The resulting data from this audit will provide you with a list of all the keywords and phrases where your content is currently ranking in the top 100 positions in Google. It will also give you data on your current rank, the total search volume (how many people are currently searching for that keyword each month), keyword difficulty (how hard it is to increase your ranking for that keyword), the amount of traffic that keyword is already driving to your site, and, most importantly, the page that is ranking for those terms.

At that point, you go through that list and select the terms that are most strategically relevant to your users (not to you!) and add those to your list of keywords to monitor and optimize.

Make sure you include your branded keywords. Those are keywords and phrases that include your business name, website, products, or brand. You want to be sure to target these terms since people are searching with them specifically to find you. Also, be sure to look for terms that you want people to be searching on to find you where you don't currently show up so that you can create new targeted content around those terms.

BUILD AN SEO STRATEGY

There are several routines you can set up within your content process that will help you develop a successful presence in search and increase your organic traffic. It starts with having a solid understanding of the content areas you focus on. You must understand your "tilt" (your differentiation area) and start collecting and targeting keywords related to that area of expertise.

DO YOUR KEYWORD RESEARCH

Keyword research is a critical component of any content strategy. You must understand which terms people are looking for related to your area of expertise and how many people are searching for those terms. This is a fundamental skill for creating content that performs in organic search, which should account for most of your website traffic.

When doing keyword research, start by creating a spreadsheet and then adding keywords, one in each row. It's a good idea to keep them separated out into questions and keyword phrases. You can do that by using two separate tabs—either by creating a column that identifies them that way or by just adding them to the document in two different chunks. Here are some resources you can use to find all sorts of keyword ideas:

- **AnswerThePublic.com.** One of the most important questions to be able to answer to create an effective content strategy is, "What questions are my users asking?" This site allows you to enter a keyword, and it will show you what searches people are doing online related to that topic. It's a great place to help brainstorm ideas.
- **Quora and Reddit.** These two sites are excellent places to research what conversations are going on related to your topic. What threads within different tools create lots of engagement and cause your potential audience to have strong opinions, one way or another?
- **Google.** Of course, go to the source. When you start typing a topic into the search field, Google will autosuggest a variety of related topics and long-tail (longer and more specific) phrases related to that

topic. These are all things that people are searching for. After you enter a search, you will see all sorts of other related searches (at the bottom of the search page), People Also Ask (PAA) questions, and different featured snippet results. Any of these that are relevant to your subject area should be added to your list.

- **Google Trends.** This is a great place to see what searches are trending on Google around a topic, and you can see how the interest in that topic changes over a particular period to look for a specific time to target that search. For example, searches for "north pole" trend upward starting in November and drop off after December 25.
- **Google Search Console.** This free tool will tell you what keywords your existing users are using to find and visit your website. These keywords are essential to add to your list because they show what people are actively searching for to come to your site and consume your content.

Once you have this list of potential keywords, phrases, and questions, open a tool like SEMrush. Then copy and paste all those keywords into the Keyword Overview database, and it will show you search volume, keyword difficulty, the trend in search interest related to that term, and other keyword ideas. Add these data points to your spreadsheet so you can start sorting and filtering your results.

Once you have that data, determine which keywords you should select from your list to start targeting. You want to select the terms that balance the highest volume with the lowest difficulty. But be careful with this. You don't want to ignore keywords with low volumes or high difficulty if they are particularly relevant to your offerings or may lead to high conversions.

You can get a template and see some of the keywords targeted at The Tilt by downloading the "keyword targeting template.xls" at EpicContentMarketing .com.

FOCUS CONTENT ON A SEARCH PHRASE

Every blog post at The Tilt has a targeted keyword phrase such as "creator economy" or "content entrepreneur." When you develop a piece of online content, try to think of the most likely keyword phrase someone would type into a search engine. Then make sure the content you create delivers on that keyword phrase.

DO A VOICE SEARCH

A report from National Public Media shows that in 2021, 35 percent of Americans owned a smart speaker, 62 percent of Americans 18+ used a voice assistant on any device, and voice shopping is projected to reach $40 billion in 2022.

According to Hootsuite, more than 24 percent of the worldwide population uses a voice assistant to find information. The convenience of not typing combined with the growing accuracy of natural language processing is making voice search more useful and more popular.

The importance of optimizing your content to be accessible through voice search has never been greater. But what does it take to capture those voice search results?

FEATURED SNIPPETS AND RICH SNIPPETS

When you do a search on Google for a popular keyword phrase, it will often return a "featured snippet" that directly answers the question that you asked or defines the term you searched for. This appears at the top of the search engine results page and is also referred to as the "position 0" result.

After the paid results and one or two organic results, you will also often get PAA results that include short questions related to your search phrase that you can click on to see short and accurate answers. These PAA results are one of several rich snippet features that Google provides.

The key findings from the SEMrush Voice Search 2019 report indicate that 80 percent of the voice search answers come from the top three search results, and 70 percent of the answers come from the featured snippets and PAA results. There are other factors that can help capture those voice search results, including page speed and a high backlink profile. Google features results from pages that load quickly, especially on mobile devices, and that have many high-authority sites linking back to them.

A great way to target those rich snippets, featured snippets, and high-volume long-tail keyword phrases is to focus on identifying questions that people are asking related to the keywords you want to target and then asking and answering those questions within your content.

REACTIVE CONTENT CREATION

It is important to look at the content that you already have out in the world and identify opportunities to optimize that content for the keywords and phrases that it's already ranking for in search. This is the "low-hanging fruit" of search optimization.

As Google gets smarter and relies more heavily on its artificial intelligence RankBrain, it will become less and less effective for you to do this sort of keyword targeting. But with the way the algorithm currently works, this is an extremely effective method to increase your organic traffic by reacting to the keywords your content is already ranking for.

You want to start tracking your rankings and organic traffic to these strategically relevant keywords and measuring how your optimization efforts are affecting those numbers. More on this in Chapter 21.

PROACTIVE CONTENT CREATION

Now that you know what content is performing, let's think about what new content you want to create. Let's not waste any of our valuable time by creating content that won't perform because our users aren't interested in it. We already know what existing content is performing, and we've done keyword research on that content to figure out how to optimize it.

Now let's look at the other keywords in our research that give us ideas for new content we can create to answer other questions that our users have on those topics. Look at the keyword list you've created, and check for strategic terms in that list that you don't currently rank for. You may initially want to focus just on the terms with high search volumes, but remember that lots of people may already be targeting those terms. First, look at the keyword difficulty around those terms, and look in Google to see who is already ranking for those terms. And then figure out if it's worth your time to target those, or maybe select some longer-tail phrases with less competition that may be more strategically relevant for your users.

Remember, even though a phrase has only 50 searches per month, you may not want to dismiss it. If those searches cause 30 people to find your site at the top of the results, consume your content, and convert into customers, it may be a better option than targeting a phrase with 20,000 searches per month that has more competition or doesn't specifically relate to the solutions and expertise that you offer.

CONTENT SYNDICATION

Are there sites out there looking for epic content in your industry? If so, there may be an opportunity to syndicate your original content on those sites.

If you are looking for additional exposure leveraging your current content, seeking out content syndication partners may be an option. You can submit your content to sites with more traffic to help increase your brand awareness. There are many sites that will syndicate your content for free, and there are sites where you can pay to have content syndicated.

CONTENT 10 TO 1

Continuous algorithm updates in search engines can make it difficult for your content to be found in a search. It's more important than ever that credible individuals share your content with others. Since our customers are completely in control of how and when they engage with our content, this means we must think from the beginning about how each of our stories will be produced and shared.

So think 10 to 1. Can you reimagine your stories in 10 different ways? Can that blog post become a white paper series, an ebook, or even a printed book? Can that video story be transcribed into a blog post, broken apart and shared via a social network, or transformed into a podcast? Think about these things up front:

- How will you preactivate the content in all situations? (Get the community involved in the content.)
- How will you share the content?
- What can the base content offering (blog, video, and so on) become?

ADD IMAGES TO EVERYTHING

Andy Crestodina does an annual blogger survey, and his 2021 survey results show that a large percentage of bloggers (47 percent) include only 1 to 2 images in each blog post, but bloggers who use more than 10 images in their posts are the ones who report that their blogs create "strong results" for their blog performance.

Images don't just make a little difference; they make a lot of difference. If we add a little common sense to the study, it seems reasonable that posts with images both perform better in search results and are shared at a higher rate than those posts without images.

Of course, this should come as no surprise. People in the magazine business had a saying that "the cover of a magazine serves just one purpose: to be opened." Design has mostly been responsible for that happening.

What are the next steps?

- Define the role of your content producer and the mix between original art and stock photography.
- Include images in all your blog posts.
- Review all your content to make sure that it is visually appealing.
- Tag all your online images with meta tags and captions when possible (millions of searches per day are image searches).

And last but not least . . .

- Build time into your content process so that design doesn't become a last-minute operation. Integrate design into the process up front.

BLOG AND SOCIAL ENGAGEMENT STRATEGY

To build a successful business, you will need to do a lot of relationship-building. There are many ways to build relationships and establish connections with other leaders in your industry, but one of the best, and easiest, ways to take that first step to connect is by engaging with that person's content.

COMMENTING ON BLOGS AND ON SOCIAL

An incredibly effective way to open the door to many relationships (and even friendships) with key industry influencers is by commenting on their blogs, engaging on social channels, and sharing their content.

Tagging an influencer on social (say, on LinkedIn or Twitter) is vastly underrated. Savvy content creators notice when they are tagged. When this is done right, it can be a real way for you to develop a relationship with an industry influencer.

Many companies and content entrepreneurs have a blog and multiple social channels, but very few of them have a social or blog commenting strategy. What a shame.

Great content alone is not enough; you must work it.

You could be the greatest content creator on the planet, but if you don't work the channels, no one will know about it, and your business won't be positively impacted. At the top of your list of distribution techniques should be commenting on the right blogs and engaging in the right social channels.

Not sure how? Here's a handy list:

- Find out where your customers and prospects are hanging out. Use tools such as Google Alerts and Twitter (or a reputation management system) to find out what blogs and social channels are making an impact on your customers.
- Develop a list of at least 10 to 15 key blogs in which you are going to be engaged.
- Make an informative comment on each of those blogs at least once per week.

Realistically, this should only take an hour or two per week, but the payoff will be tremendous. Each of those influential industry leaders will know you. After a while, some will start sharing your content. At some point, you may even become friends with them. And over the long term, it will positively affect your blogging and online marketing goals.

FREE YOUR CONTENT

I've had the pleasure of listening to David Meerman Scott, noted author and speaker, many times. According to his own personal statistics, a white paper or ebook of his will be downloaded 20 times and up to 50 times more *without* a gate in front of it. This means there is no lead form in front of the content.

You may be asking, "Why is this topic a part of this chapter?" Simple. So many times, we marketers have epic content, but we put a barrier in front of it, making it almost impossible for people to share and spread our message. Of course, there is always a time to put a form in front of one's content, but you need to understand the implications of a form or a gate. There is a trade-off.

Ask yourself, "What is my objective?"

Most people gate their content for lead or customer management purposes. This means they want the prospects' information to sell them something, or they want more information about the customers to sell to them more precisely. That makes sense, doesn't it?

This is a solid marketing objective, but is it the best or even the right one?

Shouldn't your goal with the creation of content be to spread your ideas? Doesn't it make more sense from a marketing perspective to have 50 people engage in your content instead of 1?

And here is a key point that David made clear: Who are the customers you have who will actively share your content? Bloggers and social media influencers. What customers do you have who usually *do not* download gated content? Bloggers and social media influencers.

So people who gate their content are not only limiting the people who will get access to their content; they are cutting off those customers who will actively share it with their audiences.

THE POSSIBILITIES

Let's say you received 1,000 leads via your white paper download. From David Meerman Scott's numbers, let's even take a more conservative 10 times more downloads if we remove the gate. This would give us 10,000 downloads with no lead data. Of all those people, let's say that 1 percent would share this with their blog audiences (with a very conservative audience of 100 people, although most blogs get much more).

With those numbers, the total possible content reach for gated content would be 2,000 people. Nongated content would be 20,000 people.

And take this note to heart: I haven't seen one gated piece of content marketing from a brand go viral and massively spread. If you have seen this, please let me know. What's more important to you: lead information on the few, or the opportunity to spread your brand to decision makers with whom you are not talking right now?

There are times and places to get customer information. Is the time or place to do so in front of the content you want to be shared actively? *Note:* Using this strategy doesn't mean you can't "ask" for an email address for prospects to subscribe to your content.

BRANDSCAPING

Andrew Davis's book *Brandscaping* discusses how content partnerships can work. Essentially, a brandscape is a *collection of brands that work together to produce great content* (some may call this a consortium). This is critical to the evolution of content marketing, as more brands struggle to manage the content marketing process.

It's true that many brands struggle to come up with the funding for content marketing projects. Why not work with noncompetitive partners, community members, and influencers to develop amazing and compelling content for a similar customer?

FEATURING AND REWARDING USERS

At The Tilt, influencers are featured every week in the newsletter and the blog, which is great, because they often promote that content. The community is rewarded and incentivized to create content for the blog using social tokens (more in Chapter 28), and then they have reasons to promote their content on the platform and share the social posts that feature them.

SEVEN WAYS TO TAKE THE MEDIA WORLD BY STORM

These seven tips will create a powerful concoction that will be hard for any company, including media companies and your direct competitors, to compete with.

1. **Make mobile your top channel strategy.** Traffic from mobile devices has been on a steady increase over the past 10 years, exceeding 54 percent of traffic in the fourth quarter of 2021. Google has been prioritizing mobile-friendly content in search results for the past several years and technical SEO, which makes focusing on optimizing your site performance for mobile particularly important.

2. **Hire professional journalists and writers.** According to Penelope Muse Abernathy, who at the time she wrote this was a Knight Chair at the UNC Hussman School of Journalism and Media, "Half of newspaper readers and journalists have vanished over the past 15 years. Total circulation decreased by 55 million between 2004 and 2019. During the same period, newspapers lost 36,000 journalists."

   Traditional newspapers have been struggling, and many journalists have lost or left their jobs. Lots of brands have hired those journalists to tell their stories and create content marketing. Why shouldn't you do the same?

3. **Repurpose your content.** Your users exist and consume content on many different channels online. Some people prefer YouTube videos, some read newsletters or blogs, and some listen to podcasts, and so you need to be able to put your content on all those different channels to promote it. This doesn't mean that you need to create new content for each of those channels. Focus on one channel that works for you, but repurpose your content for all the channels where your users are. This is just smart promotional marketing of your content.

   Repurposing is also a great way to revitalize existing, old, evergreen content that has performance potential.

4. **Develop rent-to-own content strategies.** As a content marketer, your goal is to own your media channels, just as publishers do. A strategy that never fails is the "rent-to-own" model. This means partnering with media companies through webinars and sponsored content opportunities to get your content in front of those companies' audiences. The goal is to convert these prospective readers into your readers. With publishing models struggling, most media companies are happy to partner with you on any number of rent-to-own strategies. Just make sure the content is helpful, not self-serving.

5. **Develop professional editorial practices.** Many brands today are leveraging employees and outside influencers as part of their content marketing programs. While this is good, there is a gaping void in the editorial arena. Simply put, brands are not investing enough in editorial and proofreading as part of their processes. Every piece of content you create should have at least two sets of additional eyes on it. Also, your employees may have the stories, but they may not be storytellers. Assign an editor to help them tell a story that works for your content marketing program. See more on the content marketing process in Chapter 17.

6. **Buy a media company.** Do an analysis of the media companies in your industry. Have a team discussion about which one is the best fit for your content marketing program. Consider purchasing that media company. (Do so even if yours is a small business.) Read more on this in Chapter 26.

7. **Make the reader your number one priority.** Commit your stories to one epic concept—what's in it for your readers (that is, your customers). This is your critical advantage, where you can and should focus all your attention.

GETTING THE ATTENTION OF INFLUENCERS

Influencers are important people. They generally have real jobs and are extremely active on social networks, spending their time sharing content and blogging. Getting on their radar is not easy. So to get their attention, you can give them content gifts. This is done in a few different ways. One of the best ways is Social Media 4-1-1.

SOCIAL MEDIA 4-1-1

Social Media 4-1-1, a term originally coined by Andrew Davis, is a sharing system that enables a company to get greater visibility with social influencers. Here's how it works.

For every six pieces of content shared via social media (such as Twitter):

- Four are pieces of content from your influencer target that are also relevant to your audience. This means that 67 percent of the time you are sharing content that is not yours, and you are calling attention to content from your influencer group.
- One piece can be your original, educational piece of content.
- One piece can be your sales piece, such as a coupon, product notice, or press release.

While the numbers don't have to be exact, it's the philosophy that makes this work. When you share the content of influencers, they notice. And you should share without asking for anything in return, so that when you do need something someday, the influencers are more likely to say yes.

EPIC THOUGHTS

- Although organic search doesn't drive the traffic it used to, it's still at the top of the content promotion list. Pay heed.

- Most organizations repurpose after the success of one content product. A better way is to plan for repurposing up front. Imagine what your stories can become and what channels make the most sense to your customers and your objectives.

EPIC RESOURCES

- Insider Intelligence, "Voice Assistant and Smart Speaker Users 2020," accessed June 29, 2022, https://www.emarketer.com/content/voice-assistant-and-smart-speaker-users-2020.

- National Public Media, "The Smart Audio Report," accessed June 29, 2022, https://www.nationalpublicmedia.com/uploads/2022/06/The-Smart-Audio-Report-Spring-2022.pdf.

- Hootsuite, "Digital 2022 Global Overview Report.pdf," accessed June 29, 2022, https://hootsuite.widen.net/s/gqprmtzq6g/digital-2022-global-overview-report.

- Orbit Media, "2021 Blogging Statistics: Blogger Data Shows Trends and Insights into Blogging," accessed June 30, 2022, https://www.orbitmedia.com/blog/blogging-statistics/.

- Andrew Davis, *Brandscaping: Unleashing the Power of Partnerships*, Content Marketing Institute, 2012.

- Penelope Muse Abernathy, "Vanishing Readers and Journalists," accessed November 20, 2022, https://www.usnewsdeserts.com/reports/news-deserts-and-ghost-newspapers-will-local-news-survive/the-news-landscape-in-2020-transformed-and-diminished/vanishing-readers-and-journalists/.

CHAPTER 20

Measuring the Impact of Your Content Marketing

BY BRIAN PIPER

I'd rather regret the risks that didn't work out
than the chances I didn't take at all.

SIMONE BILES

A year from now, what's different?

The answer to that question is the most critical element of your content strategy. Measure behavior that matters to your business.

In this chapter, you'll find a number of different ways to show return for your content marketing. Why not just one? Because there's not just one way to show return on objective. Different strokes for different folks. We've included all of them here so that you can integrate a measurement system most in line with how you currently measure your marketing. *This is key! Do not* plug in a brand-new formula to measure your entire marketing effort because you are now a content marketing believer. Instead take the best points of this chapter and insert them into what you already do.

WHAT THE C-LEVEL WANTS TO KNOW ABOUT CONTENT MARKETING

Please don't show an analytics report to your CXO. (In this case, CXO refers to the senior executive in charge. This could be the CEO, COO, CMO, or whoever else is in charge.) That person doesn't care and probably will end up asking questions that will simply waste your time. Your CXO only cares about four things when it comes to your content marketing measurement and return on investment (ROI):

- Is the content driving sales for us?
- Is the content saving costs for us?
- Is the content making our customers happier, thus helping with retention?
- Is the content growing our community and expanding our opportunities?

The reports you show the CXO need to answer these types of questions; otherwise, why show the CXO anything at all? Content marketing is all about developing content that maintains or changes a behavior. That's the focus.

RETURN ON OBJECTIVE: PART ONE

Sales lift, impact, retention, and the like are key measurements of any return on objective (ROO) program. (*Note:* I like to use ROO instead of ROI because it focuses the content marketer on the real objective.) The "measurement picture" comes into play when sales data is missing or challenging. Sometimes ROO can be determined with one metric, and other times four or five are needed to show an impact on the organization's business goals.

ROO measurements come in all shapes and sizes; they usually include multiple items to give you the complete answer to your question. The important aspect to remember is that it's not measurement for the sake of measurement. The tools and tactics in the paragraphs that follow are used to answer directly what the project's objective is. If you keep that in mind, you'll get your ROO.

Here are a few measurement initiatives to get you started:

- Tracking sales lift of those who receive the content program versus those who do not

- Tracking conversions for online content products or email subscriptions and measuring new or increased sales from that group
- Doing online readership studies to determine the impact of the content project as well as the acquisition of customer informational needs and trends (Are readers engaging in the right behaviors?)
- Measuring engagement through online research or by using analytic measures on newsletter or web portal products
- Doing a pre-awareness/post-awareness study to measure the impact of the program

THE CONTENT MARKETING PYRAMID

If you divide your content marketing measurement into a pyramid, with expanding levels of importance, you end up with three main sections. The most important thing to remember when you're building a pyramid is that every stage, every measurement you track, *must* be focused on tracking against your goals–your objectives and key results.

The three main sections are:

- **Primary content indicators.** Primary indicators are the types of measurements that the CXO wants to know about (sales, cost savings, and retention rates).
- **Secondary content indicators.** Secondary indicators are the types of measurements that help make the case for primary indicators (lead quality, lead quantity, shorter sales cycles, and so on).
- **User indicators.** These are the types of measurements that the content "doers" need to examine to help drive the secondary indicators (web traffic, likes, page views, and search rankings).

It may be easier to create an analytics pyramid for each of the goals you are trying to achieve. Everything you measure needs to start with an objective. For example:

- Build brand awareness or reinforcement.
- Create more effective lead conversion and nurturing.
- Increase customer conversion.
- Achieve customer upsell or cross-sell.
- Create subscribers to our content.

Let's say you're putting together an initiative to generate more leads for your company. Your pyramid might look like Figure 20.1.

The Content Marketing Pyramid

GOAL: Increase Leads 10% with No Increased Cost

Primary Indicators
(For C-Suite Reporting)
Converted Leads
Total Cost per Lead

Secondary Indicators
(For Managers Reporting)

Blog Subscribers	Lead Quality
Email List Subscribers	Cost per Lead
Incremental Leads	(Each Stage)
Lead Source %	Cost per Visitor

User Indicators
(For Analytics Team)

Page Views	A/B Tests	Engagement
Visitors	Conversions	Blog Traffic
Visitor Trending	PPC Bid Mgmt	Content Shares
Top Content	Page Rank	Email Subscribers
Keywords	Ad Quality Scores	Followers/Likes/+1's
Top Landing Pages	Lead Scores	
Referrers	Comments	

FIGURE 20.1 The content marketing ROO pyramid (*Source: Managing Content Marketing*)

As you can see, the pyramid is divided into the three sections previously described. Here's how to go about building your pyramid.

Step 1: Segment your pyramid. Segment your pyramid into three sections. The bottom, the widest part of the pyramid, will be your user indicators. These are the metrics that are audience-based and are meant to measure activity. You will slice, dice, add to, subtract from, and change these metrics on a frequent basis.

The second level of the pyramid will be your secondary indicators. These will be the metrics that you associate with team members and specific processes that help you reach your goals. These are generally what we think of as short-term goals.

At the top of the pyramid are your primary indicators, or the key performance indicators (KPIs) for the goal. These metrics will be very few and will be the dashboard that you present to your manager or CXO. These metrics change very rarely, if at all, and are fed by the insights, interpretation, and data from below (as well as some gut feel). The goals are what you report (and nothing more).

Step 2: Map the segments. Say that your goal is to "increase the number of converted leads by 10 percent without raising costs" and you've created a new instructional blog to help you accomplish this goal.

There are a couple of ways you can get to that number. You can improve the conversion rate of the existing number of leads by 10 percent, or you can increase the actual number of leads by a percentage so that the number of converted leads naturally goes up by 10 percent.

To build your primary indicators, you'll only want a handful of numbers in that top dashboard:

- The number of converted leads by week/month/quarter
- The total cost per converted lead by week/month/quarter

Those two numbers are the only KPIs for that particular goal that matter to the CXO.

Then, for your secondary indicators, you may want to monitor several metrics; these will give you great insights and help your team improve the process in order to reach your goals. Examples include:

- Email list subscribers versus goal
- Total number of leads by week/month/quarter
- Incremental leads from the new blog
- Lead source (for example, organic search, Twitter, Facebook)

Last, you have your user indicators at the bottom. These are the day-to-day metrics that will help you understand and get the insights to improve the process of your secondary indicators. Examples include:

- The number of visitors to the blog
- New visitors versus returning visitors
- Page views on the blog
- The number of blog comments
- Blog subscriptions
- Conversion rate from subscribers to leads
- The number of shares through social media (most shared posts)
- SEO metrics for keywords
- Twitter followers and engagement

- LinkedIn followers
- Instagram likes and engagement
- YouTube subscribers and engagement
- Social media reports (both internal and external)
- Blog comments and responses (qualitative)
- Most popular blog content/category
- Persona measurement (if you're trying to attract targeted personas)

These metrics should be monitored regularly; whether you do a monthly report or have a dashboard that you check on weekly, regular monitoring is essential for making improvements. More on this in Chapter 21.

The purpose of these metrics is to help improve your process. If you find that you're putting a lot of time into, say, Facebook but are not getting any visitors or subscribers out of it, you can alter your strategy and experiment with other social networks.

User indicators will be your finger on the day-to-day pulse of how your content is doing. Because you've taken the time to map your blog content to your personas and your engagement cycle, you'll also know where these visitors are coming into the engagement cycle.

BRINGING THE PYRAMID TOGETHER

If you spend the time to do this the right way, you will have *a lot* of tools to answer some extraordinarily complex questions about your content marketing as well as your overall marketing strategy. You may find some interesting things. For example:

- Social media channels are producing the most qualified leads.
- Email subscribers stay longer as customers than nonsubscribers.
- You're attracting way more of persona one, but persona two makes up a much higher percentage of your qualified leads.

And this is where you'll earn your keep. Once you can show certain trends with your content, then you can start to do more of what's working and less of what's not.

ANALYTICS AND TRACKING

All companies should have an analytics program such as Google Analytics that tracks visitors and visitor behavior, but analytics can go only so far. While we marketers can track general trends of all users, we cannot track the individual user without more powerful technology. There are several marketing automation systems available for companies of all shapes and sizes, including:

- ActiveCampaign
- Keap
- Oracle Eloqua
- HubSpot
- Salesforce Pardot
- Marketo
- OmniSend

Be prepared to spend between $12,000 and $75,000 per year (depending on your needs) for a marketing automation system. While you don't need one to get started, you'll quickly learn that without one you can't answer all the questions about how your individual subscribers are consuming content and what makes them different from one another. That said, the plan must come first, then the technology to support the plan.

FOUR HIDDEN BENEFITS OF CONTENT MARKETING

Joe Chernov, Chief Marketing Officer, Pendo.io

CONTENT CAN GIVE YOU A RECRUITING EDGE

In a competitive industry, recruiting top-caliber talent is a priority of the highest order. In fact, according to venture capitalist (and content marketer extraordinaire) Fred Wilson, recruiting top talent is one of only three priorities for every CEO. Yet despite the importance of recruiting, it would be easy to overlook the impact an engaging content marketing program can have on this business-critical priority.

Here's the takeaway: *partner with your HR department.* When your company onboards staff, have your recruiter ask new hires to share the reasons why they joined, and share this information with your internal teams. The ability to prove your content efforts have impacted recruiting will help make you—and your content efforts—indispensable to your organization.

CONTENT CAN HELP BOOST COMPANY MORALE

Back when I worked at a PR firm, I recall challenging a client who wanted us to help his company secure coverage in a publication that didn't necessarily influence its buyers. When I pushed back on the priority, the CEO told me, "The article isn't for our customers. It's for our staff. The place lights up when we get covered in the press . . . and I know a lot of our workers read this magazine." I've never forgotten that lesson, and content marketing can help accomplish this very same goal.

When you publish a popular asset, the cheering it receives on the social web can validate the efforts of the entire company. Your victory lap is *everyone's* victory lap, so make sure you "market" the popularity of your content to your colleagues—not to boast personally, but rather to remind them that as crowded as the social web is, your company managed to stand out.

CONTENT OPENS UP LINES OF COMMUNICATION

Remarkable content doesn't just get customers and prospects talking; it also gets your internal clients buzzing. It gives colleagues something to share with one another, something to debate, or something to challenge. It opens doors, rings phones, and makes heads "gopher" over cubicle walls. It also provides you with an opportunity to recruit advocates and participants.

When your colleagues engage with your content, it creates an opportunity to invite them to contribute to future programs. Because content marketing sits among so many different organizational functions, it is a surprisingly political role. Be sure to marshal your supporters when you have their attention.

CONTENT FOSTERS TRUST

Marketing author and leader Don Peppers convincingly argues that the key to competitive advantage is "being proactively trustworthy." *Creating content that is so valuable that people would pay for it, yet you give it away for free, is a reliable way to earn the public's trust.* This is precisely why the value transfer in content marketing should be from institution to individual, which is an upside-down model for traditional marketers. In other words, when trust is the goal, companies should strive to *sell by not selling*.

None of this is to suggest that content marketers shouldn't aspire to be measured—of course we should. But we also need to find ways to highlight the value we provide—especially if there's no KPI attached to it.

A DEEPER LOOK AT CONTENT MARKETING METRICS

Too often, content marketers tell themselves that they can't accurately measure their results, that a tactic isn't measurable, or that they don't feel comfortable measuring content.

These statements hang over your content marketing like a dark cloud. If you find yourself falling into this camp, don't worry—you still have time to get on the right track.

As with the Content Marketing Pyramid indicators, looking at different kinds of metrics—four of them, specifically—helps make the business case:

- Consumption metrics
- Sharing metrics
- Lead-generation metrics
- Sales metrics

CONSUMPTION METRICS

Typically the easiest measurements to set up and understand, consumption metrics answer the question, "How many people viewed, downloaded, or listened to this piece of content?"

These are some of the more prominent consumption metrics:

- **Page views.** These are easy to measure using Google Analytics or a similar web analytics program.
- **Video views.** YouTube Insights and similar data work best here.
- **Document views.** Platforms like SlideShare give you access to this data.
- **Downloads.** When a website is ungated (no subscription forms), measure downloads through your CRM (customer relationship management) platform or Google Analytics and other web analytics software.
- **Social listening.** Services such as Brandwatch, Meltwater, Hootsuite, Brand24, Agora Pulse, BuzzSumo, Sprout Social, and Talkwalker are all viable options for measuring social conversations.

This is the phase of measurement where some content marketers quit. But don't stop here—you've only just begun.

Revealing new questions. The consumption metrics you collect should raise several questions:

- Do people consuming this content engage in other, more desirable behaviors on your site (such as filling out an inquiry form)?
- Do they do so at a ratio different from that of site visitors overall?
- Do people consuming this content come back for more?
- Do they do so at a ratio different from that of site visitors overall?

Consumption metrics aren't everything, but they are important. To find the social impact of content consumption, let's turn our attention to sharing metrics.

SHARING METRICS

Of all the places your content resides, your site may have the least amount of traffic. Fortunately, the web has bred a culture of sharing, and this is totally measurable (if you look at the right metrics).

Sharing metrics are metrics that answer the question, "Is the content working, and how often is it shared with others?"

Your sharing metrics may include:

- **Likes, shares, tweets, and pins.** Social platforms typically keep track of these, with Google Analytics (and similar web analytics programs) offering additional insights.
- **Forwards.** If your email solution includes a "Forward to a friend" option, you can track when an email or newsletter has been forwarded.
- **Inbound links.** Tools such as SEMrush, MOZ, Ahrefs, and Majestic simplify how you measure these.

Measuring sharing metrics is important for every organization. But keep one thing in mind: sharing metrics are overvalued because they're measured publicly, in full view of prospects and competitors. Assigning an internal business value to sharing metrics is crucial to your content marketing. Otherwise you may get caught up in a competition that has no real impact on your bottom line.

That said, if you're monitoring your metrics regularly, you can tell very quickly if there is something wrong with a piece of content. Once you see that a piece of content isn't performing as well as it typically does, you can dig into the content to see whether it was the title, the copy, or the image, or perhaps we may have been too sales focused.

Boosting sharing. With a clear understanding of how sharing metrics affect business goals, your next step is to make sharing easy to help boost your numbers:

- Place easy-to-use sharing buttons on every piece of content. Configure them to focus on channels your audience uses most often. (At The Tilt, easy-to-tweet excerpts and "click-to-tweets" are placed throughout the content and have sharing buttons at the end of each article, to maximize sharing.)
- Make sure any infographics you create are easy to embed into customer or influencer content (or on Pinterest).
- Enhance your use of social proof by, for example, embedding positive Twitter comments on your website or clearly showing how often your latest ebook has been downloaded.
- Create content that's worth sharing. Every time you create a piece of content, your team needs to ask, "Will our customers share this content?"

LEAD-GENERATION METRICS

Measuring lead-generation metrics helps you answer the question, "How often does content consumption result in a lead?"

These are a few crucial metrics in this category:

- **Form completions and downloads.** Through your CRM and URL tracking, measuring how often visitors access gated content is simple. You can also measure this by setting up conversions in Google Analytics.
- **Email subscriptions.** Your email provider or CRM tracks how many visitors sign up to receive your emails. (Using a program like MailChimp or Aweber, or perhaps Salesforce for larger enterprises, will help.)
- **Blog subscriptions.** You can measure blog subscriptions through services such as FeedBlitz or your CRM system.
- **Blog comments.** A strong comment platform (like Disqus, CommentLuv, or one built into your blogging software) helps here.
- **Conversion rate.** How often do visitors who consume content become leads?

Your conversion rate is key to viewing lead generation from the highest level. It comes in handy if you're comparing your overall website conversion rate with that of an individual piece of content. For instance, if your over-all conversion rate is 2 percent, the ebook that's converting at 1 percent isn't working as well as you might think. But before you give up on the ebook, determine if prospects that download that ebook perform more positive behaviors such as becoming customers more quickly or spending more when they do buy.

Measuring indirect lead generation. Of course, not all your content produces leads directly. However, all your content can contribute to lead-generation behavior. Therefore, set conversions in Google Analytics or a similar data program to measure how content contributes indirectly to lead generation:

- For key behaviors that don't produce revenue immediately (such as email sign-up), assign a specific dollar value.
- Set up custom analytics reports showing goals for each piece of content. (Perhaps you may want to measure that white paper download separately.)

Tip: Social platforms with their own custom URL shorteners (such as HubSpot) are adept at tying social media posts to landing pages so you can track indirect lead-generation values.

SALES METRICS

The ultimate goal of your content marketing is—and always has been—to grow the business.

Measuring your sales metrics answers the question, "Did we actually make any money because of this content?"

The metrics you need to understand include:

- **Online sales.** Typically, you measure these through your e-commerce system (for example, Shopify).
- **Offline sales.** You track these through your CRM and unique URLs measured by your analytics program. Robust systems such as Oracle Eloqua, Salesforce, Hubspot, and Marketo will record which pieces of content your customers consumed, which allows you to put a dollar value on each component.
- **Manual reporting and anecdotes.** Yes, it's even important to record those handshake deals. In your CRM system (such as Salesforce.com), be sure you have your sales team report on where leads originated so

you can track this information. In some cases, they may not be known, but do your best.

Remember, if you're going to track leads and sales, you must do something trackable. To understand the impact of one blog post, you should include a call to action that is unique to that piece of content.

Keeping in mind customer retention. Your most important content audience is your current customers. Smart companies use sophisticated CRM systems to track what content is consumed by customers and measure the impact of individual content components on retention and renewal rates. When you have a new piece of content, make sure your current customers get special access to it first.

Even though customer retention is the grandparent of all goals for content marketing, most people tend to default to customer acquisition and lead-generation goals first. Don't make that mistake. If you are taking your content program to the next level, start with your current customer base. Goals to keep customers longer, happier, and/or spending more are the noblest content marketing objectives.

RETURN ON OBJECTIVE: PART TWO

Content return on objective should be calculated at the program level first. There is no inherent ROO of "content marketing." Rather, you have a ROO for each program that can then be rolled up to determine an overall return. *To understand the business impact of your content marketing, start out by calculating the investment.* Then calculate the return and use these numbers to find the ROO. Here's an example with a hypothetical blog.

Step 1: Calculate the investment.
- Multiply the hours per month needed to create the content by the hourly pay rate of the employees or contractors used to create the content.
- Multiply the result by the overhead factor. This accounts for rent, insurance, utilities, and so on. So a $30-per-hour ($57,000-per-year) employee should really be a $45-per-hour employee when overhead is factored into the equation. Whatever your hourly rate per employee is, you can add a 50 percent upcharge to cover miscellaneous expenses.

- Add all other costs, such as design fees, hosting fees, subscriptions, and software. Allocate them to a content program specifically, or amortize them monthly and spread the costs evenly across each content program.

Example: Assume 20 hours per month at $50 per hour to produce a corporate blog, multiplied by a 50 percent overhead factor. Add in $1,000 per month for design, $50 per month for hosting, and $200 per month for miscellaneous fees.

The true monthly blogging cost = $2,750

Step 2: Calculate the return. Multiply your leads per month by your lead conversion rate, average lifetime customer value, and average profit margin.

Example: You collect 40 leads per month from the corporate blog (determined by lead form, CRM system, and so on). At a 10 percent lead conversion rate, you'll generate four new customers. Assume a $5,000 average lifetime customer value and a 30 percent average profit margin.

True monthly blogging return = $6,000

Step 3: Calculate ROI. Subtract the investment from the return. Then divide by the investment.

Example:

$$\$6,000 - \$2,750 = \$3,250$$

$$3,250 \div 2,750 = 1.18$$

$$\text{Return} = 118\%$$

Sometimes, you just can't close the loop on ROI because you may not have all the data to plug into the previously given formula.

To use this measurement strategy effectively, you must:

- Track everything over a long period of time.
- Take note whenever anything changes, including PR coverage, website updates, or new ad campaigns.
- Track multiple revenue data points, including total leads, new customers, average order size, churn, and total revenue.

- Look for patterns that indicate your content is working; for example, when revenue went up, content consumption and sharing metrics also went up.

The correlation approach isn't an exact science, but it gets businesses further than doing nothing at all, making it an important alternative.

WHAT IS THE VALUE OF YOUR TIME?

Do you know the value of your time? If not, you should.

Let's look at another blogging example. Let's say that you spend two hours creating a blog post (any epic blog post should take you at least one hour) and your marketing director spends another hour editing it and inserting key links and images. You've calculated your time at $200 per hour and your marketing director's time at $100 per hour (all costs in).

Then the hard cost of creating your blog content is $200 × 2 + $100 = $500 per blog post. With that knowledge, now you can start maximizing the process. For example, what if you spent 15 minutes talking to a freelance writer who writes and prepares your blog post for distribution? The freelance writer's time is an even $50 per hour, and he takes two hours to write, edit, and link to other key documents. This also focuses your marketing director on more strategic activities. So instead of $500 per blog post, now the formula is 0.25 × $200 (your time) + $50 × 2 = $150 total. How's that for ROI?

The key is knowing what the pieces of the content process cost you and then determining if they are the best way to produce and distribute content. If you are just getting started, give it a few months, and see how things go. At first, it's always better to develop hard-hitting, epic content, and then figure out how to be more efficient after the fact.

CALCULATING THE VALUE OF A SUBSCRIBER

At The Tilt subscribers to the content are better customers. Subscribers are more likely to attend events and buy $TILT coin. Epic content does that. The goal with your content is to find out why having subscribers helps you attract and/or retain customers.

At the Content Marketing Institute, they discovered that when their customers were subscribed to the newsletter, the webinar series, and the magazine, they spent significantly more than any other group. It took CMI a few years to find that number, but when they did, it became a powerful business driver.

This is the method used by brands for over 100 years. There has never been a better opportunity than now for you to become the leading informational expert in your niche. By doing so you will grow your business.

FINAL THOUGHT ON A MEDIA BUSINESS MODEL

Even though we are focusing primarily on solving your marketing problems, we need to remember that once you build a loyal audience, you actually have 10 different ways to ultimately drive revenues.

If we use the Content Inc. Revenue Model (updated in 2021), an organization can drive six direct revenue lines and four indirect revenue lines (see Figure 20.2). Direct revenue lines look like the major revenue sources for a media business model. Indirect revenue lines are content marketing drivers.

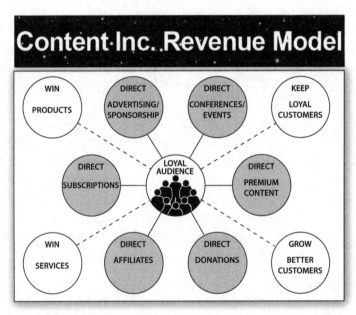

FIGURE 20.2   The potential revenue sources for content (*Source: Content Inc.*)

Direct revenue lines include:

- Advertising/sponsorship
- Conferences/events
- Premium content (like paid books or ebooks)
- Donations

- Affiliate programs
- Subscriptions

Indirect revenue (think content marketing objectives) lines include:

- Selling more products
- Selling more services
- Creating customers who continue to buy (loyalty)
- Creating customers who buy more (better customers)

The Content Inc. model is used mostly by small content creators. It doesn't get into much of the complexity we cover in this chapter, but sometimes it's important to understand that you have the ability to develop a fully functional profit machine, like Cleveland Clinic or Red Bull Media House has, if you wish to.

EPIC THOUGHTS

- What are the behaviors you need to see that lead to accomplishing your business objectives? Likes and tweets are indicators and can help us check our progress, but we should only use them if they are tied to our goal completion.

- Remember, owners and senior marketing executives only care about revenue, cost savings, or happier customers. Focus your objectives on those three things and only show the CXO reports that can help tell that story.

EPIC RESOURCE

- Joe Pulizzi, *Content Inc.*, 2nd ed., McGraw Hill, 2021.

CHAPTER 21

Using Data to Optimize Content Performance

BY BRIAN PIPER

Perhaps we could write code to optimize code,
then run that code through the code optimizer?

STEPHEN HAWKING

Let's dive into some of the places where you can find deeper insights into your data. We'll look at how you can use those insights to inspire your creative process and optimize existing content to increase performance and attain your goals more quickly.

As Chris Penn of Trust Insights says: "Here's the part that goes wrong with all content marketing analytics. You don't do anything with it." If you just collect the data and don't leverage the data to make changes and try new things, you'll never improve your process or your content.

One of the most effective things you can do with any sort of content data is to look at the performance over time and identify patterns and anomalies. Those are the areas where you can find some impactful insights.

WHERE TO FIND CONTENT PERFORMANCE INSIGHTS

Let's talk about some of the ways you can collect your data, tools you can use to track it, and places you can find insights within your data sets to provide you with useful information.

GOOGLE SHEETS AND EXCEL

What? With all the software, AI, and expensive solutions available, you're recommending Google Sheets or Excel? Yes! You may find that many of those tools don't track the data that is most important to meeting your goals. Or that one tool will provide metrics that others don't, and those will be the ones you need for a particular use case within your content.

Before putting down money on a paid solution, the best thing you can do is manually capture your data for a few months to get an idea of what you really need to track. Then you can make sure that the solution you purchase can provide you with the data you need in the way that you need it. Before you download a trial version of the software, track your data, collect different metrics, and try to establish ways to get the value you need to reach your goal. That way, when you're playing around in the trial version of some new software, you'll quickly discover if the package can provide value by automating the manual part of your data collection, or if it can automatically identify the insights and information you're looking to isolate.

GOOGLE ANALYTICS

There are several excellent paid analytics tools available that have more flexibility and functionality than Google Analytics, but you can find lots of insights and dramatically improve site performance with the data you can get from Google Analytics.

In October 2020, Google introduced its newest version of Google Analytics, Google Analytics 4. Google also announced that Google Analytics 3 (also referred to as Universal Analytics) will no longer be tracking data as of July 1, 2023. If you don't have your analytics updated to Google Analytics 4, you're already missing historical data that you could have been collecting.

Let's take a moment to talk about the differences between the two platforms and how your website measurement strategy needs to adapt to the changes.

UNIVERSAL ANALYTICS (GOOGLE ANALYTICS 3)

Universal Analytics (UA) was primarily a hit-based tool. It looked at how many sessions you had and how many users visited pages on your site. This is the convention that had been used in all the previous versions of Google Analytics, going back to the original Urchin software that Google acquired in 1999.

There are several flaws in the data that UA provided. For example, if a user visited two pages on your site, spent three minutes reading the content of each page, and then left your site, the time on the second page wouldn't count, because the code only recorded the time on page data when the user went to a new page on the site.

Also, if you had a large amount of traffic on your site, the data you got from UA was sampled, which meant that Google wasn't showing you accurate data; it was using a subset of your data to estimate the rest of your performance.

GOOGLE ANALYTICS 4

Google Analytics 4 (GA4) is entirely event-based. This means that everything that is recorded is logged as an event. So a visitor coming to a page is an event. Someone making a purchase is an event. Someone scrolling down your page is an event. While the mechanics are a bit different, you can still get most of the same information you were able to get in UA, but it may be in a different place or require you to gather it in a different way. On the plus side, it tends to be more accurate than what you got in UA.

Several of the updates to Google Analytics 4 were made with user data security in mind. For example, a new GA4 property defaults to only storing user-specific data for 2 months. You can change that to store data for 14 months, but that's the longest option available. If you often look at older, historic data within your analytics, you'll need to leverage BigQuery, which is Google's cloud-based data storage solution and is included in GA4 for free.

Another thing to keep in mind is that you can't pass data from UA into GA4, which means you may eventually lose all that historic data you have if you don't export it and back it up.

Once you have GA4 set up to track data on your site, you'll want to set up conversions (formerly called "goals") to track when users take certain actions on your site that you're driving them to, like completing a form, purchasing a course, subscribing to your newsletter, etc.

GOOGLE SEARCH CONSOLE

Google Search Console is free and gives specific data around what terms users are actively searching on to find your website. We mentioned in Chapter 19 that the search console is a great place to mine keyword data and see what sort of content your users are searching for, but it also can provide invaluable information on the performance of your website pages.

Look in the Core Web Vitals section to find performance issues that you can share with your developers that will improve your site speed and, consequently, your search rankings.

GOOGLE DATA STUDIO

Google Data Studio is a free tool that lets you easily connect to different data sources, including Google Analytics and Google Sheets, and then create visualizations to look at your data in different ways.

Google Analytics 4 has moved or removed many of the standard views and reports that marketers were used to seeing within the tool. Many experts recommend using Google Data Studio to create visualizations to help marketers interpret data without having to learn where to find or how to re-create all their standard reports in GA4.

TRACKING, MEASURING, AND OPTIMIZING YOUR ORGANIC TRAFFIC

Organic traffic in Google Analytics is traffic that is coming to your site from searches. You should be getting at least half of the traffic to your site from searches. If you're not, this is a good place to start optimizing.

In Chapter 19, we talked about doing an SEO audit and keyword research. When you look at your analytics, you want to focus on tracking which pages are getting consistent organic traffic and which pages are converting users to customers (or subscribers).

If you go to EpicContentMarketing.com, you can download a sample Google Data Studio dashboard for monitoring the amount of organic traffic to your pages and tracking what terms users are searching on to find your site.

CREATING CONTENT CLUSTERS AND EXPERTISE

Google doesn't share its ranking algorithm, but it does announce when there are updates to it and what the focus areas are for those updates. It also shares its Search Quality Evaluator Guidelines publicly. These guidelines are used by people who help determine how effective the current algorithm is and how it should be changed. One of the factors mentioned numerous times (129 times in 172 pages) in this report is EAT.

EAT stands for *expertise, authoritativeness,* and *trustworthiness.* Let's look at each of these:

- The *expertise* of the creator of the content is determined in a variety of ways. The creator can be a subject-matter expert, like a doctor or scientist, or can have "life experiences" that qualify the person to be an expert on the topic.
- The *authoritativeness,* or reputation, of the creator, the content, and the site is based on the amount of content a site has on a particular topic. That is why it is important to have key pillar pages with numerous supporting pages all relating to the same topic. It also helps to have a site with content that has been around for a longer period of time.
- The *trustworthiness* of the content can come from highlighting the credentials of the creator and the site through reviews, awards, and testimonials.

Basically, Google is looking to promote content that it considers high-quality, and the first characteristic it lists for the evaluators is EAT. This is especially true for YMYL (Your Money or Your Life) pages (mentioned 104 times in the guidelines), which offer up content that can directly affect a user's future happiness, health, financial stability, or safety.

ADDRESSING "CONTENT SHOCK"

As you continue creating content in your particular segment it's important to recognize when that area is getting filled with so much content, and high-quality content, that there is no way you can continue to compete and stay relevant.

Mark Schaefer has written several posts on the importance of recognizing this "content shock" in your industry and using that to inform your strategy. When you see the content density increasing in your segment or niche to the point where you can no longer stand out, find a deeper niche and begin to create high-quality, helpful content focused on that particular area to establish yourself as the expert there.

As important as it is to create helpful content, it's also important to create it in an area where you can differentiate yourself.

SOCIAL ANALYTICS

You can find all sorts of insights just by looking at the data supplied within your social platforms.

However, social platforms don't make it easy to collect large amounts of data or to look back over longer periods of time, two factors that are critical in identifying insights within data sets.

For example, Twitter breaks down its analytics by month. It can be helpful to look back through the past few months to see what tweets have done well and which ones haven't. It does have severe limitations on being able to look at your data over time, which is one of the most impactful methods of examining a data set for trends or anomalies. Natively, Twitter only allows you to export data one month at a time. There are workarounds to this, but you can also start with a Google Sheet (you can get a template for this at EpicContentMarketing.com) and begin adding in the data yourself.

HOW TO SELECT CONTENT TO OPTIMIZE ON YOUR RENTED LAND

Let's assume that you've been using what you've learned in this book so far and you're driving traffic from your rented land (YouTube, Twitter, TikTok, etc.) to your owned land (your website) and then monetizing the people in your audience by driving them to convert and thereby purchase products, services, courses, etc.

We talked about keyword research in Chapter 19 specific to your website. Those same keywords should be targeted across all your platforms and content. Keyword research is important for social platforms, videos, podcasts, and any other channel you choose because it can tell you what topics you need to be addressing and what sort of language you should be using.

OPTIMIZE YOUR SOCIAL PLATFORMS

Optimize your channel profile descriptions to include your keywords. Your social channels can rank on Google for keywords as well as your website pages. Look in Google Analytics to see what channels are driving the most traffic to your site, specifically to your high-conversion pages. Every piece of social content you put out should have a strategy or a call to action to drive users to some location on your website.

Any time you can include a link to your site from any social channel, use a UTM code on that link so you can see where traffic is coming from within your Google Analytics campaigns. UTM codes are very easy to create using resources like Google Analytics' Campaign URL Builder. They are an amazing way to track specific traffic to your site.

Once you're tracking your data, you can start experimenting with different techniques to figure out what works and what doesn't. Set your baseline, establish your primary channel, and put content out on it for a month. Then start experimenting with one new thing at a time, let it work for a few weeks, and then measure again. Don't get caught in the trap of assuming that the new thing you're doing is the direct cause of the change in metrics; but when you notice something spike or drop, you can double down, or you can back off on what you're trying and move on to something else.

OPTIMIZATION OPPORTUNITIES

There are so many things that you can do to affect your content performance on social channels. Follow this methodology: measure, experiment, monitor, and adjust. Measure your current content performance to get a baseline and identify trends, experiment using some of the methods that follow, monitor your data to look for dips or spikes in performance, and adjust your tactics based on what works and what doesn't.

Be consistent, be real, and be vulnerable. People love social channels that reflect real people with whom they can connect. They want to find people who consistently show up and can be expected to be there at certain frequencies with new content. Stick to three to five different topic areas so your users know what knowledge you'll be sharing with them. Record the topic area for each post in your tracking document (see our example social metric tracking sheet at EpicContentMarketing.com) so you can see which area tends to get the highest engagement and then do more of that.

Be social on social. Don't spend all your time posting your own content. Remember the 4-1-1 rule from Chapter 19, and follow, retweet, and engage with influencers in your industry. Make sure you reply to users who comment on your posts. This works for all social channels.

HASHTAGS

Using hashtags on your social posts can help make your posts more visible, searchable, and trackable. Optimize your Twitter and Instagram hashtags with tools like RiteTag (Chrome extension) or Hashtagify. Add the hashtags you use to your tracking sheet.

Consider branded hashtags if you have a following so you can let your users know how to easily find your topical content. Hashtags at The Tilt include #CreatorEconomy and #CreatorExpo for the Creator Economy Expo event.

YOUTUBE

YouTube is the second largest search engine on the internet. Optimizing your YouTube profile and content is essential for growth and increasing revenue. Make sure you include keywords in your profile, channel name, video titles, descriptions, video tags, and content.

Monitor the "average percentage viewed" metric for your videos. How long do users stick with a video? Where do they drop off? Which types of videos get the most views? Which ones drove the most subscribers?

If people aren't clicking on your videos, play with your thumbnails to see what drives more views. If they're not watching to the end, try shortening your videos or making a change in the videos at the average view duration time to pull them back into the content.

There are several ways people find videos from within YouTube—by searching, following suggestions from other videos, or browsing. You can optimize your content for each of these different discovery methods based on where they perform the best.

Tools like TubeBuddy or VidIQ (there are free Chrome extensions for both) can help you optimize your YouTube content and even perform A/B testing.

LINKEDIN

Like many social platforms, LinkedIn tends to promote posts that get high initial engagement. If you have a group of supporters or collaborators, reach out to them when you put out a new LinkedIn post and ask them to like, comment, and share your content. Do the same for them. This is a great experiment to try with fellow creators or superfans within your community.

If you're at a conference, take pictures of the speakers during their presentations and tag them in the pictures and posts.

TWITTER

Follow Twitter Business (@TwitterBusiness) for more tips and tricks to grow an audience on Twitter. Twitter Business also shares new features on Twitter that are consistently being launched.

Pin a strategically relevant, high-performing, or promotional tweet to your profile so it's the first thing users see when they visit your page. Make sure it has a call to action to a particular page on your site with a trackable link. Swap out the pinned tweet every few weeks to see which one drives the most traffic.

Use hashtags in your Twitter posts, but try to limit them to no more than two, and make sure they're relevant to your topic

Try posting every day for a month at several different times throughout the day. Look at your metrics to see what time of day and day of the week tend to have the most engagement for your audience. Then be sure to post every week at that day and time, and try to make it your most relevant post. Track to see how that day and time change. Try starting with weekdays around 8 a.m. to 10 a.m.

INSTAGRAM

Try using posts, stories, reels, and live content to see what works. Set a goal to post several ways using each channel format. If you're using stories, be sure to set a hook on the first post to keep people going through the content, and try to limit yourself to no more than six or seven posts per story. Stories tend to perform better in the late afternoon or evening, and they only remain active for 24 hours.

Use emojis. Data has shown that using an emoji or two in your posts can help with engagement. But don't go overboard; using 11 or more can have a significant negative impact on performance.

Use hashtags. There doesn't seem to be any negative impact from using lots of hashtags, and posts with more than 11 hashtags have the highest engagement rates! Just make sure they're relevant to your users and content areas. Instagram categorizes hashtags into nine distinct types, each with different purposes. There are also lots of ways to hide hashtags in posts to make them less visible but just as effective.

Mention and tag other accounts in your posts if relevant. Mentioning another account with @ will notify that account that you mentioned it.

Tagging an account in an image will notify the tagged account but will additionally cause that image to appear in a separate tab in that account's profile.

Understand that different social platforms have different audiences. Use the demographics analytics from the platforms to make sure you target the right audience with your content. As of when this book was written, you could only access Instagram Insights via mobile, but you could use several free (and paid) analytics tools on nonmobile devices.

TIKTOK

If you have a TikTok following, be sure you include a call to action in your comment and pin that comment to your video. Then create a promotional TikTok video with a call to action, driving viewers to your website, and pin that to the top of your profile. Put text on your initial screen with a hook to pull people in. Play with your titles and your content. Watch the trending videos to see what audio they're using and see what works for you.

If you're trying to increase your TikTok followers quickly, try posting three or four videos each day. They don't have to be produced or professional; they just must be on topic and relevant to your viewers.

LIVE PLATFORMS

For Twitter Spaces, Instagram Live, Twitch, Clubhouse, or LinkedIn Live, be sure to schedule your live session a few days or a week ahead and promote the event. You can stream live on multiple channels at the same time. If you're using a streaming tool (like Streamyard), you should schedule through that tool, and not through the native platform. You can use Buffer as your event calendar to schedule your live session.

Title your event strategically, write a keyword-rich description, and create a nice thumbnail. Address live comments during the stream. Outline your key discussion points so you can stay on track during your session.

PODCASTS

Jordan Harbinger is a well-known podcaster with mountains of content. He added an incredibly useful feature for his audience by creating podcast starter packs that present several podcasts focusing on one particular area. That way new listeners can listen to a starter pack on a topic they are interested in and not have to spend time searching through his thousands of podcasts. This makes the content accessible to new users and makes it easier for anyone to explore new topics. You could do this with playlists for YouTube content as well.

BUILDING ONLINE

Justin Welsh wrote a Twitter thread that shares his 15 principles for building a business online that took him from $0 to $2.4 million in three years. The steps he outlined include:

- Build a creator funnel.
- Get discovered.
- Teach people (educate).
- Be entertaining.
- Challenge people.
- Empathize.
- Learn to add value.
- Build trust.
- Write a newsletter.
- Start a podcast.
- Leverage how-to videos.
- Learn to "deplatform."
- Deepen relationships.
- Monetize.
- Explore how to use community.

Find the link to his complete thread in the Epic Resources that follow.

EPIC THOUGHTS

- Set up your data to track and monitor your performance so that you can determine what content is working for you and what isn't.

- You can't identify your "epic" content unless you're tracking the performance.

- Try the different tactics in this chapter. For each tactic, track performance for 30–60 days and see if it's worth the effort to continue.

EPIC RESOURCES

- Google, "Campaign URL Builder," accessed July 4, 2022, https://ga-dev-tools.web.app/campaign-url-builder/.

- Buzzfeed, "Justin Welsh on Twitter," accessed July 2, 2022, https://twitter.com/thejustinwelsh/status/1537409684931547136.

- Mark Schaefer, "How to Use Content Shock to Win in Business," accessed November 20, 2022, https://businessesgrow.com/2019/01/07/how-to-use-content-shock/.

- Mention, "Instagram-Report-2022-EN.pdf," accessed July 3, 2022, https://mention.com/pardot-2/files/Instagram-Report-2022-EN.pdf.

CHAPTER 22

AI and ML in Epic Content Marketing

BY BRIAN PIPER

Sometimes, I just don't understand human behavior.

C-3PO

Between the time the first edition of this book came out 10 years ago and now, there have been big advances in artificial intelligence (AI) and machine learning (ML). Computers continue to get faster and more powerful, and they can do more now than ever before.

Many people hear the term "AI," and they think of the movie *Her* or *Terminator*, basically, sentient computers. But what you should be thinking about is all the repetitive tasks that you do every day and the fact that computers can be taught how to do all those things for you. This is called "intelligent automation," and this is where you should be using AI right now to gain a competitive advantage.

WHAT ARE AI AND ML?

There are lots of terms (and acronyms) in this area. Before we can talk about how AI and ML will impact content marketing, we need to have a basic understanding of what they are.

ARTIFICIAL INTELLIGENCE

AI is the overarching term that refers to computers simulating cognitive functions that we tend to associate with people, like learning and problem solving.

At a very basic level, you can imagine this as a series of if-then statements. When you string enough of these if-then statements together and supply enough input data, it begins to simulate intelligence. AI can be used to help us perform repetitive tasks based on a set of rules that we define.

We already use AI in our everyday lives. Whether it's watching the next movie that Netflix recommends to you, looking at an ad on Facebook, or letting Gmail finish a sentence for you in an email, we use basic AI every day.

MACHINE LEARNING

ML is an advanced subset of AI and begins to integrate deeper decision-making capabilities using things like regression analysis, clustering, and classification. ML requires large sets of data and neural networks for computers to be able to "inform" themselves thoroughly enough to start seeing connections and patterns and making decisions.

Some ML applications that we use daily include Google Maps, which suggests the best route home based on time of day, traffic patterns, and driving habits; voice assistants like Alexa and Siri; and self-driving cars.

In describing the virtues of AI and ML, Christopher S. Penn, marketing and technology expert and cofounder and chief data scientist at TrustInsights.ai, says:

> AI and machine learning have done an incredible job of taking data that we collect about our content and telling us what really works and what doesn't. Savvy marketers with good in-house data teams or with the right combination of vendors and agencies can use that information in their efforts to say "we're going to do more of X and less of Y."

HOW CAN AI AND ML HELP CONTENT MARKETERS?

According to the marketers surveyed (69 percent were content marketers specifically) in "The 2021 State of Marketing AI Report":

- 52 percent said that AI is very important or critically important to their success over the next 12 months.

- 80 percent believe that more than a quarter of all their marketing tasks will be automated in five years.
- 18 percent have not intelligently automated any tasks at all.
- 56 percent believe that AI will create more jobs than it eliminates

There are many ways that AI and ML are already changing content marketing. There are tools that are writing content, predicting content effectiveness, and generating images.

DALL·E (and now DALL·E 2) from OpenAI is a system that can dynamically generate images based on the description that you provide. ImagenAI can take your Adobe Lightroom photos and automatically apply your unique editing style to new images based on what you've done with previous images.

Christopher Penn, whom we cited earlier, further explains:

> This means that you, as a marketer, still have an opportunity to have a long and rich, and fulfilling career if you create great content consistently and frequently. And if you can create great content consistently and frequently, you will remain ahead of the machines because there are not enough people like you who can make the content that these machines can learn from. They can do regression like crazy. They can do classification really well, and they can create mediocre content. And they will eventually evolve in the next few years to creating good content. But it will be a while before they create great content.

Talking about using AI for content marketing, here is what Jeff Coyle, cofounder and chief strategy officer at MarketMuse, says:

> This is how I recommend teams or businesses think about it. Go all the way from pre-ideation and document all the manual processes from research to planning, all the communications platforms you're using, all the people that touch and maintain the content, the actual writing, the editing, and then updating and maintaining existing content.
>
> Artificial intelligence technologies can fast-track all of those stages in such a dramatic form.
>
> But what it doesn't do is replace. It can augment, it can provide a way somebody could approach something, or it can provide a framework, an outline, or a structure.

CASES IN POINT

BUZZFEED

Buzzfeed is an AI-powered media company that is using AI to identify, optimize, and promote top-performing content. It is using data to determine which content to recommend to which users, and it has even created an AI-powered Good Advice Cupcake account on Instagram that has its own followers.

In his book *Marketing Artificial Intelligence: AI, Marketing, and the Future of Business,* Paul Roetzer, founder and CEO of the Marketing AI Institute, writes:

> The company uses every single publishing event as an opportunity to collect data on what drives the most engagement and revenue. This data is used to inform the next piece of content, which is iterated and improved upon based on historical data. In turn, the next piece of content generates even more data from which to learn. This data then gives BuzzFeed's AI the ability to make even better predictions about what works and what doesn't, which, you guessed it, makes subsequent pieces of content even more effective. The result is an AI-powered content machine that regularly blows the competition out of the water because it is constantly learning and improving.

THE *WASHINGTON POST*

The *Washington Post* had a problem. It needed to cover all the events at the 2016 Rio Olympics, but it didn't have enough reporters or editors to provide all the up-to-the-minute coverage its users wanted. So it created Heliograf, which generated short messages for Twitter, for the *Post's* live blog, and for the newspaper's Alexa app. Since then, Heliograf has been adapted to write entire articles, creating more than 850 articles in its first year, covering local elections in a way that wasn't previously possible.

Jeff Coyle extols the benefits this way:

> This is good for the world. Before, they can only publish articles on 15% of the Olympic events, right? With Heliograf, they publish content telling the results of all the events. Instead of only covering 8% and having a bias in your election coverage, you're covering all the elections; that's good for the world.

BLOOMBERG NEWS

In 2019, roughly a third of the content published by Bloomberg News utilized some type of automation provided by its AI system, Cyborg. Many other companies use bots to create content, but mostly these are standard, repetitive types of stories.

AI can create first drafts of content, but you still need an actual human to turn that into an interesting and creative story with the type of personality that readers want.

THE FUTURE OF AI AND ML IN CONTENT MARKETING

The future is already here. It's time to start integrating these technologies into your processes and operations.

When you start looking at where to get started, an excellent resource is the Marketing AI Institute. It has an AI Score for Marketers that asks a series of questions to find out where you are in your AI journey and can help direct you on what the next steps are. It also has a blog with incredible resources, tool reviews, and podcasts covering every aspect of AI and ML in content marketing.

Harry Syed, executive director of Innovation at Sub Rosa, anticipates:

A central nervous system will be embedded in each organization. And that nervous system will be the way in which it will constantly understand the psychology, the motivation of the people that that brand cares about and wants people to care about that brand.

Jeff Coyle has the last word in this chapter, predicting:

What we're going to see in 10 years' time is expertise drives the bus for having longevity, but also being able to package that expertise in as many formats as possible becomes the "meets minimum" for any business.

EPIC THOUGHTS

- Start looking into leveraging AI and ML solutions now to maintain a competitive edge, and let your human creators stop spending time on repetitive and mindless tasks.

- Consider one small project where you can leverage AI and ML to replace a human task.

EPIC RESOURCES

- Marketing Artificial Intelligence Institute, "The 2022 State of Marketing AI Report," accessed July 2, 2022, https://www.marketingaiinstitute.com/2022-state-of-marketing-ai-report.

- Paul Roetzer, *Marketing Artificial Intelligence: AI, Marketing, and the Future of Business*, Matt Holt, 2022.

- Buzzfeed, "The Good Advice Cupcake (@thegoodadvicecupcake)," accessed July 2, 2022, https://www.instagram.com/thegoodadvicecupcake/?hl=en.

- "The Rise of the Robot Reporter," *New York Times*, accessed July 2, 2022, https://www.nytimes.com/2019/02/05/business/media/artificial-intelligence-journalism-robots.html.

- "[The Marketing AI Show: Episode 5] Marketing AI Innovation That Could Change Everything," *Marketing Artificial Intelligence Institute* (podcast), accessed July 2, 2022, https://www.marketingaiinstitute.com/blog/the-marketing-ai-show-episode-5-marketing-ai-innovation-that-could-change-everything.

CHAPTER 23

The Creator Economy

BY BRIAN PIPER

Success isn't about how much money you make;
it's about the difference you make in people's lives.

MICHELLE OBAMA

These days, anyone with a smartphone or computer and internet access can easily create content that can reach a global audience. It's spectacular. And a little scary. According to Domo, in 2021, Facebook users shared 240,000 photos and Twitter users posted 575,000 tweets . . . every minute. That is a staggering amount of content. But even more staggering is the rate at which that content is being consumed. Each minute, users stream 694,000 hours of YouTube videos, and TikTok users watch more than 167 million videos. This has considerably muddied the waters for brands looking to have their content consumed by audiences and also for content entrepreneurs trying to make a living from their content.

When brands or content entrepreneurs create content, if they're doing it right, they're typically looking for ways to leverage that content to build an audience or a community, sell a product, increase brand awareness, or communicate key concepts of their business. When individuals create content, there are all sorts of different potential motivations. They may just be looking to communicate their opinions; they may be looking for fame or money. In fact, a recent Harris Poll survey showed that kids from eight to twelve years old are *three times as likely to want to be a YouTuber than an astronaut.*

When we use the term "creator economy," we're basically referring to the ability of content creators to make money directly from their content. This can really be any kind of content. Whether you're creating TikTok videos about how to dance to Cardi B's "WAP," putting your band's latest songs up, writing a blog, or playing video games on Twitch, there are lots of ways to use your content to generate income.

As we discussed (in Chapter 20), *Content Inc.* outlined the six direct revenue options that creators can leverage:

- Advertising/sponsorship
- Conferences/events
- Premium content
- Donations
- Affiliates
- Subscriptions

Web 2.0 opened the doors for individual creators of all types of content to create revenue opportunities. If you were a musician, you no longer had to be lucky enough to be picked up by a record label. If you were a writer, you had other options besides working for a newspaper or magazine or convincing a publisher to buy your book. There were opportunities to build an audience on different channels and then those channels would start to pay you based on how much traffic you received. When your audience was big enough, you could become an "influencer" and get sponsors and put ads on your content and make money from that.

Many content creators from brands also began trying their hand at building a personal brand and monetizing their content. Covid made this a much more appealing option to many who were working remotely, had been let go from their job, or were just looking for a way to connect with other people.

1,000 TRUE FANS

Back in 2008, Kevin Kelly wrote an article in *The Technium* called "1,000 True Fans," where he said, "To make a living as a craftsperson, photographer, musician, designer, author, animator, app maker, entrepreneur, or inventor you need only one thousand true fans."

100 TRUE FANS

Twelve years later, in 2020, Li Jin wrote an article, "100 True Fans," on how the rise of the creator economy (she refers to this as the "passion economy") allows the opportunity for only 100 superfans to power and fund a creator. In the article, Li gives numerous examples where the number of content consumers paying more than $1,000 a year has grown exponentially for creators who can deliver self-improvement, connection, recognition, or belonging.

According to Statista, in 2021 there were more than 41 million "professional" content creators worldwide with more than 10,000 followers. Based on data from Comparably, the median content creator salary is $85,000, and the range goes from $45,000 to $140,000.

According to the "2022 Content Entrepreneur Benchmark Research" report from The Tilt, more than half of full-time content creators surveyed are making enough money to support at least one person, and almost 20 percent say they earn a "substantial" income. Only 1 percent of content creators say they regret the decision they made to pursue their path.

Content creators rely on epic content marketing to build their brand, sell their products and services, and grow their communities. Just like brand content marketers, they do this on a variety of channels (see Figure 23.1).

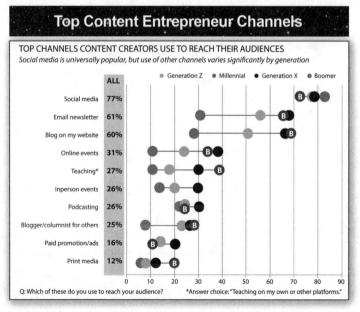

FIGURE 23.1 Different generations of content entrepreneurs use different channels. (*Source: The Tilt*)

These content entrepreneurs use a variety of monetization strategies to earn a living from their content (see Figure 23.2).

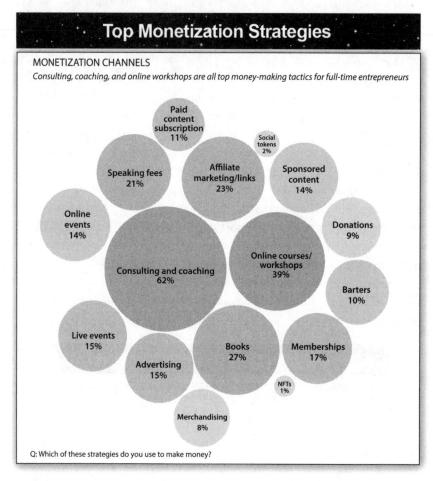

FIGURE 23.2 There are many ways to monetize content for entrepreneurs. (*Source: The Tilt*)

FOR CONTENT MARKETERS

Why is this important for brands leveraging a content marketing approach? Like it or not, the creator economy movement is only going to grow. You compete for attention, not only with your product and/or service competitors but against smaller content creators as well. Add Netflix, TikTok, BeReal,

Wordle, and a thousand other apps, and breaking through to build an audience is daunting (to say the least).

But these smaller creators and content entrepreneurs don't have to be your competition. They could be your influencer partners. They could be your freelancers. They could help you build your own subscriptions. Heck, they might even be available for purchase (we will talk about that shortly). In other words, if you can't beat them (and you can't), why not join them?

As a content marketer, it's your responsibility to leverage the creator economy whenever and however you can.

EPIC THOUGHTS

- The creator economy continues to grow as more people create content, monetize that content, and build communities.

- More creators mean more competition, but it also means more opportunity for your content marketing efforts.

EPIC RESOURCES

- Domo, "Data Never Sleeps 9.0," accessed June 29, 2022, https://www.domo.com/learn/infographic/data-never-sleeps-9.

- The Lego Group via PR Newswire, "LEGO Group Kicks Off Global Program to Inspire the Next Generation of Space Explorers as NASA Celebrates 50 Years of Moon Landing," accessed June 29, 2022, https://www.prnewswire.com/news-releases/lego-group-kicks-off-global-program-to-inspire-the-next-generation-of-space-explorers-as-nasa-celebrates-50-years-of-moon-landing-300885423.html.

- Joe Pulizzi, *Content Inc.*, 2nd ed., McGraw Hill, 2021.

- The Tilt, "2022 Creator Economy Benchmark Research," accessed July 6, 2002, https://www.thetilt.com/research.

- Kevin Kelly, "1,000 True Fans," *The Technium*, accessed June 29, 2022, https://kk.org/thetechnium/1000-true-fans/.

- Li Jin, "100 True Fans," accessed July 4, 2022, https://li-jin.co/2020/02/19/100-true-fans/.

- Statista, "Number of Digital Content Creators Worldwide in 2021, by Audience Size," accessed July 3, 2022, https://www.statista.com/statistics/1307272/global-content-creators-by-followers/.

- Comparably, "Content Creator Salary," accessed July 3, 2022, https://www.comparably.com/salaries/salaries-for-content-creator.

CHAPTER 24

The Importance of Community and Superfans

BY BRIAN PIPER

> There is no power for change greater
> than a community discovering what it cares about.
> MARGARET J. WHEATLEY

When you've built epic content that answers the questions your audience is asking and that provides value, the key to making that content effective and being able to leverage it to its full potential is by having a strong community of superfans.

As content entrepreneurs and content marketers, our initial challenge is to grow an audience, to get people to pay attention (and opt in) to our content and find value for themselves. The way we do that is by delivering the right message to the right audience at the right time . . . consistently.

Some people in our audience will get more value out of our content than others. Some of them will be at a stage where our content answers the questions that they have and solves the problems they are facing, but they want more. These people will often get more involved, look for content and connections on other channels, start sharing our content with their audiences and friends, and help us build our followers and subscribers. These are the people that we can potentially convert from audience members, to community members, and eventually to superfans.

AUDIENCE VERSUS COMMUNITY VERSUS SUPERFANS

Audience refers to the people who consume your content. They watch your videos, read your articles, absorb your knowledge . . . and move on. They may come back, they may subscribe on one or two channels, but they are primarily casual consumers of your content.

When we talk about community, we're talking about the people in your audience who engage with your content. They will most likely look for your content across multiple channels. They will often trade some of their information, like their email address, with you in order to get more content. They engage with your content, and they engage with you. They share your content, and they promote it . . . they help grow your audience.

Superfans are the "stans" in your community. They are the people who promote all the content you put out. They engage with everything on every channel. They talk about you, give you positive reviews, come to see you speak, and take your courses. They will sometimes even do work for you to help you succeed without asking for anything in return.

VALUE OF AUDIENCE

As content creators, the audience is the top of the funnel. Everything we've discussed so far about creating epic content is focused on getting users to find value in your content and become audience members.

It is much easier to get users to buy your products and services if they are part of your audience. Having people regularly consume your content, subscribe to your channels, or follow you creates the first layer of trust. They believe in the value you bring enough to commit some of their attention to you. It's up to you to deliver on that for them.

VALUE OF COMMUNITY

There is something inherently beautiful about having a community and being part of a community. The support and sense of belonging are empowering. The connection, transparency, and ability to share and be vulnerable create a stronger bond than you can achieve with an audience.

When it comes to the importance of community, there are few people that understand that better than David Siegel, the CEO of Meetup. Meetup is a company whose entire mission is to help people connect and build community.

David says:

> In my opinion, everything is more effective when you're dealing with other people. Learning is better with other people. Community decreases ignorance, decreases xenophobia, it decreases hate between people, because you learn about them, you realize they're not so different than you. It's literally a magnifier for all the great things and the antidote for all the challenges.
>
> Community is the greatest basis for retaining top talent. It's also an important basis for recruiting top talent. And if you're a content entrepreneur, and you're looking to build a team, well, the best way to build a team is through tapping into your community.

VALUE OF SUPERFANS

When you start looking at those very engaged community members who are your true stans, you're talking about your superfans. And Pat Flynn literally wrote the book. Author of *Superfans* (and *Will It Fly* and *Let It Go*), host of the *Smart Passive Income* podcast (and *AskPat 2.0*), and creator of the Pat Flynn YouTube channel (and Deep Pocket Monster), Pat has created a guide to creating superfans.

Superfans walks the reader through building the Pyramid of Fandom, which includes steps to convert the casual consumer to an active audience, then into a connected community, and finally to superfans.

I had a chance to interview Pat, and here's what he shared related to the value of community and ways to build superfans with content marketing:

> In *Superfans* I talk about the idea of creating memorable moments by surprise. I think that is something that big brands have the money and the capability to do, but they're just not thinking about. I think brands need to get smarter by hiring people who care about their people. Because a lot of people at those companies care about other things, from the content generation to the bottom line, to HR and management. . . . But who are they actually caring about—you know, Joan, who lives in Oklahoma

254 I EPIC CONTENT MARKETING

and just lost her mom? Well, that's where you can come in for support. And even just a note or a video from a company goes a very, very long way. You don't have to send free products to be able to make a huge impact on people's lives; you just have to know where they're at and what they're going through. This is why it's important to have brand community managers and community directors, who are there to get to know their customers.

That's when a few things happen. Number one, those customers feel more connected and tied to the brand, which then influences their amplification of that brand to others to bring people in, and they're not coming in cold anymore; they're coming in warm, because it's coming in from a recommendation. But I also think that's where you get a lot of your best affiliates. If you want to talk business and bottom line, it's not just about making people feel good. Sometimes those people are going to be the most loud-spoken people that you could ever ask for that may have brands or connections that can help the brand, and everybody wins. That's important to me.

I think that is the difference between being on stage and saying, "Welcome to the concert; we hope you enjoy it today," and then you sing your songs versus going out in the crowd, shaking hands and talking to people individually, and realizing that not everything has to be scalable, not everything has to be automated, nor can everything be scalable and automated.

When it comes to the human-to-human connection, I think that's really what it's going to come down to, and what's going to help brands thrive. No matter what happens with technology, no matter what content mediums are out there when you can get to the human-to-human connection, you're going to win as long as humans exist.

BECOMING A SUPERFAN OF YOUR FANS

There are few better examples of the power of superfans than the Savannah Bananas baseball team. Jesse Cole, owner of the Savannah Bananas and author of *Fans First*, is a proponent of becoming a superfan of your community, and the mission of the team is simple: "Fans First, Always Entertain."

At the beginning of each game, as fans enter the stadium, they're greeted by players delivering the H3: hugs, high-fives, and handshakes. Not only does this connect the fans with the players, but it connects the players with the fans. It lets the players see the people that they're entertaining and gives them the inspiration to deliver.

In an interview, Jesse says:

> I look for every unremarkable moment. You put yourself in your customer's shoes. Every night, someone on our team goes undercover as a fan. At the end of the night, we tell everyone, "what were the fan's first moments and what were the friction points, what were the frustration points, and what was unremarkable."

By focusing on the fans and making them the most important thing about the event, the team has sold out every game, has a 50,000-ticket waitlist, and has more than 1 million social media followers.

"When you think about marketing," Jesse says, "everything is marketing. Every touchpoint, every interaction with your customer is marketing. So how do you make every interaction remarkable?"

When you really start to leverage the power of your superfans, you can start to create a much broader impact than just the success of your business.

In *Superfans*, Pat Flynn says:

> No matter your size, you can also use your following to help serve the community outside of the arena of your brand, to move your superfans to make positive change in the world.
>
> Your fans want to feel like they're making an impact and are part of something bigger than themselves. When you facilitate and make that happen, you can make great change and service happen, and strengthen those superfan bonds in the process.

EPIC THOUGHTS

- The key to building a strong and loyal customer base is to look for opportunities to convert your audience to community and your community to superfans.

- The connections you create with your superfans can open doors and create opportunities much larger than just helping your business.

EPIC RESOURCES

- Kelsey Reidl, "How to Be SUCCESSFUL by STANDING OUT!," YouTube, accessed July 4, 2022, https://www.youtube.com/watch?v=uXo_ZrcGxk4.

- Jesse Cole, *Fans First*, Lioncrest, 2022.

- Pat Flynn, interview by Brian Piper, June 6, 2022.

- Pat Flynn, *Superfans*, Get Smart Books, 2019.

CHAPTER 25

Selling Your Content Company

BY JOE PULIZZI

If you can do it, do it. If you can achieve it, achieve it.
BESSIE BLOUNT GRIFFIN

When we're working on building our content company and creating epic content, we rarely think about our exit. I mean, we're just getting started, so why should we already be looking at our exit? Well, here's why. All business owners are going to have an exit from their business; it's just a matter of how much control they have over that exit.

At the end of this chapter, we've included the step-by-step process for how I sold Content Marketing Institute back in 2016, which I outlined in detail in *Content Inc.* In this chapter, we'll hit on some of the key concepts and most important things to understand as a content entrepreneur.

Simply put, if you've built a valuable audience, there will always be a buyer. Some companies will want to buy your content business for the audience access alone. Others will judge you on your revenue and profit. Some will want to buy your content brand because it's meaningful in your particular marketplace.

Note: This chapter leans toward smaller creators, but it's important for content marketers to understand the motivations of content entrepreneurs toward an exit (see Chapter 26 for more).

Where do you start?

Start with your end goal in mind. What do you want your exit from your business to accomplish for you? Look at some of the types of companies being bought and what the deals included at TheyGotAcquired.com.

Thomas Smale is the CEO of FE International and has helped with more than 1,200 successful business sales. He says that most people frame their exit goals based on time or money. When do you want to exit your business (in 5 years, when you're 50, etc.), or how much do you want to make when you sell (enough to retire, $5 million, etc.)?

Here are a few key terms that will be used in any business sale that you need to understand from the beginning so you can factor these into the decisions you make as you grow your business and continue to build your strategy:

- **EBITA** (earnings before interest, taxes, and amortization). This is how a company's profitability is measured by investors. Larger companies with more physical assets will also factor in the depreciation of those assets (EBITDA, or earnings before interest, taxes, depreciation, and amortization), but that doesn't typically affect content entrepreneurs.
- **SDE** (seller's discretionary earnings). This is net income adjusted to include discretionary income. Your business may be showing a zero profit for tax purposes, but the valuation will factor in your expenses (vehicles, travel, conferences, training, etc.). This differs from EBITA because it includes the expense of replacing the owner within the business.
- **LOI** (letter of intent). When you're ready to sell your business, buyers will submit a nonbinding document with informal agreed-upon terms and pricing, and then they will begin to further examine your business.

As a content entrepreneur, what can you do to set yourself up for success?

Let's start off by talking about some numbers. When talking about small businesses, we're generally referring to businesses making less than $2 million a year in revenue. This is not net income; it is SDE. Generally, the larger the business, the higher the valuation curve is going to be. But on most small business sales, you can figure a three to five times sale value based on your SDE. So if your business is making $500,000 a year, you could expect to sell the business for around $1.5 million to $3 million.

Is it just revenue?

You may be thinking, "Hey, I've got 100,000 TikTok followers; that's got to be worth something, right?" Well, yes, it is worth something to a purchaser, but you're not going to be able to harness the true value of that audience in the sale if you haven't monetized that audience. You will be leaving money on the table if you don't put in the time to grow your revenue before you sell.

That being said, some buyers are more interested in acquiring your community, and if the perceived value to them is high enough, it might not matter as much that you haven't taken the steps to monetize. Your best bet, if you don't want to put in the work to monetize your content, is to try to get several potential buyers interested in the hope of creating a bidding war.

PRICING FACTORS

Many factors can affect the final price of a sale. Some things can help your bottom line, and some things can hurt it:

- **Growth rate.** If your business is growing quickly, you can often get a higher multiple. If your growth rate is flat or declining, that will generally drive the price down.
- **Figurehead.** If your business is built entirely around your personal impact (your talent, knowledge, ideas, etc.), it can be much more difficult to sell because the buyer is basically hiring you and not really buying your business. If this is the case, you need to think of ways to start removing yourself from the business and putting mechanisms in place (cohosts, courses, etc.) that will allow you to extricate yourself from the company.
- **Type of revenue.** Some of the higher multipliers for selling content businesses can come from having revenue based on subscriptions and events. Buyers see those recurring revenue streams as easy ways to continue generating revenue that they don't have to work as hard for.

As you know from the previous chapter, David Siegel is the CEO of Meetup, and he is also the author of *Decide & Conquer*. What you may not know is that David also ran Virgin Acquisitions for 1-800-Flowers, and during his time there, he purchased at least a dozen companies and had over $1 billion worth of spend.

According to David, for a content business, an acquiring company is typically looking for either volume or rabid users. In either case, you want to be sure you're tracking the right metrics so you can include those in the bargaining. For volume, you obviously need to be able to show the number of followers. For rabid users, there are a few indicators. The net promoter score is a good metric. Also, repeat visitors and the amount of time they're spending with your content. Are they coming every day? Once a week?

IT'S ABOUT MORE THAN JUST THE BENJAMINS

There are many factors besides the money to consider when thinking about selling your company. There are many questions you need to ask yourself:

- What do you want for the future of the company? How will you feel if your business is bought and a year later the buyer decides it's not worth the investment and shuts it down?
- What do you want for your staff? What if the buyer fires all the people you've worked with and built relationships with as soon as the deal is done? Sometimes, the team is the heart of the business. In this case, you may want to look into an acquihire. This is basically selling your whole team to a purchaser, with employment contracts included as part of the sale.
- How long are you willing to stay? Some deals include a set transition period where the buyer wants you to stay and manage the company but without the autonomy or level of operational control you're used to.
- How much control do you want? If you're going to stay on with the business for a set amount of time, how much decision-making ability do you want to have while you're still there?
- How much cash do you want up front? OK, so this is all about the Benjamins, but it's also about timing. You can negotiate the terms to allow you to get more money up front and less on the back end.

These are all things you can include in the negotiation and things you should consider.

WHERE DO YOU GET BUYERS?

Finding a buyer for your business can be challenging if you don't start creating connections early. Of course, you can always hire an M&A (mergers and acquisitions) firm that will help you find buyers, but there will be a fee for that expertise.

There are way more types of buyers of content businesses than you may be aware of. Obviously, there are big brands looking to acquire audiences, but there are also private equity groups who may be looking to add value to something in their portfolio, partnership groups, and even just high-net-worth individuals who happen to be passionate about a particular niche and want to invest.

Lots of business owners don't think about selling their business until someone comes knocking on their door looking to acquire it. At the selling stage of the process, it's always better to have more buyers than fewer. A little competition can do great things for your sale price and leverage when negotiating.

FORM RELATIONSHIPS

Many of the buyers for content companies come from contacts you already have. So as soon as you can, begin to create connections with people who could potentially buy your business. We sold Content Marketing Institute and Content Marketing World to UBM (now Informa). Before we even started talking about selling, I found out who the M&A person was and reached out to offer some free tickets to Content Marketing World.

More and more, for content companies, the buyers will come from sponsors. Look at HubSpot buying The Hustle or JP Morgan buying The Infatuation and Frank. You can also look at other media companies, and other influencers, who may be interested in your audience or community.

HIRE A NEGOTIATOR

Every negotiation will, at some point, have some friction. There will be issues; there will be rejections and unacceptable offers. When that happens, it's always better to have a third party negotiating for you so the friction is coming from the third party and not from you.

IDENTIFY BUYERS—A CASE STUDY OF CMI

By 2010, our Content Inc. model started coming into form. The revenue opportunities were presenting themselves, and I could envision the company we would become. I could also envision what types of companies would want to buy us.

Over a few months, I began to list the types of companies that could possibly buy us in the future. I only listed strategic buyers (not financial buyers) since my goal was not to stay with the business too long after the sale.

I added pure media companies, event companies, education and training companies, consulting companies, and even a few of our sponsors to the list. After compiling what I believed was an all-encompassing list, I narrowed it down to my top five.

How did I do this? I looked at those companies that I believed (1) would keep the mission of Content Marketing Institute strong and alive and (2) had the funds to purchase us at or over our asking price.

COMPLETE THE DETAIL

Once you have your top five, fill in the gaps. A spreadsheet works best at this point. Complete these columns:

- **Parent company.** List the parent company.
- **Acquiring brand.** Does the parent company have a sub-brand or brand extension that would be integral in the purchase? For example, is Alphabet/Google (the parent company) buying you directly, or is the purchaser Nest (a sub-brand of Alphabet)? In the latter case, it probably would still go through Alphabet, but Nest is the one in the negotiation room.
- **Rationale.** Why would each one want to buy you? Does your Content Inc. model satisfy a content gap for the buyer? Do you have access to an audience it desperately needs? Have you developed a product that would complete its portfolio?
- **Key contact(s).** Who is the decision maker? Who are the gatekeepers to get to the decision maker? Is this one person's decision, or are there multiple team members who will make the decision? If multiple, list the team.

MEET AND GREET

Now the work begins.

Your quest, over the next 12 to 18 months, is to meet and/or chat with each of the key contacts on the list. That doesn't mean you mention anything about selling the company. At this point, just get to know them and start forming a business relationship. Maybe (just maybe) there is a project both companies could work on together (a win-win).

For our list, I was able to set up appointments and meetings at trade shows and events. Do the research and find out what events your contacts speak at or attend. Send the email and set up the appointments. Something like:

> Hi Sue,
>
> Not sure if you know me, but my name is Joe Pulizzi, founder of Content Marketing Institute. I'll be attending XYZ event and would love to buy you coffee if you have 30 minutes. Would just be nice to meet, catch up, and talk shop. I have XYZ times and dates available. If that doesn't work, shoot me some alternative times.

Keep your email short and to the point, and always include times and dates (executives hate back-and-forth emails). You'd be surprised how many meetings you'll get this way. If you don't have an email address, try a direct message through Twitter or LinkedIn.

NURTURE THE RELATIONSHIP

Once you've met the contacts, the nurturing process begins. Every other month, send them an important link or report. It doesn't have to be much, but a "Thought this report would be of interest. Check out page 4" goes a long way.

FINALIZE YOUR LIST

Some exiting entrepreneurs do not limit the list. They like having more companies and the possibility of diverse offers. My preference is six to eight companies, but if you need a few more on the list, that is fine. You aren't sending a tweet out to the world that you are for sale. You are approaching a few trusted people and businesses that should very much be interested in purchasing your business. You have done your research and know there is a fit.

GROW TOWARD THE GOAL

My wife and I wanted to close a deal in 2015. The problem? By the end of 2014 we did not have the financial numbers to justify a $15 million valuation (more on valuation in a second or so). Because of this, we made multiple decisions in 2014, including purchasing two small properties and an email database. We believed that those purchases, along with continual organic growth, would get us to where we needed to be.

At the beginning of 2015, everything was in place, and we were ready to execute the rest of the strategy.

GET YOUR HOUSE IN ORDER

You have two meetings to take. First, with your attorney.

What needs to happen to protect you and your family? Are there any legal issues you need to be aware of?

Now is also the time to check through all your partnership, vendor, and employee agreements. Are there any problem areas?

Do this:

- Make copies of every agreement you have, and place them in a folder (paper or digital).
- Pay your attorney to review (or rereview) all agreements to spot problem areas.
- Fix anything that needs fixing.

After the meeting with the attorney, your next stop is to visit the accountant.

The big issue is that, most likely, the way you produce your financials will probably not be the way the buyer needs them for analysis purposes. This is something to keep in mind now (more on that later).

Your accountant needs to review all tax implications with you. Is there a better time to sell? A better type of buyer? Make sure the accountant lays out everything so you can confirm that your final list is correct and your timing is in the ballpark.

FIND A FINANCIAL ADVISOR

The best advice I can give you: *do not go through this process yourself.*

That means finding a financial advisor that can run point on all correspondence and negotiations. Unless your deal is expected to be for more than $50 million, I recommend hiring an independent financial advisor (not a larger firm).

This is something you should be researching as well. For about a year before we put the selling plan in action, I researched financial advisors. Besides scouring Google, I asked industry friends (in confidence) and attended event sessions on mergers and acquisitions. The advisor we chose used to be the CFO at a large media company and had 20 years of experience working on small acquisitions like ours. I approached them after seeing them speak at an event, and we hit it off immediately. But how do you price such an arrangement?

According to Hal Greenberg of The Riverside Company, most media businesses use what's called the "Lehman formula" when hiring a financial advisor. It looks like this:

- 5 percent of the first $2 million
- 4 percent of the next $2 million
- 3 percent of the next $2 million
- 2 percent of the next $2 million
- 1 percent of the next $2 million and up

On a $10 million deal, the fee would be $300,000, or 3 percent, plus 1 percent above $10 million. For our deal, we agreed that:

- Financial advisor receives 2 percent of the sale price up to $10 million (only on the up-front sale price, not on earnouts or bonuses after sale).
- Financial advisor receives 1.5 percent of anything over $10 million.
- Fee for a successful sale would be capped at $300,000 total.
- Financial advisor receives $150 per hour if there is no deal. In this case, we had our financial advisor keep track of the hours.

FINALIZE THE LIST

If you have chosen wisely, your financial advisor will have some thoughts about your list. Make sure your advisor reviews the list and confirms your hypotheses.

My initial list of four potential buyers grew to eight after discussions with our advisor. We entered each possibility into a spreadsheet, did a complete analysis of each opportunity, and agreed that we would approach those eight companies.

THE OFFERING MEMORANDUM

After agreeing on a final list, we put the calendar together, leading up to sending out the investment memorandum. The sections of the investment memorandum include:

- Executive summary
- Investment highlights
- The company
- Overview—Content Marketing Institute
- Financial summary
- Product offerings (break these down)
- Audience/database
- Marketing and sales
- Production
- Growth opportunities
- Market overview
- Competitors
- Management and ownership
- Executive management
- Employees and contractors
- Ownership
- Conclusion

Keep this document to no more than 20 pages. I agonized over our document, spending more than three months going through multiple drafts. You probably will as well.

THE NIBBLE

For all the contacts with whom I had a direct relationship, I sent a quick email:

> Hi Bob,
>
> I'm in the process of selling Content Marketing Institute. Would you be interested in seeing the Offering Memorandum?

When someone said yes, I introduced our financial advisor, who quickly took me off the email chain and proceeded with the process.

In situations where I did not know the main contact, our financial advisor found the correct contact and worked to set up a quick call discussing the opportunity.

Once we knew which parties were or were not interested, we proceeded to the next step.

THE NONDISCLOSURE AGREEMENT

Five of the eight companies were interested in taking a closer look at our financials and asked to see the full offering memorandum. Our financial advisor received each main contact's signature on a basic nondisclosure agreement and then emailed over the memorandum.

The financial advisor also sent over dates when we could take calls and answer questions, as well as a deadline for receiving letters of intent from interested buyers.

THE LOI

From the five potential buyers, we received two letters of intent (LOI). An LOI is a short, nonbinding contract that precedes a binding agreement, such as a share purchase agreement or asset purchase agreement.

An LOI typically includes:

- Transaction overview and structure
- Timeline
- Due diligence
- Confidentiality
- Exclusivity

An LOI is not binding in any way. It is like a marriage proposal. Sure, you are serious, but we are not really married yet.

The first LOI we received was a genuinely nice package, but below what we were looking for in terms of the purchase price. The second one I will never forget.

I had just finished a workshop in New York. I had a voicemail from my financial advisor, who told me to check my email. This one was from a global events company.

I opened it. Read it. Read it again. Then I called my wife. When looking back, this was our moment, the moment when we cried and told each other that "we did it." Financially, it was everything we could have asked for. From an operations point of view, we needed some clarifications. The company was asking for a lot in return for its investment, and rightly so.

Over the next two weeks, there was back-and-forth on several issues, culminating in the formal pitch meeting.

THE PITCH MEETING

Exactly one month after receiving the LOI, we had our first in-person meeting. My wife, our financial advisor, and I reserved a small conference room in New York City for our meeting with two of the buyer's senior executives. One was in charge of M&A for the division, and the other ran the actual division.

To prepare, I put together a presentation based on the offering memorandum and worked hard to address the concerns the buyer had raised. The meeting was intense. The buyer challenged many of our growth assumptions. It lasted about three hours, and I was exhausted when we were finished.

THE SIGNED LOI

How silly I was to think the LOI we received meant something. It does not. It is like Play-Doh in the can before sculpting a piece of art. It's the signed LOI that counts. That becomes the template used to build the final asset purchase agreement.

After the pitch meeting, we received a number of requests from the buyer, including all our past financials, our updated projections based on the meeting, our sales pipeline, and our organizational structure. This was the moment we discovered that our taxes and accounting setup were completely different from the buyer's. *Word of warning:* Get your accountant involved as soon as possible in the process.

Approximately seven weeks after the pitch meeting, we received an amended LOI and I signed it. Although the overall financial number did not change, some money was moved from the up-front payment to the earnout (money we get based on performance up to three years after the sale). We were happy with it, but here is the truth: you should only count on the up-front money when selling your company. Anything could happen after the deal goes through. An earnout or bonus, while great in some cases, may never materialize. My wife and I signed the deal because the up-front number met our objectives.

FINANCIAL HELL AND NEGOTIATIONS

The next four months were some of the worst of my life. My wife and I completed literally hundreds of spreadsheets and operational documents. I started to despise the person who invented spreadsheets. If you want to sell, especially to a global corporation, as we did, be aware of what can happen and the things you must do.

Some of our event registrations were tracking below pace, and the buyer was concerned. That said, all the buyer's questions had been answered, and it was time to see the final agreement. Weeks went by. No word. No agreement. I was getting concerned.

Walking out of a meeting in downtown Cleveland, I received a call from my financial advisor. He told me to sit down.

Apparently, the buyer was going to send us the final agreement with some major changes. First, the buyer reduced the up-front payment again. Second, the buyer lowered the total financial deal.

I was deflated. Exhausted. Frustrated. I took down all the details from my financial advisor, ended the call, and sat in the middle of Tower City in downtown Cleveland trying to figure out what to do. After all, the ball was still in our court. We could always say no.

I called my wife and relayed the details. I told her I was thinking about canceling the deal. She said she would support whatever decision I made, even though she really wanted to sell the business.

Instead of feeling sorry for myself, I looked at this as an opportunity. If the buyer wanted to spend less money, maybe I could ask for other things in exchange for lowering the price. I started scratching out notes. I created a new plan.

I would accept the terms with provisions. First, I wanted it in writing that no person would be fired or let go without my permission while I was still with the company. Second, I was concerned about staying on with the company for three years after the deal was signed. If the buyer wanted to lower the deal, I wanted more freedom. I asked the buyer to cut my time from three years to a year and a half. (My wife would leave after six months.) Third, if the buyer was going to cut the up-front payment, I wanted to accelerate the earnout. I asked for a higher percentage on the initial parts of the earnout to make us whole, if we hit certain sales targets.

The buyer agreed to each of these clauses. The first two (keeping the team intact and shortening my stay) were absolutely worth every penny we did not receive in up-front payment. Never be afraid to ask for anything. The worst that could happen is that people say no.

NOTIFYING THE TEAM

A month later, the deal was finalized. The sale took 6 months from receiving the LOI to a signed asset purchase agreement, and exactly 12 months from when we started the selling process.

Once we received the final signature, my wife and I eagerly anticipated the up-front deposit. I almost dropped the computer when I saw all the zeros in my online banking statement. When we received the money, the deal was officially done. Our bank account showed an additional $17.9 million.

Now came the hardest part. My wife and I split up the calls to our team members and notified each one. Those who received a large bonus payment were ecstatic about the bonus, but still they and most of the other team members were sad. They did not want to see things change. It helped that they all knew the goal was always to sell, so they were not completely surprised.

It has been more than four years since the deal went through, and almost every person from the original team is still employed at Content Marketing Institute. Of all things, this might warm my heart the most. It means we did something right.

EPIC THOUGHTS

- As more large brands and companies realize the time investment involved in building an audience, and recognize how owning their audience can lower the cost of acquisition and increase the lifetime value, more media companies will be acquired.

- Selling your content company doesn't just happen. It's a process, and it takes time. Exit planning starts at the beginning . . . so your journey begins now.

EPIC RESOURCES

- They Got Acquired, "Resources Archives," accessed June 23, 2022, https://theygotacquired.com/category/resources/.

- Matt and Liz Raad, "Thomas Smale of FE International Shares His Insights into Buying and Selling Websites," YouTube, accessed June 23, 2022, https://www.youtube.com/watch?v=hEZOPUFC4fM.

- Hal Greenberg, interview by Joe Pulizzi, April 2020.

CHAPTER 26

Buying a Media Company and Audience

BY JOE PULIZZI

If you don't see a clear path for what you want,
sometimes you have to make it yourself.

MINDY KALING

We're seeing more and more brands spending money to acquire media companies with existing audiences and communities instead of spending the time to develop their own. And it's going to continue as other businesses recognize the value and potential revenue these audiences bring compared with the time and effort that it takes to create these audiences from scratch.

There are several reasons your company may want to investigate purchasing a content business. You may be looking to increase your revenue by adding a new product or expanding into a new market. But the primary reason that will drive a merger or acquisition is speed.

When a brand is trying to decide on whether it should buy or build, Thomas Smale says:

Acquiring a business is a shortcut to growth. If you have the capital, it is much faster than building something from zero, particularly if it is a content business that may rely on organic traffic sources such as Google. If you have a team that is strong at operations but not so strong at creative, acquisitions can make even more sense—you can build on something someone else has already built and got off the ground and not incur the risk of a new project being built from zero not taking off.

How much capital to risk should be a business decision when budgeting each quarter or year. This will vary by company or individual but, as a general rule, never invest more than you are willing and able to lose.

Eugene Levin from SEMrush shared a diagram (see Figure 26.1) to show some concepts that SEMrush considers when deciding if M&A may be appropriate. SEMrush weighs three key factors when looking at adding a new solution to its business. Is the new solution strategic, unique, and time sensitive? The solution only falls into the M&A model if it checks all three of those criteria. If it doesn't, there is generally another solution that is more effective than an acquisition.

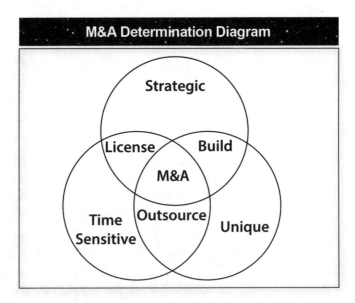

FIGURE 26.1 Consider the different strategic needs to determine the method to use to add a new service or solution. (*Source: SEMrush*)

Having worked with content entrepreneurs and built audiences for many years, we know that it takes, on average, 12 to 24 months to build a minimum viable audience (one that generates revenue or return on objective). For content entrepreneurs who are building their audience and community while they slowly introduce different monetization opportunities, this isn't a substantial amount of time. For large businesses that could be leveraging that community immediately to add revenue and grow their existing network, this time could represent a significant loss of potential capital.

In the past few years, particularly after Covid drove so many businesses and workers online, more and more companies began looking to acquire content businesses, digital products businesses, software, e-commerce, etc. TheyGotAcquired.com is an excellent site with numerous stories of content (and other) businesses that have been purchased for six to eight figures. Empireflippers.com and Flippa are two communities that have additional information (and do transactions) on buying content-based websites.

PRIMARY CONSIDERATIONS

When looking to acquire a content business, there are some key factors to consider.

Thomas Smale emphasizes the importance of making sure the company is a good strategic fit and the purpose of the acquisition is clearly understood:

> This comes down to what you are trying to achieve or gain from the acquisition. Is this purely a financial acquisition? Is it just for the audience or email list? Don't buy a business without a plan and a core goal in mind.
>
> Media and content businesses, by their very nature, depend heavily on the quality and quantity of content produced. An ideal deal will include the current content team (or founder if they are producing content) transferring as part of the sale. If they are not, this can add operational complexity and reduce the likelihood of it being a successful acquisition.
>
> Once a deal is complete, the success of acquisitions is ultimately down to how well you operate the business. A great business operated badly will not succeed, and vice versa, a bad business can succeed if operated well.

David Siegel stresses the importance of ensuring that the culture of the company you're looking to acquire fits into your culture. Even if you're buying a small company, a mismatch in culture can create a significant barrier to a smooth integration.

The other aspect David warns about is making sure that the customer base is the right fit. It's about more than just demographics. It's important to understand why the community is engaging with the content and what people in the community are getting out of the relationship.

If you're looking to acquire a business to build your community, it's vital that the community you're bringing in really wants the solutions you're providing. There are several different ways to test an audience out, and oftentimes the business you're looking to acquire will help facilitate such a test. If the business has spent years earning the trust of its community, the last thing it wants is to alienate everyone by having the new owners suddenly start selling the members something they don't want or need.

CASE STUDY: ARROW ELECTRONICS

Arrow Electronics is a $35 billion global engineering distribution firm whose products span from hardware to software and data. In 2015 and 2016, Arrow spent millions to purchase more than 50 media properties to acquire their audience and editorial staff. Victor Gao is senior vice president and chief marketing officer at Arrow Electronics.

INTERVIEW WITH VICTOR GAO

Brian: Tell me about how Arrow started purchasing media companies.

Victor: We started with a simple observation, that if our customers were engineers, then the more engineers, the better for Arrow. How can we access more engineers? Further, how can we reach more engineers that are not only good with their individual work but good at lifting up others, good at creating a community and educating others, improving themselves, and improving others?

We saw the premium titles in our industry buried in the bowels of larger media conglomerates who have way sexier consumer titles. These hugely storied and respected titles were underresourced and not as much of a focus for management. That was the second observation.

Next, we thought, for the sake of the industry, somebody needed to go in there and help shape an economically sustainable path for those media assets for the long run, but it has to be the right buyer. Our view was, if not us who? The way we could approach these media assets with our intimate knowledge of the industry they serve would be a key part of their future sustainability.

We were not taciturn about the benefit this could accrue to our core business, but we knew that we had to preserve the editorial integrity, the independence, and in fact, the journalistic tradition of these publications to make this place somewhere that journalists would love to work. Only then will you have all the downstream benefits.

After we identified this strategic direction, it was just a matter of execution. Conversations happened at the right level between us and our friends at the large media conglomerates. They were glad we could take this off their hands and take care of the people that are in these portfolio companies. It was a win-win situation.

But we really focused on the trust the audience had in the coverage and analyses. We focused on the community, and the organic engagement between our readers. After we took over control of these companies, we set up a firewall (between Arrow and the media brands). We then invested additional resources to streamline the tech stack and launched a series of industry-first flagship products such as five weekly radio shows and a weekend edition newsletter, which further attracted editorial talent from the markets we served.

Brian: Were you doing content marketing at Arrow before you started looking for these acquisitions?

Victor: Yes and no. As a sage brand, Arrow has always placed tremendous value on providing the most helpful information to our customers, but it wasn't always systematic, and the lens was more traditional marketing than journalistic. If you want to do something new, where speed to market is important, you go and you buy the biggest, most respected properties. The editorial talent is already there. It's way easier to go that route. It's not for everybody; you have to be well resourced. If I was at a startup, I may not have pursued this strategy. But for other companies like Arrow in a corporate context that has the scale and integration know-how, I would implore every CMO to look at media acquisition as one of the options in your toolbox.

In a world where third-party cookies are phased out, doing content marketing without an in-house editorial team is going to be more and more difficult. For return on capital invested, measured by any marketing metric you can imagine, especially the ones that ultimately matter, that are your bottom line, your P&L, it pays for itself over and over. It's worth consideration.

Brian: It sounds like you gave autonomy to a lot of these publications after you brought them in.

Victor: Yes. But it's more than an altruistic desire to preserve editorial independence for its own sake. There is self-interest here for sure, but there's a public service alignment to this kind of strategy. Because in a world where customers and employees are looking to a brand to serve a greater purpose, and you're providing a service of widely acknowledged value, why wouldn't you want to pursue it? It's a great thing for the brand to be known as providing a public service.

Brian: You bought more than 50 different media properties. What were the biggest lessons you learned?

Victor: First, I cannot stress enough the importance of keeping the editorial side independent. I'll say that three times if needed. The second is to focus on running a good media business. If you need to update the tech stack, consolidate processes; then figure out what works for you quickly, and what your outlays are going to be. Define a road map, and sell it to whomever you need funding from, especially your customers. Don't delay that.

Brian: What sort of benefits have you gained that you can point at and bring up if you had to go to another company and make the same business case to acquire a media company?

Victor: My advice is not to be too focused on the bottom line of the media assets themselves right away, because that's how you kill the goose that lays the golden eggs. If you do right by the media business and give it the editorial autonomy it needs, the media business will do right by your core business, and it will be sustainable because it's authentic. Because as ever, with any media business, the audience looks for that authenticity and credibility. Ultimately, what you want to do is to just run a good media business and the rest will come. The details are more involved, but the strategy is straightforward.

PRIVATE COMPANY VALUATIONS

When private companies are purchased, the numbers are all over the board. According to the *Wall Street Journal* and *PitchBook*, Spotify bought Gimlet (the podcast company) for 15 times revenue, or a $230 million purchase price on $15 million in revenue. PopSugar sold to Group Nine for three times its revenue.

Smaller media enterprises are often valued at less. The company's value depends on the revenue, the profit, and the content the business sells. After we worked out all the back-and-forth, I ended up selling Content Marketing Institute for about 2.5 times revenue and 10 times net profit. Since CMI was mostly an events company (the majority of our revenues came from paid event registrations and sponsorships), that was the agreed valuation between me and my prospective buyer.

Companies get higher valuations on subscription and event revenues because they are more predictable revenue streams. Valuations for online education are comparable to software-as-a-service models, where the multiples seem to be around eight times revenue. Membership models, like Netflix, are glorious because of the automatic monthly or annual billing (similar to models such as Slack or Salesforce).

Businesses where most of the revenue is from advertising or sponsorship receive lower multiples. A few years back, a colleague of mine sold their print magazine property for 1 times revenue, while another sold their regional event business (generally 100 people at each event) for 1.25 times revenue. The valuation depends on the business but also on what the exiting founder wants to do and how badly the founder wants to sell.

Industries matter, as does consumer versus business to business. Media mergers-and-acquisitions and marketing consultant John Blondin uses EBITDA to value the companies he advises. John says:

> Within Australia and New Zealand, a reasonable consumer title would command a multiple of 5 to 25 times EBITDA. High-profile titles [go] at high multiples. With business-to-business media operations, the values used to sit at between 3 and 5 times EBITDA. However, over the past five years I have sold several titles for $1 million or more based on 0.85 to 1.75 times EBITDA. I also sold a title to a Travel Company that saw the database and digital brands as valuable to their business. The company was sold for $1, with the new owner taking over the existing staff liabilities. Deals are deals are deals. It comes down to finding a buyer who is interested in the sector and can recognize an upside for their model.
>
> All this means that a content or media business should be valued anywhere from 1 to 3 times revenue, with between 2 and 2.5 times being a fair starting valuation. If you are looking at EBITDA, look at 5 times for an unloved industry (or a nonrecurring revenue model) and 10 to 15 times for a recurring revenue model.

EPIC THOUGHTS

- Before you make the decision to purchase a company, ensure that it supports your strategic goals and aligns with your brand culture.

- If you're buying a media company for the community, give the acquisition the latitude it needs to continue engaging the members the way it has.

EPIC RESOURCES

- Duda, "We Are SaaS: Mergers & Acquisitions," YouTube, accessed June 23, 2022, https://www.youtube.com/watch?v=hEZOPUFC4fM.

- They Got Acquired, "Resources Archives," accessed June 23, 2022, https://theygotacquired.com/category/resources/.

- Victor Gao, interview by Brian Piper, June 24, 2022.

- John Blondin, interview by Joe Pulizzi, April 2020.

PART V

Web3

CHAPTER 27

WTH IS WEB3?

BY BRIAN PIPER

> Don't be intimidated by what you don't know.
> That can be your greatest strength and ensure
> that you do things differently from everyone else.
> SARA BLAKELY

You may have heard all sorts of discussions and references to Web3, blockchain, and NFTs. These terms may be new to you, you may have a general awareness of what each of these terms means, or you may already be deep down the rabbit hole.

You may also be one of the many people who dismiss the entire concept of Web3 as nothing more than overpriced JPGs and fake money. Understandable. Just remember what people thought when the personal computer was invented, or the internet. While many of the projects that have been created in the current iteration of Web3 will fail and go the way of Pets.com, the fundamental technology that powers these projects is here to stay. And it will change the way we live our digital lives.

Note: You may be wondering why we are covering Web3 in a content marketing book. Simply put, we believe that several blockchain projects are going to have a major impact on how your audience interacts with your content. As of this writing, we are in the very early stages, but we are already seeing promising applications in this area, especially around privacy and ownership. If you already understand Web3, feel free to skip to the next chapter. Otherwise, here we go!

HOW WILL WEB3 TRANSFORM THE CREATOR ECONOMY?

The growing use of blockchain technology provides a decentralized way to monetize and create previously unheard-of opportunities for everyone, particularly for creators.

Web3 provides content creators and entrepreneurs the ability to build and connect with a community, not just an audience, and communicate with them directly on their own channels, without relying on rented land where someone else can control your presence, frequency, and content.

Web3 gives creators the opportunity to build their community the way they want, and the way the community wants. We believe this next phase of community "ownership" is critical for content creators, both content marketers and content entrepreneurs, to understand.

THE BASICS

Let's start off with a high-level introduction to Web3, then go to the terms we'll be using and the technology behind this new model. There are many new terms in the Web3 landscape, and we're only going to address the ones most relevant to content creators and content marketers. You can find a more thorough list of Web3 terms at The Tilt, https://www.thetilt.com/industry-news/web3-term-definitions.

WHAT IS WEB3?

Marc Maxhimer, director of growth at The Tilt, describes Web3 this way: "Web3 is the internet owned by the builders and users, orchestrated with tokens."

In this chapter, we'll talk about the changes in the functionality of the internet. In the beginning, the internet was just a bunch of computers connected by a bunch of wires that could send information back and forth. It started back in the 1960s as a military experiment called "ARPAnet."

Let's start with some semantics and caveats before we get into this. When developers talk about version control and revisions, they typically use version numbers (whole numbers—for example, Windows 1 and macOS 10) and build numbers (decimal numbers—for example, Windows 1.01 and macOS 10.12). Version numbers indicate large changes to the system or code base.

There are many ways to break down the difference between web 1.0, web 2.0, web 3.0, and Web3, but the one that makes the most sense from our perspective is this:

- **Web 1.0—read.** The creation of the internet gave us access to an incredible amount of information, but it was difficult for nondevelopers to easily share their content and ideas without an investment in time or money to build a website. Web 1.0 was basically about consuming content that other businesses and people who hired developers were putting up on their websites.
- **Web 2.0—read/write.** This is where nondevelopers started getting access to CMS platforms and could create their own websites and put their content up. Email protocols became standard. Once social networks came along, we suddenly had a place to share our opinions, ideas, and content. We quickly learned that you had to be careful what you said, however, or you could lose your right to publish and exist on those channels.
- **Web 3.0.** This can be a little confusing, and this term is often excluded from most explanations, or it is interchangeably used to refer to Web3 (which frustrates some Web3 purists immensely). Web 3.0 refers to the linked or semantic web and was coined by Tim Berners-Lee in 2006. Berners-Lee's vision is that all the raw data would live in one central place and be accessed by users through their WebID.
- **Web3—read/write/own.** We have reached a point where the technology exists for content creators to put their content up on their own platforms or on publicly shared platforms, and with a small, loyal audience (Kevin Kelly's 1,000 true fans or Li Jin's Superfans model), they can build a financially sustainable model of creating content and engaging with their community members.

One of the fundamental strengths of Web3 is that it's decentralized (or leans in that direction). In web 2.0, much of the content that is created lives on second-party platforms like Twitter, Instagram, Snapchat, etc. All the content goes to their server and is shared (and controlled and monetized) by them. In Web3, most of these platforms are peer-to-peer networks, meaning that the content isn't posted on a single company's server. It is shared on a global network of computers.

286 Ⅰ EPIC CONTENT MARKETING

The ability to create a community where the members can benefit from the content in multiple ways is a game changer for content creators. More on that will follow, but first, there are some terms we'll need to define that will help provide clarity as we move forward. We could provide a list of hundreds of new terms that are cropping up around Web3, but we'll stick to the ones that are most essential for our discussion.

Let's start with defining some of the key terms that creators will need to be aware of if they're interested in leveraging Web3 technologies and entering the Web3 creator economy. We'll try to define these in the order that you need to understand them. These explanations are very high level, and you can dig much deeper into each one of these terms.

WHAT IS BLOCKCHAIN?

Blockchain technology basically refers to a type of database—one that can't be rewritten or edited once it's created. At a high level, the information is contained in blocks of information. When a block gets full, it is closed, and the information starts going into the next block. These blocks are joined together by cryptographic "chains" that are created using a complex algorithm.

Functionally, it's a permanent, public ledger that can be used to store information in a way that is extremely difficult to change.

Some popular blockchains are Bitcoin, Ethereum, Polygon, and Solana. Some blockchains allow creators to add a layer of code, called a "smart contract." These smart contracts can include certain parameters that can be activated when needed. For example, a smart contract can programmatically unlock new benefits for the owner when they take a certain action. So, if owning multiple different digital assets gives you access to different content or courses, those will be automatically unlocked for you as soon as you purchase the additional assets. And that access will be automatically removed and transferred to someone else if you sell them the assets.

WHAT IS FIAT CURRENCY?

Fiat currency refers to a currency that gets its value based on government backing. It is not backed by a commodity (like gold), only by the trust in the government (a sovereign entity) that issued it. Some examples of fiat currency include the US dollar, the euro, and most other physical currencies. So while the US dollar is sovereign (controlled by a government), something like Bitcoin is nonsovereign (not controlled by a government or individual entity).

WHAT IS CRYPTOCURRENCY?

Cryptocurrency is a digital currency that is created on the blockchain. Most people are familiar with Bitcoin, which was the first digital currency created. Back in 2008, Satoshi Nakamoto (an anonymous developer, or group of developers, whose identity is still unknown) wrote the Bitcoin whitepaper, "Bitcoin: A Peer-to-Peer Electronic Cash System," which described the theory of cryptocurrency.

Some of the highest-volume cryptocurrencies (at the time of this writing) are Bitcoin, Ether, and Solana.

Crypto is not fiat because it's not backed by a government. It only has value because the people who own it attribute value to it and can use it as a store of value or to exchange as payment. Crypto only has value because of the strength of its community.

Cryptocurrency has created the previously nonexistent idea of digital property. The fact that you can now create a scarce digital asset that has value is a true innovation. Bitcoin is an example of this since there is a limited supply of it and the record of the supply is contained on a public blockchain and not held by a bank or government intermediary. If you understand the concept of physical real estate ownership, think of crypto as digital real estate ownership.

WHAT ARE CRYPTOCURRENCY EXCHANGES?

An exchange is a place where you go to buy, sell, trade, and hold crypto. There are several exchanges out there. Some of the most popular ones are Coinbase, Binance.US, and Crypto.com.

Exchanges will typically charge you a small fee for purchasing and withdrawing crypto.

WHAT ARE CRYPTO WALLETS?

When you purchase crypto through an exchange, the exchange stores that crypto for you. You do not have direct custody of that currency. A digital wallet provides you with a more secure way to privately store your crypto on your own device.

When you set up a digital wallet, you are given a seed phrase. This phrase is usually a set of 12 or 24 words. This phrase is the key to unlocking your wallet. This phrase should *never* be shared with anyone and should not be stored online. The only time you should use this phrase is when you're setting up your wallet on a new device.

Digital wallets also have a public address that you can share with other people so that they can send crypto and other assets to your wallet.

WHAT ARE HOT WALLETS?

A hot wallet, or software wallet, is a digital wallet where you can store your crypto assets. Hot wallets are generally installed as a browser plug-in and require an internet connection to be able to use. Some of the more popular hot wallets are MetaMask, Phantom, and Coinbase Wallet. They are "hot" because they are immediately usable and accessible via a website, app, or plug-in.

WHAT ARE COLD WALLETS?

A cold wallet, or hardware wallet, is a physical device (most look like a thumb drive) that provides a slightly higher level of security for your digital assets than a hot wallet provides. It is "cold" because it cannot be accessed immediately by the owner or anyone else without entering a passcode on the physical device (thus it is more secure).

WHAT ARE CREATOR COINS/SOCIAL TOKENS?

Creator coins (like $TILT and $PIPER) are social tokens that provide ways for creators to reward users who bring value to their community and to provide levels of access based on the users' interest in the community. If the users put more time and resources into the community, they get more out of it. Users can get access to different channels and different conversations based on their contributions. Community owners can also provide rewards to members for participation. You can "level up" within the community and earn different badges, roles, and features.

Social tokens are considered "fungible," meaning "not unique." Think of them as you would a dollar. I can trade you $1 for another, and we believe the value is the same. But with tokens, the value is typically based on the utility, or benefits they can provide, and not the monetary value.

WHAT ARE NFTS?

NFTs, or nonfungible tokens, are unique digital assets that users can purchase, typically by using cryptocurrency. They can provide unique utility, including access to events, one-on-one time with creators, and other rewards.

NFTs exploded in 2021, most notably with the sale of Beeple's NFT at auction for $69 million. Since then, the NFT market has seen incredible growth and activity.

NFTs typically contain smart contracts that can activate upon certain actions. For example, if you hold the NFT for a year after purchase, a reward could be automatically given. This reward can come in a variety of formats. Some creators have provided special access, coins, vacations, and even other NFTs.

You can also include other requirements in your smart contract. For example, many NFT creators have it written in their smart contracts that each time the NFT is sold, the creator gets a percentage of that sale. This is an incredible change for creators, who, previously, would sell a piece of art or music and would only get a piece of that initial sale (minus what their agent, promoter, record label, etc., would take). Now artists can continue to get revenue as their art is sold and increases in value.

NFTs can also provide utility. For example, Creator Economy Expo (CEX) is an event where you can purchase your pass the traditional way using fiat money, you can purchase using $TILT coin (fungible tokens), or, using crypto ($ETH), you can purchase an NET (a Never-Ending Ticket NFT) or lifetime pass. This pass can be sold, traded, or used for as long as someone owns it and the event continues to run. Some CEX NFTs have special features. For example, one of the passes gives the holder the ability to introduce one of the keynote speakers to the main stage at the conference. The passes give you access to special events at the conference and a special channel within the Discord group.

NFTs can act as publicly verifiable transaction records. Think of your car title, your house deed, control of your medical records, your education records, your degrees and certifications. All of these could be NFTs that you could store in your digital wallet and control access to.

WHAT IS A METAVERSE?

There are many definitions of what the metaverse is but the most comprehensive and accurate one I've found comes from Matthew Ball in his book *The Metaverse: And How It Will Revolutionize Everything:*

> A massively scaled and interoperable network of real-time rendered 3D virtual worlds that can be experienced synchronously and persistently by an effectively unlimited number of users with an individual sense of presence, and with continuity of data, such as identity, history, entitlements, objects communications, and payments.

Current web 2.0 metaverses include environments like Second Life, Fortnite, or Roblox. Web3 metaverses are virtual environments where assets are managed as NFTs on the blockchain. Examples of Web3 metaverses include Decentraland and The Sandbox, which are both developed on the Ethereum blockchain.

WHAT IS DECENTRALIZED?

You will hear the term "decentralized" often in Web3. This refers to the fact that many of the applications (DApps) and data are housed on peer-to-peer networks of computers instead of being owned by a single company that controls the data, access, and network.

Cryptocurrencies sit on decentralized blockchains that aren't controlled by any one institution or government. Crypto has value based on the size of the community that holds it.

This can apply to content as well. For example, when you post something on Twitter or YouTube, that content lives on the company's network. The company can choose to pay you or not, share the content that it sees fit to share with whom it wants to share it, and only show you the data it wants you to see.

On a network like D.tube, which is a blockchain-based video network, you own your content; everyone can see that content is connected to your digital wallet. You earn DTube Coins as other people view or interact with your content, and everyone can see your viewing data.

In publishing, Mirror.xyz is a decentralized Web3 publishing platform. It is a user-owned, blockchain-based, decentralized environment that allows writers to monetize their content and connect with their audience in a variety of ways. They can turn their content into NFTs, embed their own NFTs into their content, leverage crowdfunding to give your community a say in what you create, and then share a portion of the profits.

WHAT IS OWNERSHIP?

Another key of Web3 is verifiable ownership. If your content exists on the blockchain, or the record of ownership of your content exists on the blockchain, it is a public record of who created that content and who owns it. You can sell that ownership, you can transfer usage rights, and you can set it up so that every time ownership of that piece of content is transferred, you get a percentage of the sale value.

WHAT ARE DAOs?

Decentralized autonomous organizations (DAOs) are organizations that are governed by rules written in code on the blockchain. Think of a DAO as if it were an LLC or other business, but instead of being controlled by shareholders or investors, it is controlled by an automated and crowdsourced system.

The Constitution DAO was formed by a community that brought more than 17,000 people together virtually to raise capital to attempt to buy a copy of the US Constitution that was being auctioned at Sotheby's. They raised more than $47 million in a week and were outbid at the auction.

CASE STUDY: SALESFORCE AND WEB3

Known for its cloud-based business software, Salesforce is embracing Web3 technology and creating the first enterprise tools for the space. This is another example of a large brand entering Web3 and investing heavily in the new paradigms that it creates. Mathew Sweezey is a cofounder of Salesforce's Web3 Studio and helps drive Salesforce's Web3 vision.

INTERVIEW WITH MATHEW SWEEZEY

Brian: How do you see Web3 technologies impacting content marketing for brands?

Mathew: I think from a high level, people need to realize why brands do content marketing in the first place, and fundamentally how that shifts. Seth Godin wrote a book called *Permission Marketing,* in which he says we need to have a value exchange to get an email address. Brands understand email addresses are valuable, and to get that we need to create something of value to exchange for them. Many times, we create a piece of content to exchange for the email. This changes with Web3.

One of the big key tenets of Web3 is ownership of personal identity, which is stored in a wallet. And email is no longer the primary identification of an individual. That becomes a wallet, which individuals connect to your website bringing with them their own private data. Regardless of whether content marketing changes, what the brand will be receiving in return is very different. We won't be receiving an email address; we'll be receiving a wallet ID and a trove of zero-party data the consumer may choose to share with us in real time as well. This is the first major change.

The next major change is the personal ownership of that data. The individual will have control over that data, and the brands will literally just be renting that data from them. This is the power of the wallet. The consumer knows who is connected to their wallet and what data they are receiving. They control it and can turn it off at any point. They do not need to ask you to unsubscribe them; they simply click a button and you're disconnected and no longer have access to the data. It'll be a very different relationship for brands and data.

For the majority of content marketing, it will function much as it does now, but rather than asking for an email, you'll ask for a wallet connect. You'll still be hosting the content on your site, doing blog posts, etc. SEO will still be powerful. However, with Web3 there are also new mediums that come into play, which will change the face of content marketing.

New mediums like metaverses open a new type of experience brands can create. It is a new value for consumers. Where we create content to transfer knowledge, and to help improve our SEO rankings in the metaverse, we'll be creating immersive experiences. Brands will build immersive experiences, just as they do websites, and will ask consumers to connect their wallet as an exchange for the experience.

As we think about the future of content marketing and a metaverse, we're building experiences. But we need to also realize the ethos of Web3 is co-ownership and collaboration. Brands must embrace this as well. It's much more likely that a brand is successful by building a world that they cocreate with others, just like Roblox. If your kids go to Roblox, they're not playing games that Coca-Cola made; they're playing games that the girl two doors down made, or their friend in some foreign country made. Brands must learn to cobuild with their communities.

Imagine that you as the brand aren't creating the content; rather, you have a DAO of people that create this content for you. And then based on how many people download the content, that is how those people get paid. Based on performance. We could see content marketing become a performance marketing methodology, which would be rad.

Brian: If you're a brand, a big company, how do you start thinking about using Web3 and integrating it into your content marketing?

Mathew: It's a sliding scale. At the far end, you could be Web3 native, which means that you were born out of the Web3 world, you were born out of Web3 ethos, and you've built and are structured in a completely decentralized fashion. That's a full Web3, native.

All existing brands are web 2 that are going to have to embrace elements of Web3. They will not ever give anything up in exchange to become Web3; instead they will just simply add things to do what I call "Web2+."

The most basic thing that everyone's going to have to do is understand that for these things, you have to have the technology to do it. You're going to have to be able to connect wallets on your website, step one. You're going to have conversations about how you deal with this data. What are the ethical implications that you even have to understand? And these are things that all have to happen before we ever even build a program.

We have to talk with our financing teams. How do we accept crypto? How do we think about crypto on our books? Going back to the data ethics, because we can see a person's chain and what happens on chain, do we look? Do we buy data from data brokers that scrape things on chain? What are the ethical implications that we now have to put in place that we didn't have to before?

Once you have those questions answered, you should next look to your community. Just like any other product, you need to talk to the customer to know what to build. This community isn't just there to answer questions; you need to involve them deeply in the process, and give them ownership if possible. In Web3, the community is your defensibility. You need your community. They're going to be the ones that help you ideate what you're going to build; they're the ones that are going to help you market what you build, and they're going to be the ones that help you service what you build.

And my favorite example to illustrate this point is to look at the two biggest Web3 brands and compare them with two mega web 2 brands. Instagram and TikTok are two of the biggest web 2 brands. If we look at the combined market cap of those two, it's $500 billion. If we look at the two biggest brands currently in Web3, Bitcoin and Ethereum, the market cap is a combined $1.5 trillion. Those are two brands that already have three times the valuation of the two largest web 2 brands.

And then the point is, how big is the marketing department at Instagram and TikTok versus how big is the marketing department at Bitcoin and Ethereum? And the answer is, there is no marketing department at Bitcoin or Ethereum. And these two companies have created three times the size of the market cap of the two biggest companies with massive marketing departments of hundreds of people.

Web3 isn't just an iteration; it's a revolution. We need to approach it differently. We need to build it with our community. Web 2 taught us the basics of user-generated content and influencer marketing. This is the next evolution of those ideas.

EPIC THOUGHTS

- Web3 has the potential to create new paradigms in content marketing, but at the core, it's still all about delivering value to your users.

- Brands need to consider the new methods that Web3 innovations can provide that will allow them to connect with and empower their communities.

EPIC RESOURCES

- The Tilt, "Content Creators: 70+ Web3 Definitions," accessed July 4, 2022, https://www.thetilt.com/industry-news/web3-term-definitions.

- PWC, "Estonia—the Digital Republic Secured by Blockchain," accessed July 10, 2022, https://www.pwc.com/gx/en/services/legal/tech/assets/estonia-the-digital-republic-secured-by-blockchain.pdf.

- Mathew Ball, *The Metaverse: And How it Will Revolutionize Everything*, Liveright, 2022.

- Mathew Sweezey, interview by Brian Piper, June 15, 2022.

CHAPTER 28

Social Tokens, NFTs, and the Metaverse

BY BRIAN PIPER

Innovation is the ability to see change
as an opportunity—not a threat.

STEVE JOBS

There are numerous innovation opportunities within the Web3 space for creators and content marketers. There are three areas that are particularly relevant for content creators and brands: social tokens, NFTs, and the metaverse.

In the last chapter, we briefly defined each of these terms. In this chapter, we're going to dive into these in more depth and focus on the benefits and uses each of these has for creators and content marketers.

THE POWER OF TOKENS

Chris Dixon is a digital futurist and leads a16z Crypto, a Web3 investment company. He describes tokens as digital primitives, "the atomic unit around which a new era of the internet is organized."

Tokens are the building blocks of Web3. They provide a programmable layer that can be owned by individual users but exists on a public network that no one owns.

Tech billionaire, entrepreneur, and venture capitalist Naval Ravikant says, "There's just this huge opportunity now to make every person a worker, an investor, a shareholder, an evangelist, an owner, a creator, a designer. We can fold it all into one."

At this time, there are three major applications for tokenization: social tokens, NFTs, and the metaverse.

SOCIAL TOKENS

Social tokens, also called "creator coins," are custom-branded cryptocurrencies. When creators launch their own coin on the blockchain, it gives them opportunities to connect with their community in a new way. By purchasing or earning these tokens, community members gain partial ownership in the community that is not available in a Web 2.0 environment.

As we discussed in Chapter 24, communities are members of your audience who have become connected with the creator or brand in a larger way than just being an audience. There are limited ways to do that in web 2.0, such as engaging with your content through commenting and sharing or by purchasing your courses, products, or services. Even memberships are particularly transactional. Community members pay a set fee every month or year, and they expect to get something in return for that investment. If they don't, they just cancel their membership and they're out the money they've already spent.

For members of a Web3 community, they spend their fiat money or crypto, or invest their time, to get a certain amount of coin, but they also expect to get something additional in return because many Web3 users don't purchase coins specifically for the financial value. There are many coins that don't have any financial value at all, only the value that is attributed to them within that particular community. This is where it's different in Web3.

First, with coins that do have a financial worth, members may notice an increase in the value of the coin (token) they're holding. As with any economy, as more outside money flows into it, the value increases. The increase in value isn't always apparent in cryptocurrency tokens because many people look at the dollar value of the token, which is tied to the dollar value of the cryptocurrency that it is bonded to. So if the overall cryptocurrency decreases in dollar value, the social tokens will also decrease in dollar value, even if the community is growing.

However, if the holders look at the value of their tokens relative to the value of the cryptocurrency economy in which the tokens exist, the holders will see that the value of their coin is increasing. Basically, that translates to "What can you do with the token?" They can spend their coin on merchandise, on gated content, or as a tip or donation, but they get more value through access just by holding it.

Second, they'll notice that the creator is adding more ways to leverage the coin. New functionality is becoming active in the community based on feedback from the holders on what they want, what would be helpful for them, and how they see the community growing stronger. Many of the greatest benefits of social tokens have come as recommendations from the holders because they think of something that could benefit them and that would benefit the other community members.

Third, and most importantly, as with any community, the more people who join, the more benefits everyone gets from the new ideas, connections, and collaborations. It's a network effect. The relationships formed among individuals who come together, while sharing ownership of pieces of the community, grow extremely quickly and are very strong.

Joe has said this about his $TILT coin community—that a token community can be the "ultimate loyalty and referral program." Having subscribers is great ... but not necessarily powerful. Those subscribers who also hold $TILT coin are, in essence, superfans. They contribute to the community in many ways and work hard to get more people to join the community. Why? Because they know that the more people who hold and use the token, the better it is for everyone involved.

When you bring new users into a Web3 community, the language is all about being stronger together, building together, and owning the community together. One of the common sayings in Web3 is WAGMI (We're all gonna make it). This incentivizes members to build the community and to stay actively involved and engaged, all while holding or growing the amount of coin they have.

And then if they decide at any point that they're not getting what they need from the community, they can sell their coin and leave. That's why Web3 is often called a "hold economy" instead of a "market economy." Coin holders can leave anytime they don't feel like they're getting value, or they can continue to hold and not feel like they're consistently being forced to pay for something they aren't using.

NFTS

NFTs can work much the same way as social tokens by providing access to certain areas of the community, events, and content, but they also add the elements of scarcity and uniqueness.

The fundamental appeal of an NFT is the fact that it's unique. Each one is different. That's what makes it nonfungible (not interchangeable). Through leveraging this, creators can form desired subgroups or create benefits within their community based on certain traits in their NFTs. These can be activated through a smart contract (every NFT is represented by a smart contract underneath). For example, your smart contract could specify that all NFT owners who hold their NFT for a certain period of time could automatically be rewarded a certain amount of your coin or are awarded an additional NFT.

Kevin Rose is the creator behind the Moonbirds NFT project. Any community member that owns a Moonbird can "nest" their NFT. This basically means the owner won't sell it. By "nesting," the owner gets benefits as time goes on, including access to events or airdrops of newer NFT projects.

Gary Vaynerchuk, also known as Gary Vee, is a social media influencer and serial entrepreneur. He created the VeeFriends NFTs in 2021. These NFTs provided the only entry method into his VeeCon conference for three years.

VeeFriends featured several different types of tokens that provided different levels of access to different experiences and personal time with Gary. VeeFriends made more than $90 million in the first 90 days after launch between primary and secondary sales.

Kings of Leon has dropped two albums as NFTs and created "golden tickets" that provide holders additional benefits, such as four front-row spots to any show for life, a VIP experience that includes hanging out with the band before the concert, and individual art pieces. The band has created millions of dollars of revenue in its initial sales and is getting ongoing passive income every time one of its NFTs is sold.

Chris Dixon says, "NFTs are artifacts of networks. You have your own community and the NFTs you're creating will be artifacts for that community. And they derive value to the extent that they reinforce that community's values and norms and language and memes . . . you're owning a piece of this community that has importance in the history of the Internet and the history of crypto."

Tokens, fungible or nonfungible, can be used by brands and creators in a variety of ways. According to Jeremiah Owyang, there are at least five distinct strategies that content creators can leverage, including:

- **Reward fans for engaging.** Provide tokens as they consume or engage with content.
- **Use membership models.** Provide access to content, events, or services.
- **Redeem tokens for perks.** Trade tokens for physical merchandise or experiences.
- **Upgrade the relationship.** Get personal access or participate in community decisions.
- **Grow a peer-to-peer ecosystem.** Build your network or support group causes.

Larger brands, such as Adidas and Anheuser-Busch, have already jumped on the NFT train. Initially these use cases looked more like glorified marketing stunts. But we are advancing rapidly. Robert Mondavi pairs up exclusive wine bottles with NFTs for proof of ownership. Coachella uses NFTs for ticketing. Tommy Hilfiger uses NFTs for digital merchandise.

This is just the start. NFTs (and tokens) need to have a strategy, just like everything else. What's the purpose of your NFT project? How will you integrate it with your content? What does the token provide to your audience? What's the behavior you want to see from your audience? How can you execute this best with a tokenization strategy?

THE METAVERSE

When most people talk about the metaverse, they're referring to an immersive virtual space where people can connect and communities can grow. Some "metaverses" have existed for some time. Think of communities like Roblox and Minecraft. In this case, we are talking about a metaverse driven by tokens, both fungible and non-fungible.

This metaverse can include a variety of different experiences and formats. You can interact with the metaverse using a two-dimensional display like your phone or laptop with augmented reality overlays, or you can have a completely immersive virtual reality experience that can even simulate touch with mechanical devices that create tactile feedback.

The thing to remember as content entrepreneurs and content marketers is that these environments are going to need to be filled. And people will be looking to acquire goods and services in these new environments. Those goods and services will be run by a token economy. For example, land in The Sandbox, a popular virtual community, must be purchased with $ETH or $SAND tokens. Once purchased, the owners build out their land by providing additional or different tokens to users. And there will be more opportunities for epic content in these virtual spaces than we've ever seen before.

RISKS

There are several things to be aware of for new brands and creators looking to start leveraging Web3 technologies. Government regulations and tax laws haven't caught up to the financial aspects of these new technologies yet. The language and strategies that you use with your community and within your project could have a financial impact down the road based on what regulations and tax laws get created. Many advisors recommend *focusing on the utility aspects of any tokens that you create* and making sure that your community knows that the value of the tokens comes from the benefits you receive from holding them.

The Financial Action Task Force (FATF) is the international organization that regulates anti–money laundering. FATF currently regards NFTs as "crypto-collectibles," which places them in a different category from that of standard cryptocurrency.

As with any new technology, there are new opportunities for scams and fraud, and there are new security issues. There have been several cases of people's digital wallets being compromised, code being hacked, and data being stolen. Blockchain security makes it very difficult to hack; but user error, phishing scandals, and malicious code have resulted in billions of dollars of losses.

The potential to operate as an anonymous agent and create scam projects, trick people into buying in, and then take the money and run has resulted in the creation of a new term in Web3, the "rug pull."

And there are also environmental impact issues to consider. Some of the blockchains operate on the "proof-of-work" model, which requires large amounts of electricity to process the calculations necessary to validate the transactions. There are other blockchains that rely on "proof-of-stake" models that greatly reduce the impact these transactions have. These are all considerations for anyone looking to get into Web3, and it is important that you do your own research before getting into this space.

Our short recommendation is this: before you proceed with any token project, consult both your attorney and your accountant. If you're going to take on a Web3 project, be sure you create a solid strategy, goals, and expectations around it, as you would do with any content marketing project.

If you're going to create NFTs, have an NFT strategy. If you're going to use social tokens and launch a creator coin, have a token strategy. Understand your priorities, and track your data.

WEB3: JUST THE BEGINNING

Mathew Sweezey explains:

> If you move into this place, it can be expensive, or not. There are many paths. POAPs [Proof of Attendance Protocols] are free to create, but if you want to build a full NFT product line, you must consider a community and a team of builders. This is not a simple flip of a switch. I've seen quotes for building and running enterprise Web3 communities that are seven figures. That's just to run the community. If you want to have a developer and build NFT products from scratch, you'll need specialized programmers, and those aren't cheap. A good one is a half million per head, and you'll probably need a minimum team of five to do a full NFT project. Then there is the strategy and advisory to ensure you know what you are doing. All in, you're talking multiple millions of dollars to create a full NFT product line, and probably 6 months to get your first out the door. Even though it's digital, it is still a product line.

> As time progresses, we'll see many uses for NFTs, from tickets to songs. Consumer brands will be one of the pioneers of the space, as they have the easiest use case. Digital wearables. Sure, the fashion houses will sell expensive NFTs, but most brands will create lifestyle NFTs. Meaning that they will be a high volume and a low price point, with simple utility that will be extended over time.

CASE STUDY: GARY CLUB

Gary Club is a Web3 community powered by $GARY coin and the Giraffe Tower. $GARY coin is a creator coin, which sits on the Solana blockchain, and Giraffe Tower is a sold-out project with 10,000 NFTs. Founded in 2021, Gary Club has built a community of creators and helped launch more than 30 individual coins. Gary Henderson is the founder of Gary Club, $GARY coin, and Giraffe Tower. He is also author of *The Clubhouse Creator* and the owner of digitalmarketing.org.

INTERVIEW WITH GARY HENDERSON

Brian: What are some of the differences you've seen in building a community in traditional web 2.0 formats and what you've done in building your community using tokens and NFTs?

Gary: With building on web 2.0, there's a lot of, "You do this for me, I'll do that for you." When I got into Web3, at first, I didn't understand what it meant to do gamification strategies. What it meant to reward people for making micro-commitments. I didn't understand that process. But as I leaned in, I realized that as a community member, they own an asset, cryptocurrency, a token, or an NFT—they have a pride of ownership. It's theirs, and they get access to something that they've never been able to get before. We're able to find what it looks like as a community to win together, and incentivize people to do just that, using that token or using that resource. What it's done is it's built a super-tight community.

We have a coffee shop that runs in the metaverse every morning, and the only way you get in is with a giraffe, and we get 60–70 people to show up for coffee at 5 a.m. Eastern Time. If I were trying to get people to show up to a real coffee shop, I would have to beg, borrow, and steal and plead to get people to show up. But because they own the giraffe, because they have the access, and because of the energy that's in that room, everybody wants to show up.

Web3 is about pride of ownership. It's about wanting to be there. It's about building uniquely but winning together.

Brian: Could you talk a little bit about some of the different ways that you're creating recurring revenue streams, not only for yourself as a creator, but for other people in your community?

Gary: It's about access and proximity. In the past, creators would have to get an influencer deal. They would have to try and sell their following something. If you want access to me, if you want my courses, if you want my content, then you'll own my assets. Now I'm not dependent on the value of the US dollar. Because I've built my own intrinsic value within my economy, $GARY coin has a value within the community; giraffe has a value within the community. And we've enabled 20+ creators to create their own tokens, and now they have value. And they're using those tokens to buy real-world stuff. They're using their tokens to pay for their haircuts. They're using their tokens to buy their dinners. They're using their tokens to grow their community. And it's so different because it's not a transaction anymore. It's a relationship.

You build your income by deepening your relationship with your audience. In a normal economy, you build your income by transacting in a relationship with your audience; and in Web3, you build it by deepening the relationship.

As they hold your coin or NFT, what it ultimately does is decrease supply. As you have more demand, it increases the price. And you control what that looks like. Because you control the demand. And your community controls the demand. You're creating a microeconomy that you operate on your own. And anyone can do it. It's not just me.

I think the average creator probably wants to make, I don't know, maybe 60 to 120 grand a year. Five to ten grand a month. In Web3, growing a small community, if you can get about 100 true fans, you can make five to ten grand a month.

If you're a TikTok creator, just do more stuff with TikTok. I can give early access to my TikToks, Q&A time with me, extra live streams with me. I'll pin your comment. I'll retweet you. I'll follow you. Those are all monetizable elements of a creator.

If you have a blog post, I'll talk about you. I'll review your content if you're a writer. If I believe in your software, maybe you can write on my blog, and you can be a contributor. If you're a writer, you can earn tokens. Living in this world of being a creator, and just getting paid to create, getting paid to grow your community, it's extremely simple in Web3 to replace your current income, leave your full-time job, and get your base built.

For some of you, that's all you want. For some of you, you want more. The beauty is that it's at your control; you're not limited anymore. When you're working for someone else, they're making money on top of you. They're making profits. There's a reason they're paying you. If you could do that same job for other companies and they could transact in your own currency, you could maintain that profit yourself. It's simple to replace your current income.

Brian: Could you talk a little bit about the software that you've created to help reward your communities for engaging and participating?

Gary: As a software, Social Connector connects your community. It's my opinion that Web3 is not about building a fan base on Clubhouse, and building a fan base on TikTok, and building a fan base on Twitter. *Web3 is about building your fan base no matter where they exist on the web.* So Social Connector connects you, the creator, to your fans wherever they are. And we're bridging gaps. We go to email; we go to Discord; we go to Clubhouse; we go to Twitter.

We do fun things like if you come to the Clubhouse room and you stay a half hour, we'll pay you a little $GARY coin. If you read the blog posts, we'll pay you $GARY coin. If you retweet the tweet, we'll pay you $GARY coin. If you wear a giraffe as your profile photo, we'll pay you $GARY coin. If you show up to the training, we'll pay you $GARY coin. By the way, the only way you get the training is if you also have $GARY coin. You have to own so much to get in. And then we'll give you some more when you show up.

I do all of this because I need you to consume the content. Your attention span is low. I need you to read the book. And if I can get you to read the book, if I can get you to consume the content, I can get you to be in the room.

All I did is ask, "How do I connect with my community in all the places that I want to go create?" And as I go create there, I find a way to connect with them.

Brian: What sort of advice would you give content marketers on how to start leveraging Web3 technology to build their brand?

Gary: For the brand, it would be loyalty. How do we reward our most loyal people? And how do we use that loyalty, use the token, and use the assets that we give them? Or that we allow them to acquire?

I'll give you an example. Gary Loveman was the CEO of Caesars, and he told a story at VRMA several years ago in Atlantic City. He said, when you go to a Caesars venue, you can never buy front-row seats to a concert. They're not for sale. He said the only way you get a front-row seat is if you're in the casino and you're one of our best customers; then we will reward you with a front-row seat. You can't buy them. He went on to share how you reward your best customers with things that they can't buy.

And he shared how he got it wrong for years. He said for years he tried to say, we'll come to pick you up; we'll fly you to the casino. And everything was focused on their business. And he finally figured it out. He said our best customers are already going to spend money on our business. Now let's give them something that they want. He found out that one of his best customers liked to go visit her grandkids. He flew the Caesars jet to pick her up and take her to visit her grandkids, and then he takes her back home. So that's what he did. That's what we have to do. Brands that are launching or wanting to play in Web3 must find their nonbuyable moments, and they have to allow their best customers to do their desired actions and earn those nonbuyable moments.

Now that could be a private label release. It could be a party. It could be a gift. It could be early access. There are so many opportunities there for a brand to lean in.

Brian: What would be your advice to a new entrepreneur looking to start leveraging Web3? Would you recommend building a community first, getting a coin, or doing NFTs?

Gary: Coins, and day one. As content creators, you build fans every single day. And I think content creators need to embrace having fans. I think that's odd to people. They say, "No, I'm a fan of LeBron James, or I'm a fan of this musician, or I'm a fan of this." But you know what, you have fans too. There are people that are just like you. And when you embrace that, and you lean into that, they want to support you. I think every creator should have a token wrapped around their name. As you meet people along your journey, whether you go fast or you go slow, those people are able to build a connection with you, and they're able to build a relationship. They're able to put your assets in their wallet. It's not about getting their email. It's not about getting their phone number. It's about getting their wallet address, so your assets are in their wallet. And now if they forget about you, when they check their wallet, you're still there. You have a relationship; you met this person. I would encourage every content creator if you're a blog writer, if you're creating on TikTok, if you're creating on YouTube, if you're writing on Substack or Patreon, don't charge people monthly. That's the wrong model. It doesn't work; it's broken. You won't survive. Patreon will tell you to charge five bucks a month, get 1,000 people, and make $5,000. If you can get 1,000 people to pay you $5 a month, I could do 10 times that in Web3. Because the relationships are different. It's not transactional anymore. Start day one. Lean into building a fan club. And gate their access points to the content that you're already creating. And then grow your superfans from the very first moment you start.

EPIC THOUGHTS

- Web3 creates new ways to use the internet that haven't been available in previous versions.

- As content entrepreneurs and brands doing content marketing, it is important to look at ways to leverage these technologies to grow our communities, connect with our users, and build trust to create superfans.

EPIC RESOURCES

- Future, "Tokens: A New Digital Primitive Future," accessed July 7, 2022, https://future.com/tokens-are-a-new-digital-primitive/.

- Rattibha, "20 quotes on Crypto, Web 3, NFTs, and Decentralization from Tim Ferriss, Naval Ravikant, and Chris Dixon," accessed July 7, 2022, https://rattibha.com/thread/1454466351624511491?lang=en.

- Gary Henderson, interview by Brian Piper, June 3, 2022.

PART VI

What's Next?

CHAPTER 29

The Future of Content Marketing

The future belongs to those
who prepare for it today.

MALCOLM X

We asked some of the leading experts in the content marketing industry
what they think the future holds and what content marketing will look like
in 10 years. These insights may inspire ideas for where to focus your marketing efforts and whether you should treat your content like a product. Here is
what they said:

> Ten years ago, Joe and I predicted that we'd see content marketing just
> become a core tenet of marketing more broadly. In much the same way
> that digital marketing is now. Arguably it always has been—but it's been
> seen (rightfully I believe) as different because of the differences in the
> core values of the content itself. As I describe it—content that has value
> in and of itself, without describing the value of the product, service, or
> brand of the originator. Put simply, the content doesn't describe the
> value (or lean on the value) of the brand providing it, but instead is valu-
> able outside of that context.
>
> But arguably—this approach is becoming a core business strategy—
> content is product, product is content—thus it becomes a key piece of
> the business—and so where do you put it? Marketing seems the logical
> place. So—content marketing simply becomes a chapter in Kotler's next

book. Maybe it's the fifth "P": product, price, place, packaging, and publishing . . . I just came up with that—and I kinda like it . . . so if you use that last bit, make sure Pulizzi doesn't get credit for it . . . LOL.

—ROBERT ROSE, THE CONTENT ADVISORY

Should we all be depositing poop emojis in our pants at the idea that artificially intelligent robots will take over all our marketing writing jobs in 10 years?

No.

The smartest writers will learn how these tools and technologies will help us be more creative.

There's a problem with that, too. But first, let's talk about marketing in 10 years, because that's what Joe & Brian asked.

In 10 years, AI will take over a lot of the mundane, data-driven repetitive tasks most of us don't enjoy anyway.

Like researching audiences and content. Analyzing data for content strategy. Optimizing email (subject lines, send times, personalizing newsletters). Helping to generate social content, templated writing (basic boilerplates, for example). And some initial drafts.

Scary? Not really.

Another way to think of it: AI increasingly helps us be more creative and strategic, letting us focus on the parts we love while outsourcing the stuff we don't.

It's not that the robots are coming for us; it's that we will use them.

Of course, they might also just decide to kill us all.

(Just kidding.)

(I think.)

So what's the problem I foreshadow above?

The problem is that marketers need to work their storytelling, writing, creative muscles until they're tight and toned as a CrossFit disciple's muscles.

We need to understand how to tell great stories. Create a warm and accessible brand voice. Pull emotions out of our organizations. Find the human beings at the center of our work.

We need to let go and dream. Imagine. Create.

We are capable. But we haven't prioritized our creative fitness in the past few years, and we've become flabby and weak and deconditioned.

I worry we aren't preparing the next generation of marketers. We aren't empowering them for a time when creativity, storytelling, and writing will matter more than ever.

—ANN HANDLEY, MARKETINGPROFS

The big will get bigger. And the smaller publishers will continue to struggle to get visibility. But smart strategists aren't alarmed. Content programs with big audiences are at risk to changes in algorithms. And content programs with small audiences can drive amazing results by focusing on quality and relationships. It will be stressful for anyone who doesn't see the big picture.

—ANDY CRESTODINA, ORBIT MEDIA STUDIOS

I would say that content needs to continue to make emotional connections. In the next 10 years, I expect holograms to become more prevalent. I anticipate some new and innovative ways to deliver and to consume content through holograms. How? No clue, but I think the potential for epic content is fascinating!

—BERNIE BORGES, IQOR

We'll stop using the term "content marketing" in 10 years, which means that it will also disappear from job titles. That might make some sad, but what it signals is that the discipline has grown up and is deployed everywhere.

—DENNIS SHIAO, ATTENTION RETENTION LLC

The amount of information being generated continues to increase exponentially. That is true; it's verifiable. The devices that we use to create content are getting better, faster, and cheaper every single day. Our ability to create immersive content used to be extremely expensive. Now you can buy a 360-degree camera off Amazon for less than $500 and have quick good results that you can use in a virtual reality headset. There's no way to know what's going to happen in 10 years, even 5 years; we just don't know. But what we do know is what's not going to change. We know people will always want things better, faster, and cheaper. People always want to be educated, to be entertained, to be engaged emotionally in the content they consume; those things are not changing. And if we focus on fulfilling those needs, we will do well.

—CHRISTOPHER PENN, TRUST INSIGHTS

I think the line, insofar as one exists today, between content marketing and entertainment will be increasingly blurred or probably fade away. Increasingly, I think the content that is content marketing and content that is just content will be the same. There will be TV channels that are just content marketing. There will be magazines that are just content marketing. This idea that media companies and non-media companies will be standing shoulder to shoulder is absolutely the direction that this is headed.

—JAY BAER, COAUTHOR, *TALK TRIGGERS*

Over the next 10 years, content will move from something we consume to something we experience. Experiential marketing and content marketing will grow closer together as technology pushes us into more virtual experiences.

We will begin to consider virtual experiences to be in person, and content will be something you do as much as something you see.

—A. LEE JUDGE, CONTENT MONSTA

Content of all forms is facing an existential crisis due to the ability of dark forces to create bot-generated content, misinformation, and deep fakes with almost no effort. All marketing is based on trust, and we are in a world where trust is falling off a cliff.

In this environment, our only hope is to create an uncompromising brand of trust. Branding is more important than ever, whether you are a corporate brand or a personal brand. The only remedy is to establish and maintain an effective digital base of trust so people know what to believe.

On the positive side, there will be so many opportunities for content creators in the future. The escalating content arms race will create an insatiable demand for talented people. The technology enabling Web3 and the metaverse will unleash an unparalleled opportunity for creativity! The future of content marketing is going to be driven by 12-year-olds.

—MARK SCHAEFER, SCHAEFER MARKETING SOLUTIONS

So many people are worried that AI will make marketing obsolete, it will make content creation less personal, and more. What I'm seeing is that AI can take the repetitive, data-driven tasks off my plate so I *can* be more human. I can focus on things I love doing—talking to customers, growing community, and being creative. So what I see happening is a shift to content marketing aligning more with IT and technology teams to build MarTech stacks that take the burden off marketers where it makes sense for them/their company. Marketing will have a bigger seat at the table with technology decisions within organizations.

—CATHY MCPHILLIPS, MARKETING ARTIFICIAL INTELLIGENCE INSTITUTE

Personally, I'm excited to see how creators and marketers approach content marketing in the age of Web3, AR, VR, NFTs, and the Metaverse. I know that's a lot of buzzword soup, but I've always felt one of the best parts of content marketing is that we get to be the brave explorers who set out to learn how to tell stories in new and interesting ways whenever new tools and platforms become available or gain popularity.

—MELANIE DEZIEL, THE CONVOY

I think what it will take to be successful with content marketing in the next 10 years will go beyond what a "T"-shaped professional can deliver. The breadth keeps expanding, everything from empathy to AI. Strategy to measurement. Technology to talent. Privacy to purpose. And the depth of all of these areas is unfathomable, not to mention how they intersect. All of this in the context of building audiences and growing customers along their journey. Content marketers will have to look like a platypus rather than a unicorn.

—CARLA JOHNSON, RE:THINK LABS

I can't predict the platform or even the medium by which content is being shared. I mean, things change so quickly. It could be anything from going into the metaverse and having it be a 4D experience with haptic sensors, or I could see it going back to how it was with newspapers because that was lost and now it's coming back. Everything else seems to come back, so I can't really comment on the medium.

What I can comment on is an understanding that it is continuing to become more and more important to personalize. The more personalized that material is, the more it's going to connect with people because there's so much noise. The more I can find a piece of content that's relevant to me, the more likely I am to consume it. If I find that it's more general, it's probably not for me, or it's not going to help me as quickly as possible. That's the other thing that we all are feeling now. People want answers quickly, and our attention spans are much shorter.

I think that the communities that come along with these platforms are going to be key. It's not just content that's generated from a leader or an authority; it's content from somebody who's literally in the thick of it with you. That is often more valuable because now you have a partner to go through with. Now there's support, and there's also accountability. I think that more of that is coming. And it's probably going to be more micro niche than ever.

—PAT FLYNN, SPI MEDIA

Number one, I doubt we call it content marketing. Number two, a lot of it stays the same. I've never seen one marketing methodology take another marketing methodology away. I've seen them take the budget away. Content marketing is not going to go away; it will still be relevant; it will just be extended into new formats and forms and new places. But the fundamental aspect of value exchange between brands and consumers will always exist, period. It will just depend on the mediums that we use and the technology in place of how that exchange actually takes place.

—MATHEW SWEEZEY, SALESFORCE

While a lot will change in 10 years, some things will remain the same. People love to be taken on a journey and love the "story" behind the story. While the current trend has been for short "TikTok"-type content, I think that people will migrate back to wanting to see longer stories, from *real* people that they can connect with. While famous people will always be around, content marketing from the "influencer" type will be gone as people get tired of the BS surrounding it. Web3 will be well established and mainstream. Even mums & dads will have a crypto wallet!! Connecting with everyday people, on their level, will be back big time!

—MICHELLE PETERSON CLARK, GHOSTMARKET.IO

In the last 10 years, content marketing has become considerably more sophisticated, with a huge number of platforms to communicate through, SEO practices and ever-changing algorithms to constantly adapt to, and a slightly more skeptical general public to contend with. More than ever, it's important to know the clients, where they spend their time, and use the right touch and on the right platform(s) to reach them.

In the present climate, a key consideration and best practice has been to get customers off platforms that we as marketers don't own or control (like social media). I think this trend will continue to increase, with greater attention paid to fostering communities whose members feel they are a part of the process and whose voices are heard. People are craving ownership and discussion rather than being shouted at through the void. Having authentic discussions with clients and customers through these communities will allow marketers to create products and services that serve their audience better than ever.

—NORA DUNN, THE PROFESSIONAL HOBO

The future of content marketing is personal.

When the answer to practically any question can be looked up in an instant—what do people still rely on when making decisions? The opinions of people they trust.

What software to use.

What vendor to hire.

What to make for dinner.

People trust people they can relate to—and who share their experiments, wins, and failures.

And personality-driven content deepens the connection between the audience and the creator.

The lines grow ever more blurred between what content is considered personal versus business. The audience hears about your pets, your hobbies, your favorite hacks—all the things that make you you (and all the things that could help them be successful). It's no longer a one-way push—now audiences can interact (and react) with creators all over the internet—from DMs, to emails, to tagging and sharing memes.

In the last few years we've seen the rise of the personal brand, not just celebrities and "influencers," but the small business owner who shares the behind the scenes of their daily grind and passion projects.

Showing your personality is no longer seen as a bad thing—it's an asset that makes you stand out in a crowded marketplace.

People want to know that you're real—that you're trying things and sharing what shakes out. They want to know that it doesn't always have to be perfect—and that you'll share how you got there so they can do it too. Above all, they want to connect with a real person.

And when you build a loyal audience that trusts you, they'll be there when (and if) you pivot—as long as you take them along for the ride.

—MICHELLE MARTELLO, MINIMA DESIGNS

Content marketing has always been driven by powerful storytelling, and over the next 10 years, those stories will ripen into well-developed worldviews.

GenZ is maturing into a pragmatic generation that prizes autonomy and has limited patience for authority or platitudes. They'll look for content marketing stories to become more global, more credible, and more holistic. The drive to Net Zero carbon emissions will play an increasing role in marketing stories, as organizations that lack a credible climate plan start to lose customers, as well as access to capital. And as implementation of those plans touches every element of a business's operations, the most adept organizations will turn their reworked business models into compelling, shareable stories.

The most savvy companies, particularly social enterprises, will realize they can work with complementary organizations to nurture digital ecosystems, defined by shared values and identities. Content creators will be the bards of these global villages, telling and retelling the most important stories that underline those values.

The seeds of these trends are everywhere today. They come from companies like Apple that are incredibly good at fostering a sense of shared identity, and also from the profusion of independent content creators weaving the story threads that reinforce that identity and make it relevant and personal.

—SONIA SIMONE, REMARKABLE COMMUNICATION

Ten years from now, I can't imagine that humans have to write the first drafts for certain kinds of content. I think there are going to be forms of content that the machine is way beyond just being an assistant and an editor. But I think content will be very different 10 years from now. Machines are going to get very good at doing the things we do as writers, as content strategists, as content creators, as people who promote content. It's just hard to overestimate the impact AI will have on content marketing in the next decade. That's it. It's going to be significant. It will be very weird to look back 10 years from now and see it looking anything like it does today.

—PAUL ROETZER, MARKETING ARTIFICIAL INTELLIGENCE INSTITUTE

At Cleveland Clinic, I see us becoming the undisputed leader in the space, because the plan is working, and the scale is there. And we're gonna continue to invest and do all the optimization work that we need to. I also think that when you look at consumer behavior, search is not going away, especially as it relates to health. I think we've seen this evolution over the last 10 years from what was going on with social to search. But having search available on your phone, at your fingertips at all times, is just going to increase. And I think as you see more and more of that, how you connect those users through to the actual end game, which is making an appointment and seeing a provider.

With the rise and emergence of technology on the clinical care side of things, it totally changes the game for us. If you can see a doctor right now virtually, what we're able to offer you in that moment when you're reading our article is drastically different than a phone number that I can put there right now. I think that there's going to be even more importance placed on what we're doing. And I think that the content is going to continue to be a larger front door for us. I think that's true of a lot of industries. In healthcare, the damage that's been done by Covid in the last couple of years, to the industry, to the credibility of science, I think is something we're going to be overcoming for a little while. And content is the best way to do that. It's grown in significance and importance in the past 10 years, and I think that's just gonna continue into the next 10 years. And the opportunities from a revenue- and business-driving perspective are going to exponentially increase over time.

—AMANDA TODOROVICH, CLEVELAND CLINIC

I think a couple of really meaningful things are going to happen in the next three to five years that will dictate where we land in ten. First, con-solidation in publishing is going to have to be dealt with. How are the search engines going to deal with someone who buys up thousands of websites and can buy real estate in organic search? Second, there's going to be a reckoning on privacy and ads. The best place to watch for what 10 years will be, is going to be privacy-focused search engines. I think in four years, we'll have an Apple search engine. We'll have another privacy-based search engine that's actually private. And there will be tremendous restrictions on advertising, especially in your money or your life zones. In 10 years, I think we're going to be so worn out on traditional content marketing, that quality and expertise will have to be what's driv-ing the bus, and there will be standardized metrics and methodologies for assessing true expertise.

And those will be the only people still thriving and living. The other side of that is the youth of today. The way that they consume content will have to reconcile with business publishing. I've seen studies show-ing that consumption of mid- to long-form content is demographically skewed, in a horrifying way. So repurposing. I'd say repurposing will be one of the most desired skills on teams. What we're going to see in 10 years' time is expertise drives the bus for having longevity, but also being able to package that expertise in as many formats as possible becomes the meets minimum for any business.

—JEFF COYLE, MARKETMUSE

Over the next decade, there will be a collective awakening that the highest-leverage thing you can do online is content marketing for your-self, not someone else's business.

If you're a creator, freelancer, or knowledge worker, sharing, curating, and expressing unique ideas will become your vital insulation from the impending tidal wave of banal content posted by others to appease the social media algorithm gods.

—JUSTIN MOORE, CREATOR WIZARD

Content isn't king; it's not even air; it's strategy. In the future, most content will be produced via AI, but the content strategy still resides with the brand. The key will lie in a brand's ability to create massive amounts of first-party data that not only reveals a true content journey but also uncovers the hundreds of ways that customers move through that journey. Possessing that data will allow brands to create many more segments and personalize content at increasingly granular levels. The content itself won't matter as much as when the content is put into context. I know marketers have been saying this for a long time, but the advancement of AI-aided technology will make it so automated that any business can and frankly must employ this tailored approach. It will be like free shipping—everyone is doing it.

—JOHN JANTSCH, DUCT TAPE MARKETING

I first learned about content marketing in 2017 when I left teaching. I knew I needed to earn additional income but wasn't sure where to even start. I stumbled on a few podcasts that ultimately changed the course of my life. From my first email subscriber to a list that now reaches over 90,000—I couldn't have done this without all of the content marketers generous enough to share their knowledge with me. In the next 10 years, I believe content marketing is going to become even more common as a source of income for the average household for two reasons. First, simply due to the demand, which is not going away anytime soon. But more importantly due to the abundance of amazing content marketers willing to support one another and grow together. There are so many in this community who are completely changing lives like mine.

—DAPHNE GOMEZ, TEACHER CAREER COACH

Since the digital divide has disappeared across age and demographic groups, people will move from keyboard computers and other forms of swipe devices to wearables and the Internet of Things. In terms of content, people will use their voices to accomplish actions more quickly and easily.

From a content marketing perspective, this has complex implications across your organization requiring senior management support to succeed. Why? Because it requires investment in bringing existing technology and information up to current standards, as well as additional librarians to supply the related metainformation to keep the content useful across formats.

To start, the human, technical, and data silos across the entire organization need to come down so businesses can supply blocks of content in the mix and format requested by the user as quickly as possible. All systems and people should be able to communicate across product, operations, pricing, etc. This includes legacy systems and external systems.

Successful organizations must be able to select units of content or information from across their full technology and data offering based on the user's questions. In other words, your content marketing must be able to adapt to respond to questions about the minutest detail and recombine the answer for a different inquiry. Further, to retain their trust with consumers, content marketers will need to be transparent in their use of customer data and privacy.

This requires appropriate, quality metadata based on an organizational content strategy to quickly locate micro information from across the organization regardless of the age of the content and last update. Then this information must be able to be converted back into the content format that the user needed.

—HEIDI COHEN, ACTIONABLE MARKETING GUIDE
AND RIVERSIDE MARKETING STRATEGIES

I think you're going to see even more marketers taking to heart their societal responsibility. I think even more journalists are going to see the power of leveraging private funding to do what they need to do. And I think this respect between the two is only going to grow, the more they understand what the other side does. You are going to see more of that on both the media community front and the marketing community front. I'm an optimist. I think this will be good for us, for our society.

—VICTOR GAO, ARROW ELECTRONICS

In 10 years, I think content marketing is going to become more natural. I think the algorithms are going to get smarter. I think it's going to become more global. I think we're going to transact in a new way, commerce in a new way. I think content marketing is going to be about reaching your audience at the right time for them. It's going to be less about "let me optimize for the search engines," and there will be more natural processing that ends up happening.

I think content marketing in the future is going to be about getting your superfans because they're going to look at the engagement metrics you get at the beginning; and when your people are engaging in it, when your people are loving it, when your people are consuming it, then content marketing engines are going to reward you in a big way. It's about genuine engagement with your community.

—GARY HENDERSON, GIRAFFE TOWER AND DIGITALMARKETING.ORG

The future of content marketing is community. No matter what changes in technology, whether we're in a fully immersive virtual world or an entirely connected Internet of Things physical world, what will matter for brands and content entrepreneurs is building trust and forming connections with other people.

Establishing that trust and authenticity and creating content that helps others succeed and solves their problems is how we show people that they can believe what we say.

Web3 is a mindset change. The blockchain is a tool that can provide more transparency, more authenticity, and can be used to build that trust. AI and machine learning provide insights and opportunities that will empower us in ways we can't even imagine.

Working on this book, talking to such talented people, and looking back at the previous 10 years has been amazing. The next 10 years are going to be epic.

—BRIAN PIPER, UNIVERSITY OF ROCHESTER

WRAPPING IT UP

Most people focus on what has changed in the last 10 years. What's interesting to me is what has not. To build an audience and community, you still need to deliver valuable, relevant, and compelling information to a targeted group of people over time. That content needs to be differentiated in some significant way.

That is how the *New York Times* did it when it started its newspaper. That is also how the latest TikTok influencers made their way. So while the types of content and the platforms have changed, the "how" has essentially remained the same.

Over that time, we've learned that content marketing and the development of loyal audiences is extremely difficult. Most organizations either give up too soon or never start out differentiated enough. That means two things will happen. First, almost all innovative and successful companies will have a content or media division. Doesn't matter whether that's a product or service company like LEGO or a media company like Morning Brew. Both brands will seek out loyal audiences, and those will be built by delivering amazing content experiences.

Second, because it's hard, more brands will buy up small content creators and influencers. As we noted in this book, that has already started, but I could see that some brands will go on a buying spree in the next couple of years . . . especially once they realize that they need a content marketing practice, want to get one, and then realize how long it takes.

So when the next edition of this book comes out in 10 years, the front half will remain essentially the same, while the back half will be completely and utterly different (just like the previous 10 years).

Yours in Content, Joe Pulizzi, The Tilt

CHAPTER 30

The Evolution of Your Epic Story

BY JOE PULIZZI AND BRIAN PIPER

We've only just begun . . .
THE CARPENTERS

There are so many additional concepts to cover in this book, but as we've discussed with content marketing, there is no perfection, and as Seth Godin says, shipping the product is the most important.

We begin this last chapter with epic examples to inspire you. We go on to address the critical questions that get asked on a regular basis and that we feel the book would be incomplete without. And then we leave you with a bit of motivation at the end of this chapter.

EXAMPLES FOR INSPIRATION

Although there are dozens of them already in the book, you can never have a shortage of content marketing examples. The following are some epic examples of content marketing and a few smaller content projects collected throughout the years. Enjoy!

- **Airbnb.** Its design personality quiz is a short, eight-question quiz that is easily shared on social and via email. The quiz asks the users to make a series of choices based on their personal preferences about their dream house or ideal space. In the end, Airbnb presents them with a variety of vacation choices that match their needs as well as design tips from its partner, Domino. https://bit.ly/ECM-Domino.

- **Apple.** The Shot on an iPhone campaign was launched in 2014 as a billboard campaign featuring photos that customers had taken with their iPhones. Since then, it has become an annual contest with images posted on social and featured in print ads, digital videos, and TV commercials. This is a great example of user-generated content with incredible sharing potential that has turned into a cultural phenomenon. https://apple.co/3NZ1YwC.
- **Adobe.** The #CreativityForAll campaign features tweets meant to spark creativity for designers and offer tips to creators. Adobe has expanded the program by asking for creators to share gratitude for who inspires them and donated $500,000 to @TeachForAmerica. https://bit.ly/3IwgmeG.
- **University of Chicago.** Big Brains is a podcast that features the research and breakthroughs from the University of Chicago. It has won numerous awards and is monetized with sponsorship opportunities, merchandise, and donations. https://bit.ly/ECM -Chicago.
- **Planters.** Telling the story of the death of Mr. Peanut, and his miraculous rebirth as a Baby Nut, the "A Nut Above" campaign committed to giving away $5 million to people doing charitable acts. https://bit.ly/ECM-Planters.
- **WarnerMedia.** HBOMax created the TikTok #LegendaryChallenge to promote its ballroom dance show. The challenge has generated more than 4 billion views and 450,000 videos on TikTok. https://bit.ly/ECM-WarnerMedia.
- **Mailchimp.** Whether it's the company's free Content Style Guide or its "All in a Day's Work" campaign, Mailchimp has content marketing programs to both educate and entertain its customers. https://bit.ly/ECM-Mailchimp.
- **Monster.** When a pandemic changed the world, Monster saw the need to support employers and employees and launched the Work in the Time of Coronavirus microsite. The site evolved as the virus did and drove an average of 2,500 monthly B2C visits and had a 52 percent click-through rate from visitors. https://bit.ly/ECM-Monster.

- **TD Ameritrade.** *thinkMoney* is an award-winning magazine created for active traders. The usefulness of the magazine was under review in the early days, but after two years of publication, the data showed that subscribers and readers of the magazine traded five times more than nonsubscribers. https://tickertape.tdameritrade.com/trading/thinkmoney/.
- **HubSpot.** The INBOUND conference attracts more than 26,000 attendees from 110 countries to hear thought leaders and celebrities talk about marketing, sales, customer success, and revenue operations. https://www.inbound.com/.
- **Google.** Letting creators build, edit, and host videos on their own sites is the goal of Google Web Stories. It provides Google with more searchable, indexable content and increases potential organic traffic and engagement for the creators. https://stories.google/.
- **ZocDoc.** This website helps patients find doctors and schedule appointments. It discovered that employees weren't scheduling preventive care visits so it launched the UnsickDay microsite to encourage employers to give employees a day off to see a doctor. The campaign created more than 70 million social media impressions in its first few weeks and had 12 new employers sign on as sponsors. http://unsickday.com/.
- **You Suck at Cooking.** This funny take on cooking recipes and techniques has created millions of subscribers to its YouTube channel, tens of thousands on other social channels, a book, and numerous sponsorship opportunities. http://yousuckatcooking.com/.
- **Dasha Kennedy.** Dasha launched the Broke Black Girl Facebook group in 2017. She grew her Facebook audience to more than 60,000 followers in the first year and has since expanded to Twitter, Instagram, and her own website. https://www.thebrokeblackgirl.com/.
- **Simran Kaur.** Leaving her optometry career, Simran launched the Girls That Invest Instagram account and podcast in 2020 and has grown her audience and her revenue. She had more than 500 people sign up for her first online class, earning more than $149,000. https://girlsthatinvest.com/.
- **Alisha Ether.** When she was laid off from her bartender/server job during Covid, Alisha started playing video games on Twitch and

launched Leesh Capeesh. She expanded into TikTok and is now a full-time content entrepreneur. https://www.leeshcapeesh.com/.

- **Zach King.** After being rejected at film school, Zach launched the FinalCutKing YouTube channel in 2009 with videos like "Jedi Kittens Strike Back." His channel has acquired more than 14 million subscribers and has over 69 million TikTok followers. https://www.zachkingmagic.com/.

- **Ann Handley.** An author and content marketing expert, Ann launched her *Total Annarchy* newsletter in 2013. Her funny, personal, and creative writing style has grown her subscribers to more than 40,000. https://annhandley.com/.

- **Nora Dunn.** Nora sold everything she owned in 2006 and followed her travel dreams. She launched *The Professional Hobo* blog to chronicle her adventures and now offers guides, courses, and e-books. https://www.theprofessionalhobo.com/.

- **Wally Koval.** In the summer of 2017, Wally and his wife, Amanda, started Accidentally Wes Anderson. AWA is now a design/media powerhouse with over 1 million followers on Instagram, a *New York Times* bestselling book, and 50,000+ email subscribers. https://accidentallywesanderson.com/.

- **Nigel Ng.** A Malaysian standup comedian, Nigel launched his YouTube channel, Uncle Roger, in 2020. He has more than 6 million subscribers. https://nigelngcomedy.com/.

WEB3 EXAMPLES

- **NBA Top Shot.** NBA Top Shot launched a line of NFTs featuring images and videos of top plays in NBA and WNBA history. A LeBron clip sold for $387,000. https://nbatopshot.com/.

- **Coca-Cola.** A special "Coca-Cola Friendship Box" was sold for $575,000. The "loot box" contained four unique NFTs, and the proceeds of the sale went to Special Olympics International. https://maketafi.com/coca-cola-nft.

- **Lacoste.** A collection of 11,212 NFTs, UndW3, is being launched and will provide digital and physical benefits to holders. After announcing the project, the brand gained 30,000+ Discord members in 48 hours. https://undw3.lacoste.com/.

- **Chainsmokers.** The band created and gave away 5,000 tokens to its biggest fans. These tokens gave the owners a share of the streaming royalties for the entire *So Far So Good* album. The band also decided to give the royalties from the secondary sales of the tokens to other songwriters that helped with the album. https://bit.ly/ECM-Chainsmokers.
- **Adidas.** In 2021, Adidas launched its "Into the Metaverse" NFT project, which sold out in a few hours for more than $22 million in funds. https://www.adidas.com/metaverse.
- **Alivia.** "Buy My Cancer" is an NFT project that combines contemporary art, modern medicine, and the blockchain to raise money to provide cancer treatments. https://www.buymycancer.org/.
- **3LAU.** Justin Blau, better known as 3LAU, is a DJ who launched an album in 2021 as a 33-piece NFT collection, which sold for $11.7 million. He has cofounded a company, Royal, that works with other musicians (like Chainsmokers) to sell tokens that provide a portion of the streaming rights from their albums. https://royal.io/.

A REVIEW: TOP 25 CONTENT MARKETING QUESTIONS ANSWERED IN 140 CHARACTERS OR LESS

Sometimes you just want quick answers. Not a whole explanation; just the answer, and get on your way.

In that spirit, here is a list of the top content marketing questions we receive on an ongoing basis. We've briefly answered them next.

If we missed any questions that you'd like answered, please let us know.

1. What are some of the best B2C content marketing examples that you like to reference?
   Sweet Farm, Red Bull, *New York Times* Wordle, and Cleveland Clinic.
2. How about B2B content marketing examples?
   Adobe, Arrow Electronics, HubSpot, and Salesforce.
3. Who are some of the best examples of content entrepreneurs?
   Wally Koval, Zach King, MrBeast (Jimmy Donaldson), Amy Porterfield.

4. How do I integrate content marketing in my own company?
   Use the SAAS model—get the leaders from each department (through email, search, PR, and so on), and have them meet weekly to coordinate content activities.

5. Where do I start with my content marketing strategy?
   Develop your content marketing mission statement. There you can have an impact as an authoritative voice. Do this before you develop any more content without a strategy.

6. What's the most underutilized content distribution tool?
   Email. Most companies don't hold their email newsletter in high enough regard.

7. How do I create more content?
   You most likely have enough content assets. First, look at stopping some things that aren't working and reallocating those resources to quality content initiatives.

8. But what if my content is not in story-ready form?
   Most companies have content assets that aren't in a compelling form. Hire or contract out a journalist, editor, or natural storyteller to help get those assets into shape.

9. Should I insource or outsource my content?
   Most companies do both. It doesn't have to be an either-or proposition, and there is no silver bullet. Find the resources necessary to get the job done. It will never be perfect, so don't wait.

10. Should I place my content behind a form or set it free?
    It depends on the goal. If the metric you are using is a lead, there has to be a form somewhere. That said, if you use a form, you might get less sharing and awareness . . . and that may be OK. As a rule, free your content!

11. Do I need a newsletter?
    Email is possibly the greatest owned media channel for brands. To keep that channel alive, you need a consistent flow of amazing content.

12. Why in the world would I give away all our knowledge for free?
    As the great Don Schultz has always said, communication is the only true competitive advantage. If you don't help your customers reach greater heights, who will? Your competitors?

13. Do I have to be on Facebook, Twitter, or TikTok?
No, you don't. But if you are, ask yourself why you are using those channels. In fact, ask yourself why you are using any channel.

14. How do you get all your content creators on the same page?
Make sure *every* one of your content creators has a copy of your content marketing mission statement. In most brands, content creators never know what the true reader or company content mission really is.

15. What is the best way to figure out my customer's pain points?
First, talk to your customers. Then talk to more customers. Then listen on Twitter and launch some surveys. Then talk to sales and customer service. Then talk to your customers.

16. How do I measure ROI?
You don't. Figure out what the specific content marketing objective is, and then measure your return on objective. Use the four types of content marketing metrics for guidance as addressed in Chapter 20.

17. What kind of content works best?
According to Julie Fleischer (formerly at Kraft), the keys to creating the most effective content are: (1) have a purpose, (2) be captivating, (3) go where the customer is, (4) be aware that timeliness matters, and (5) know your metrics.

18. What is the difference between *content* and *content marketing*?
Content marketing must work to enhance or change a behavior. If it doesn't, it's just *content*.

19. How do I get C-level buy-in for my content marketing?
First, you may not need it. The CEO might not believe you can do it. That said . . . Start a pilot. For television shows to get approved, they need a pilot; you should do the same. Create a six-month pilot period using agreed-upon metrics.

20. What is the biggest reason why content marketing initiatives fail?
First, the creator or brand stops producing the content (campaign mentality). Second, there's inconsistency. Third, it's not remarkable content.

21. How important is design in your content marketing?
What is the purpose of a magazine's cover? To get it opened. Much of that depends on design. If your design doesn't compel people to engage, what's the point? Invest in design.

22. What is a no-brainer issue that some marketers don't deal with but ought to?

    Updating old content. Get a plan to make sure content that is still being found is up-to-date.

23. Will brands start doing content creation and distribution better than publishers?

    In certain niches, some will. But publishers and brands are better together. Brands have more resources, but the media model is changing, we think for the better. Traditional publishers will always be needed.

24. Can't I just create one content platform for all my customers?

    How are broad, horizontal news sources doing these days? Look at what Patagonia does and how many different content platforms it has for different editorial interests. Start with one platform, and be amazing; then diversify.

25. Should I stop everything else and just do content marketing?

    Do you want to be fired? Content marketing works *with* your other marketing, not in replacement of it. Nowadays, the issue is that most brands are underdeveloped in content marketing and need to catch up.

CONTENT MARKETING COMMANDMENTS

If you're a content marketer or content entrepreneur, these should be printed on your wall as a reminder of the content marketing revolution and its importance to your business. Enjoy!

- The content is more important than the offer.
- A customer relationship doesn't end with the payment.
- Printed marketing doesn't stop with full-page advertisements.
- "Being the content" is more important than "surrounding the content."
- Interruption isn't valued, but engagement is.
- A blog can be and should be a core part of communicating with and marketing to your customers.
- Internal marketing always takes precedence over external marketing.
- A brand, or personal brand, is a relationship, not a tagline.
- Focusing on what the customer wants is more important than what you have to sell.

- A news release isn't meant to be picked up by the press but rather to help customers find your great content on the web.
- Communicating directly with customers is the best choice.
- Marketers can and should have a publishing mindset.
- Today's traditional publishers are worried about how many resources brands have.
- Without content, community is improbable, if not impossible.
- The marketing brochure should be stricken from all strategic marketing plans.
- Content without design doesn't look appetizing (or deliver on marketing goals).
- Lead generation is only one small part of the marketing picture.
- Hiring an editor is not a want, but a must, for all organizations.
- No matter the medium or the provider, someone is always selling something.
- The long tail of search engine optimization is driven by consistent content on your corporate blog or website.
- Ninety percent of all corporate websites talk about how great the company or product is and forget about the customer.
- Ninety percent of all corporate websites are terrible.
- Ninety-five percent of all personal websites are terrible.
- Data without strategy or goals is just numbers.
- Buyers are in control; the traditional sales process has changed; and relevant content lets organizations into the buying process.
- Long-form branded content can be created anywhere your customers work, live, or play.
- The chief content officer is the CMO of the future.
- Customers want to be inspired. *Be the inspiration!*
- There is no one right way to do content marketing. Be willing to experiment.
- In-person events continue to be one of the best ways to connect with your audience.
- We have learned how to do virtual events better, and they can be extremely powerful.
- Never overlook the power of simplicity.
- Content marketing success in your organization means having the right process.

- There are no shortcuts to great content marketing; it takes a lot of elbow grease.
- Don't rely too much on search engines to bring traffic to your site. Don't be too reliant on any one thing to bring traffic to your site.
- Content curation is important, but it is not a strategy. To be the trusted expert in your industry, you must create your own content.
- Don't wait for perfection. Great content doesn't have to be perfect. It will never be perfect.
- Outsource effectively or be effectively outsourced.
- If you don't have scaling problems with your content, you aren't moving fast enough.
- Before you create your content masterpiece, first figure out how you are going to market it.

GO TELL YOUR STORY

We believe that you will do great things with content marketing. We hope, after reading this book, you have the tools you need to create and distribute epic content that will transform your customers and your business. Here's an epic list to help keep you focused:

1. Develop and refine your content marketing mission statement.
2. Find one or multiple partners, and launch a content marketing program together.
3. Consider that maybe *less* content will mean *more* impact.
4. Find at least three thought leaders in your organization, and build them into your content plan.
5. Send those thought leaders to Toastmasters to work on their public speaking skills.
6. Define your most valuable audience, and consider a targeted print publication.
7. Assign one employee to LinkedIn, and figure out how to leverage this tool as part of your content marketing.
8. Develop a series of stories for your industry or niche on an aspect that has never been covered before.
9. Make sure that every content landing page you develop this year has only one call to action.
10. Stop one content initiative this year.

11. Write your book.

12. Update your social media influencer list before the end of the year.

13. Compile a substantial piece of influencer content (for example, an e-book of influencer insights).

14. Get at least five employees who are not in marketing involved in your weekly content plan.

15. Make it a priority to personalize your content by persona.

16. Start a podcast series.

17. Sit down with every salesperson and ask each one what their customers' biggest pain points are.

18. Develop a list of the top 100 questions coming from your customer base.

19. Commission a piece of art from a local artist to use in your next content piece.

20. Target one traditional marketing initiative that can be enhanced with content marketing.

21. Set a goal this year to double the number of e-mail subscribers to your content.

22. Attend Creator Economy Expo. (Okay, that's a blatant sales pitch.)

23. Read one nonmarketing book each month during the year. (It will open up new content marketing ideas.)

24. Develop a content marketing metrics plan for your CEO or supervisor that includes only those metrics that will make the case for company business objectives.

25. Stop doing the same old press releases, and instead create them as engaging stories.

26. Find a way to work with the leading trade magazine in your niche on a joint content effort.

27. Commission a piece of research that is important to your customers.

28. Use your research findings to build a six-month campaign with at least 20 independent content pieces.

29. Commit to smarter usage of images in your content.

30. Do an audit of all your blog posts to determine which types of titles lead to the right reader behaviors.

31. If you have the budget, start identifying media companies in your industry that may be ripe for acquisition.

32. Make sure your content is easy to read on both smartphones and tablets.

33. Set up an editorial leader in each of your silos, and plan to meet with that person at least once per week.

34. Develop a customer event that doesn't talk about your projects but rather educates customers on where the industry is going.

35. Create a piece of content this year that would be completely unexpected and see what happens.

36. For every story idea you have for next year, plan on developing 10 pieces of content from it.

37. Send a videographer and journalist to the next industry event to cover it.

38. Give out quarterly awards to all internal content creators based on number of content shares. Make it public.

39. Choose 10 of the top influencers in your industry and sponsor a one-day brainstorming session on how you can all help each other.

40. Ask whoever oversees customer service what the top 10 complaints were last year. Build a content program to help with answers.

41. Get a digital wallet and buy some crypto. Experiment.

42. Buy an inexpensive NFT and some social tokens (maybe some $TILT and $PIPER).

43. Whatever you do this year, make sure you are telling a different story than everyone else in your industry is telling, not just the same story told incrementally better.

THE FINAL WORD

You have made it to the end of this book. We've obviously said enough, but we wanted to say a final "thank you." We truly appreciate the time and effort you put into this piece of work.

Of course, your journey is just beginning, and content marketing continues to evolve. If you'd like to keep up with everything going on in the art and science of content marketing, we would like to urge you to subscribe to our newsletters for regular updates on TheTilt.com and brianwpiper.com. You won't regret it.

Now go out and change the world by giving your customers the best storytelling on the planet. Be epic!

Life is either a daring adventure or nothing.

—HELEN KELLER

Index

About the Authors

JOE PULIZZI (he/him) is founder of multiple startups including the content creator education site The Tilt and the content entrepreneur event Creator Economy Expo (CEX). He is also the bestselling author of seven books including *Content Inc.* and *Epic Content Marketing*, which was named a Must-Read Business Book by *Fortune Magazine*.

Joe is best known for his work in content marketing, first using the term in 2001, then launching Content Marketing Institute and the Content Marketing World event. In 2014, he received the Lifetime Achievement Award by the Content Council. He successfully exited CMI in 2016 and subsequently wrote an award-winning mystery novel, *The Will to Die*.

He has two weekly podcasts, the motivational *Content Inc.* podcast and the media news and analysis show *This Old Marketing* with Robert Rose.

His foundation, The Orange Effect, delivers speech therapy and technology services to over 300 children in 35 states.

Joe and his family live in Cleveland, Ohio.

BRIAN PIPER (he/him) is an author, keynote speaker, consultant, and Director of Content Strategy and Assessment at the University of Rochester. Brian has been doing SEO and web content optimization since 1996. He has created online training programs for hundreds of companies including Xerox, L3Harris, IBM, and Volvo. He has spent the last seven years focusing on data analytics, digital marketing, and content strategy. Since 2021, he has been diving into Web3, community building, NFTs, and social tokens. He is the founder of $PIPER coin.

When he's not creating data visualizations, he teaches wingsuit skydiving and spends time with his wife and six children in Rochester, New York.